Catching a wave

CATCHI

AI

EDITED BY RORY DICKER & ALISON PIEPMEIER

Catching a Wave

reclaiming feminism for the 21st century

NORTHEASTERN UNIVERSITY PRESS · BOSTON
Published by University Press of New England
Hanover and London

Northeastern University Press
Published by University Press of New England,
One Court Street, Lebanon, NH 03766
www.upne.com

Printed in the United States of America   5   4   3

ISBN–13: 978–1–55553–570–4
ISBN–10: 1–55553–570–4

Library of Congress Cataloging-in-Publication Data
Catching a wave : reclaiming feminism for the 21st century / edited by
Rory Dicker and Alison Piepmeier.
    p.   cm.
Includes bibliographical references and index.
    ISBN 1-55553-570-4 (pbk. : alk. paper)—ISBN 1-55553-571-2 (cloth :
alk. paper)
    1. Feminism—United States. 2. Young women—United States—
Attitudes. 3. Women—United States—Social conditions—21st cen-
tury. 4. Feminist theory—United States. 5. Social change—United
States. I. Title: Reclaiming feminism for the 21st century.
II. Dicker, Rory Cooke, [date]. III. Piepmeier, Alison.
    HQ1426 .C284 2003
    305.42'0973—dc21   2002153489

 University Press of New England is a member of the
Green Press Initiative. The paper used in this book
meets their minimum requirement for recycled paper.

Acknowledgments

⸻⸻Any book is a collaborative effort, and this has certainly been the case with *Catching a Wave*. We have had much help in developing this book from its origins in a conversation we had after Rebecca Walker gave a talk at Vanderbilt. Along the way, we have attended regional and national conferences and symposia, conventions and panel discussions; in so doing, we have become part of a community of scholars and activists working on and in the third wave.

One of the wonderful fringe benefits of editing such a collection is the opportunity to get to know feminists in various fields from around the United States and Canada. Our contributors have been ideal, steadfastly revising based on our comments and undaunted by last-minute e-mail requests. They have taught us much about the third wave, and we feel lucky to have been able to work with them. We'd especially like to thank Jennifer Baumgardner and Amy Richards, who have shared their advice and experience and have consistently offered us generous assistance whenever we asked for it. Their willingness to advise us at the beginning of this project—when they didn't even know us—demonstrated for us their commitment to creating feminist community. Thanks to Jennifer Baumgardner for connecting us to a larger feminist community through her work with Katha Pollitt on the book's afterword. We appreciate the time and care Jennifer and Katha took in crafting such an insightful coda to *Catching a Wave*.

Many people have helped us improve the text. We'd like to thank our two outside readers for Northeastern University Press for their helpful and thoughtful feedback. We also appreciate the suggestions of Walter Biffle, Alyssa Harad, Astrid Henry, Amanda Kinard, Deandra Little, Eliza McGraw, and Tracy Moore, all of whom offered thoughts and advice that helped shape the introduction. (It goes without saying, of course, that all flaws are ours alone.) Also, many thanks to Michael Ames for helping us when we first began the process of navigating the publishing world.

We have had a great deal of hands-on assistance throughout this process. We are grateful to Stacie Furia, Liz Royal, Jen Howard, Whitney Bullock, and Nikki Williams for their attention and care to the manuscript. We couldn't have done it without you. Thanks to Gayle Parrott for her enthusiasm, encouragement, and love. Thanks, too, to Ronnie Steinberg and Beth Conklin for their support, both personally and financially. A summer research award from Westminster College also helped to defray expenses.

We have been pleased to work with Elizabeth Swayze at Northeastern University Press; her enthusiasm for this project from our initial meeting has encouraged us as the project has progressed. She is a wonderful hands-on editor who has been available and supportive throughout this process. We would also like to thank Ann Twombly, the production director at Northeastern, for her careful and meticulous work during the production of the book. Her attention to detail has strengthened the book.

I (Rory) would like to acknowledge the many friends whose provocative conversation and (sometimes) outrageous behavior have challenged my feminism over the years: thanks go to Cathy Wasserman, Amanda Kinard, Laura Kinard, Lady Smith, Carol Manthey, Antonia Moser, Lucy Appert, and Rebecca Shapiro. I thank the many feminist mentors I've been lucky to encounter and learn from, including the late Nancy A. Walker, Cecelia Tichi, Ronnie Steinberg, and, most recently, Carolyn Perry. My family has never stopped being a nurturing support system for me; I wouldn't be the person I am without the love of Ellen Dicker, Saul Dicker, Moira Mosco, John Dicker, Ella Mosco, and Alice Cooke. I also wouldn't be as sane, healthy, and happy without the love of Paul DeHart, a true friend. Finally, though, it is my great pleasure to thank Alison, whose humor, insight, and inspirations have reminded me what I love about scholarship and what scholarship should be about.

I (Alison) would like to thank the many wonderful feminists who have formed a community of love and political solidarity for me: thanks to Catherine Bush, Jay Crockett, Deandra Little, and Eliza McGraw. I have been fortunate to have teachers and mentors—including Cecelia Tichi, Ronnie Steinberg, Connie Hood, and Margery Hargrove—who have provided me with models of female empowerment. My students have been an inspiration—I can't imagine a better job than getting to talk to them about feminism every day. Thanks to my family for everything they give me: to mom, who gets more radical as she gets older; to dad, who always points out sexist commercials; and to Trey and Aaron, whom I would like to publicly "out" as feminists. Thanks to Walter, who is working with me every day to forge a new kind of marriage, one that is as feminist as both of us. Finally, I am very grateful that my partner in this project has been Rory, who balances me out, attends to details I miss, laughs with me, and helps me to work through my personal and political life. Who knew when we started this project what good friends we'd end up being?

Contents

CATCHING A WAVE

RORY DICKER & ALISON PIEPMEIER

Introduction

"As far as I can tell, the third wave is just the second wave with more lip gloss."
—Young woman at the National Women's Studies
Association conference, June 2001

We are tired of waiting. Sick and tired.

At Vanderbilt University's graduation ceremony in 2002, the top students in each of nine schools received awards. These were exceptional students whose accomplishments in scholarship, service, and leadership distinguished them from thousands of their peers who were also graduating on this day. Of these nine honorees, six were women. Presenting the awards were the deans of the students' schools. Of these nine deans, two were women—unsurprisingly, they were deans of the education and nursing schools. The remaining seven deans were men.

"So what?" you might say. If you'd been there, you might not even have noticed. Scenes such as this are so commonplace that they seem unremarkable, perhaps because, even thirty years after the start of the women's movement, we are still used to seeing men in positions of power. Although the presence of these six talented, achieving female students reveals the success of feminist efforts, the scarcity of highly placed women in university administrations, corporate America, and government—to name only the most obvious institutions—demonstrates our very real need for continued feminist activism. Young women today have more options available to them than at any other time in history, and because of these options, they feel, as we ourselves have felt, that not only can they accomplish anything they want to but there are no gender-based barriers; sexism, these young women are sure, is a thing of the past. Yet, as the above example illustrates, in spite

3

of these beliefs, societal structures have not changed as much as feminists might have hoped or expected.

When we point out these kinds of structural inequalities, we generally receive one of two responses. Some people dismiss us as hyperanalytical, oversensitive "feminists with a capital F" who are only wallowing in victimhood. To these people, there's really no need for feminism, anyway, so the subject of inequality seems irrelevant. Other people, those who are more sympathetic to the idea of women's empowerment, try to assuage us by telling us that things are getting better and have changed so much already. If we wait twenty years, they say, things will be much more equal.

This is what they were saying twenty years ago. We are tired of waiting.

In fact, if we were to be as patient as our sympathetic listeners, we might be waiting a long time. Although women have now entered traditionally male professions with such regularity that it may appear that there are no barriers to women's success, the fact remains that women are dramatically underrepresented in decision-making, power-brokering positions. To look at only one professional realm, top management: "Twenty-five years ago, graduating business school classes included 20 to 25 percent women; today, 99.94 percent of the CEOs, and 97.3 percent of the top earners are men."[1] These statistics reveal that women entered the corporate world in reasonably large percentages and with competitive educational backgrounds a generation ago. These women should be in the pipeline, assuming or being ready to assume significant leadership roles. They should be university deans, bank presidents, and members of Congress, but they are not. The solution to this lack of women in power is not to continue to wait. Indeed, as Susan Estrich informs us, if we keep waiting, "at the rate we're going, it will be another 270 years before women achieve parity as top managers in corporations and 500 years before we achieve equality in Congress."[2]

We can't wait that long. The alternative to waiting is waking up, recognizing the inequalities that surround us, and figuring out what we can do to redress the balance. To do these things, we need feminism, a social philosophy aimed at eradicating the pervasive sexism of our culture. The point is not that all women need to be CEOs or senators (as if they could) or that female leaders would necessarily have the interests of women at heart; instead, the point is that the lack of women in the pipeline is one sign of a deeply patriarchal culture that perpetuates sexist ideologies and systems. To combat this sexism, *Catching a Wave* contends that this generation needs a politicized, activist feminism that is grounded in the material realities and the cultural productions of life in the twenty-first century. We need a feminism that is dedicated to a radical, transformative political vision, a feminism that does not shy away from hard work but recognizes that changing the world is a difficult and necessary task, a feminism that utilizes the new technologies of the Internet, the playful world of fashion, and the more clear-cut activism of protest marches, a feminism that can engage with issues as diverse as women's sweatshop labor in global factories and violence against women expressed in popular music.

Though we often refer to our feminism as the third wave, we want to render problematic an easy understanding of what the third wave is. Typically, the third wave is thought of as a younger generation's feminism, one that rejects traditional—or stereotypical—understandings of feminism and as such is antithetical or oppositional to its supposed predecessor, the second wave. The feminism we claim, however, aligns itself with second wave strategies for recognizing and addressing structural inequalities. One such strategy is consciousness-raising, developed in the 1960s and 1970s. In their heyday, consciousness-raising (CR) groups offered a space for women to discuss their life experiences and feelings. What women often discovered in these groups was that problems that they thought were particular to them were shared by many others and were, in fact, part of a larger system of sexist practices. These groups launched much feminist activism and social change. We wanted to continue this activist tradition by using a consciousness-raising format in this book: rather than being organized into topical units, the essays in *Catching a Wave* are grouped in a way that mirrors the process of consciousness-raising itself. We decided to use this organizational pattern as a way first to highlight the social inequalities in the world today and then to politicize our readers to take action. Because these inequalities are so often obscured, the first step to a feminist consciousness is to recognize the status of women in the world.[3]

If you think that there's no need for feminism because the world is basically equal, consider this: women are 51 percent of the U.S. population, but only 13 of 100 U.S. senators and only 59 of 435 representatives are women. This means that women occupy only 13.8 percent of the seats in Congress. Only 2 of the 9 Supreme Court justices are women, and we have never had a female president or vice president.

Our lack of political power translates into economic inequality. Today, nationwide, when you control for factors such as age, experience, education, occupation, and industry, women earn around seventy-three cents on a man's dollar.[4] In fact, although we like to believe that we're making progress, the wage gap between women and men in managerial positions actually widened between 1995 and 2000.[5] As of 2002, only six women are CEOs of Fortune 500 companies.[6] Worldwide, when a woman does a job, even if that job is virtually identical to one performed by a man, the man's work is more valued and better compensated.[7] Women tend to be concentrated in the lowest occupational sectors; as a result, women and children constitute 70 percent of the world's impoverished people.[8] In the United States, "welfare reform" in the 1990s disproportionately affected women, shunting them into low-paying "women's" jobs—even when they were qualified for other kinds of work.[9]

Just as women's economic inequality reveals their low status, so does their treatment in personal relationships. Violence against women is a worldwide epidemic, affecting the health and well-being of countless women. In fact, according to the United Nations Population Fund, at least 1 in 3 women in the world has been physically or sexually abused by a man at some time in her life.[10] Every year, 700,000 women are raped in the United States, a country that claims to value women and provide for their safety; in this allegedly civil society, a woman is more likely to be killed at the hands of a man she loves than by anyone else.[11]

Worldwide, women's and girls' bodies are prey to abuse. More than 130 million women globally are affected by female genital mutilation (FGM), which involves the excision of the clitoris without anesthesia, and sometimes the slicing and sewing up of the entire vaginal area, leaving only a small hole for the elimination of urine and menstrual blood.[12] In some cases, the exploitation of female bodies becomes part of global economic strategy. For instance, many Western men travel to Thailand to participate in the thriving "sex tourism" industry there, paying to have sex with girls as young as six. The World Bank and the International Monetary Fund encourage this tourism as part of Thailand's "development."[13] Up to 4 million women and girls around the world are bought and sold into marriage, prostitution, or slavery every year.[14]

Our bodies are under attack in other ways as well. Reproductive rights for women in the United States are more threatened now than they've been in thirty years. Although abortion is technically legal, its availability is severely limited, with 86 percent of U.S. counties providing no access to abortion.[15] This is only going to get worse if the Supreme Court overturns *Roe v. Wade,* which seems likely if President Bush gets to nominate a new justice. The right to abortion is under attack, and, ironically, so is contraception: insurance companies in the United States cover half of the prescriptions for the erection-inducing drug Viagra, but only one-third of the prescriptions for birth control pills.[16]

Although the United States likes to tout its "family values," it has the worst parental leave policy of any industrialized nation. Only 50 percent of new parents in the United States are guaranteed parental leave—and legally they're guaranteed only twelve weeks, unpaid. Compare that to eighteen weeks in Great Britain, ten months in Italy, and almost a full year of paid parental leave in Norway and Sweden.[17] Given its policies, it comes as no surprise that the United States is the only industrialized nation in the world that has not signed the United Nations' Convention on the Elimination of All Forms of Discrimination Against Women (CEDAW), putting it in the company of countries such as Saudi Arabia and Sudan.

Being confronted with such sweeping inequalities may be surprising, given that many of us view injustice as something that happened in the past; if injustice does occur in the present, we assume it is an aberration, not a widespread or systemic problem. The facts we've just listed would suggest otherwise. We present these facts because a recognition that inequality not only exists but is indeed pervasive is necessary to an understanding of feminism. So is anger. Feminists have often been ridiculed for their anger, but this anger comes from an acknowledgment of social problems and a desire to improve the world. If we don't identify the ways in which women and girls are exploited globally—if we don't realize the reasons for feminist anger—then feminism, a movement concerned with eradicating inequality, will seem irrelevant, irrational, or even passé. Yet this movement is not at all out of date; in fact, *Catching a Wave* argues that, as we enter the new century, we can create a world we want to live in only with the help of a feminist consciousness.

The anger and passion that feminists express on behalf of women lead many people to label them man-haters. However, most feminist praxis operates not out of hatred of men but out of a deep commitment to women's lives and to redressing the injustices that they face. In its most basic sense, feminism calls for the social, political, and economic equality of women. While feminists have traditionally sought equality for women, more recently they have realized that the term "woman" is an inadequate category because of the many differences among women; to be effective, feminist practice must take these differences into account. The influential black feminist writer Barbara Smith encapsulates the multi-ethnic, multi-issue approach that must define feminism: "Feminism is the political theory and practice to free all women: women of color, working-class women, poor women, physically challenged women, lesbians, old women—as well as white economically privileged heterosexual women. Anything less than this is not feminism, but merely female self-aggrandizement."[18] As Smith notes, feminism is not simply about women's issues but is a broad-based political movement that seeks freedom for all those who are oppressed. *Catching a Wave* is a call to action for all of us who have benefited from feminism's gains; as we discuss later, we believe that political engagement and activism are crucial components of a feminist consciousness in the twenty-first century.

THE WAVES: UNDERSTANDING FEMINIST HISTORY

The history of feminism in the United States is often explained by using the metaphor of waves. According to this language, the first wave of the women's movement began in 1848 at the women's rights convention in Seneca Falls, New York, where Elizabeth Cady Stanton and her colleagues wrote the "Declaration of Sentiments." The central goal of this wave was gaining a legal identity for women that included the right to own property, to sue, to form contracts, and to vote. Although this wave is widely assumed to have ebbed with the ratification of the Nineteenth Amendment in 1920, feminist historians such as Sheila Ruth remind us that women from the 1920s to the 1960s simply channeled their energies into other social justice and activist work.[19] Spurred by the civil rights movement, countercultural protests, and the publication of crucial texts, including Betty Friedan's *The Feminine Mystique* (1962), feminist awareness and activism gained momentum in the 1960s. This heightened activity, referred to now as the second wave, focused on gaining full human rights for women: some of its central demands were equal opportunities in employment and education, access to child care and abortion, the eradication of violence against women, and the passage of the Equal Rights Amendment. Second wave activists critiqued the notion of biological or inherent differences between the sexes, contending instead that these differences are socially constructed.

In the 1970s and 1980s, U.S. women of color and lesbians, responding to their marginalization by the mainstream white, middle-class women's movement, extended the insights of second wave feminism by theorizing about their experiences. They called for a recognition that identity is intersectional—in other words, that gender, race, ethnicity, class, and sexuality are interlocking and that oppression is not experienced simply along one axis. These women, who labeled themselves U.S. third world feminists, questioned the tendency within the second wave to reduce the category of "woman" to its essence. In their writings, U.S. third world feminists moved the concepts of difference and diversity to the foreground, reminding us that even if sisterhood is global, not all women's lives and experiences are identical. As Leslie Heywood and Jennifer Drake have asserted, U.S. third world feminism created the space for the emergence of a third wave of feminism: "[T]he definitional moment of third wave feminism has been theorized as proceeding from critiques of the white women's movement that were initiated by women of color, as well as from the many instances of coalition work undertaken by U.S. third world feminists."[20] The third wave thus recognizes that the differences among women are as substantial as the differences between women and men: the category of "woman" is no longer the only identity worth examining.

Third wave feminism represents a reinvigorated feminist movement emerging from a late twentieth-century world. Many of the goals of the third wave are similar to those of the second wave, though some, such as its insistence on women's diversity, are new. *Catching a Wave* contends, however, that third wave feminism's political activism on behalf of women's rights is shaped by—and responds to—a world of global capitalism and information technology, postmodernism and postcolonialism, and environmental degradation. We no longer live in the world that feminists of the second wave faced. Third wavers, who came of age in the late twentieth century and after, are therefore concerned not simply with "women's issues" but with a broad range of interlocking topics—topics, as Jennifer L. Pozner notes in her essay in this volume, ranging from protests of the World Economic Forum and welfare reform to activism on behalf of independent media outlets. Just as it is interested in a multiplicity of issues, the third wave operates from the assumption that identity is multifaceted and layered. Since no monolithic version of "woman" exists, we can no longer speak with confidence of "women's issues"; instead, we need to consider that such issues are as diverse as the many women who inhabit our planet. Although third wave feminists have a reputation for sexiness and frivolity—a reputation voiced in our epigraph—this doesn't represent the heart of the third wave as we see it. At its best, the third wave engages with a diverse spectrum of issues in ways that are passionate as well as playful, inclusive as well as rigorous, making use of the best of second wave theory and strategy as well as critiques of second wave feminism. *Catching a Wave* identifies and calls for a third wave of feminism that is politically conscious, grounded in the realities of life in the twenty-first century, and willing to engage in collective action in order to address injustice.

Rebecca Walker coined the term "third wave" in "Becoming the Third Wave," an essay published in *Ms.* magazine in 1992. Walker's essay was a response to the Clarence Thomas–Anita Hill hearings and the media's claim that we had entered an age of postfeminism. Indeed, the early 1990s was a pivotal time for young women and men who, after a decade or more of the conservative policies of Reagan and Bush, were introduced to feminism by books such as Susan Faludi's *Backlash* (1991) and Naomi Wolf's *The Beauty Myth* (1991) and then were galvanized to action by the sexism revealed in the Thomas-Hill hearings. This inspiration and outrage began to be channeled into new forms of feminist activism; for instance, in 1992, Walker, Amy Richards, and others, including some men, started the Third Wave Foundation, the only organization devoted to feminists between the ages of fifteen and thirty. Other young feminists, like the Riot Grrrls based in Olympia, Washington, used their punk sensibilities to create music that proclaimed their defiance of sexist norms and confining gender roles. Young women who wanted to read edgier publications—magazines that represented their lives in ways that the older, less playful *Ms.* couldn't or didn't—created *Bust, Bitch,* and countless 'zines.

These examples illustrate the third wave's creation of an activist culture. Despite this activism, third wave work hasn't coalesced into a larger, easily definable movement. This is one reason that older feminists and the media alike have criticized younger feminists for their lack of political involvement and even for their apathy. Another reason, of course, is that many of us today—women and men, feminists and nonfeminists—are less politically energized than previous generations, perhaps in part because third wavers have benefited from the results of second wave activism, almost without realizing it. Third wave feminists may be less active because, for their generation, "the presence of feminism . . . is taken for granted." As Jennifer Baumgardner and Amy Richards explain, "For our generation, feminism is like fluoride. We scarcely notice that we have it—it's simply in the water."[21] Although not all populations receive this water equally, as a whole, this explanation captures the chronological and ideological distinction between the second and third waves.[22] Because those of us who have reached adulthood in the late twentieth century have grown up in a world not only shaped by feminism but also saturated with backlash rhetoric and politics, we see the world differently from the way previous generations have. We experience hard-fought feminist gains as fundamental rights, without recognizing the efforts that went into securing those rights. We expect many feminist ideals to be part of our culture, but many of us have no idea whether these ideals are being met or how, even, to agitate for change.

The third wave has been around for ten years now. During this time, it has been written about in various ways. Much third wave discourse has been personal and anecdotal; indeed, two of the best-known works on third wave feminism, Barbara Findlen's *Listen Up: Voices from the Next Feminist Generation* (1995) and Rebecca Walker's *To Be Real: Telling the Truth and Changing the Face of Feminism* (1995), are collections of first-person narratives. In both books, the use of a personal-essay format was deliberate. As Findlen explains in her introduction, "Individual women's experiences of sexism have always been an important basis for political awareness and action. This collection gives voice to young feminists' personal experiences because they have often been, and continue to be, our point of entry into feminism."[23] Both anthologies avoid the emphasis on white women's experiences that was prevalent in much second wave writing; the diverse essays show their authors exploring their own intersectional identities. The essays, particularly those in *Listen Up*, are engaging self-examinations that often point to broader cultural and social problems. As early works of the third wave, *Listen Up* and *To Be Real* helped to articulate a third wave identity, giving voice to the third wave and thus introducing readers to this feminist generation and its problems. However, neither anthology offers a sustained analysis of how these personal stories fit into a larger political picture. Because these collections fail to employ the second wave tenet that the "personal is political," an entire element of potential analysis is elided. While these anthologies do engage in the first step of consciousness-raising, *Catching a Wave* contends that it is time to move beyond personal accounts to political and collective action.

Later writing has begun the process of analyzing, theorizing, and historicizing the third wave.[24] A project that has proved influential for scholars of the third wave is *Third Wave Agenda: Being Feminist, Doing Feminism* (1997), a collection edited by Leslie Heywood and Jennifer Drake. The book's introduction offers a useful theoretical foundation that includes a definition of the third wave "as a movement that contains elements of second wave critique of beauty culture, sexual abuse, and power structures while it also acknowledges and makes use of the pleasure, danger, and defining power of those structures."[25] According to Heywood and Drake, because of its willingness to use beauty, sex, and power strategically, even as it criticizes traditional definitions of or approaches to them, the third wave occupies a space defined by seeming paradox and contradiction, an idea that has become a refrain throughout third wave discourse.[26] In *Manifesta: Young Women, Feminism, and the Future* (2000), Jennifer Baumgardner and Amy Richards situate the third wave in the context of feminist history, noting young feminists' debts to previous generations. Perhaps the main contribution of *Manifesta* is its emphasis on activism; in particular, its thirteen-point agenda reveals the authors' investment in teaching others how to transform the world that they live in. In so doing, Baumgardner and Richards refute the common assumption that today's youth are apathetic and unwilling to expend the energy it takes to make lasting change. Baumgardner and Richards reflect on activism and leadership in an essay in this volume.

Catching a Wave continues the discussion begun in all of these books.[27] Unlike texts such as *Listen Up* and *To Be Real, Catching a Wave* offers essays that use personal experience as a bridge to larger political and theoretical explorations of the third wave; these essays function as the very tools we need to effect change. In the essay "'That's Not Fair!' Nurturing Girls' Natural Feminism," for instance, Nancy Gruver demonstrates the way in which a personal reaction to the inadequacy of girls' magazines led her and many others to become active advocates for change. Similarly, in her essay on feminism and Judaism, Alana Suskin shows how her own feeling of exclusion from Jewish worship practices prompted her both to question the egalitarianism of her faith and to channel her energies into political protest. Just as important as these individual essays, though, is the argument that they make collectively about the need for a feminist consciousness. Arranged in a consciousness-raising format, the essays in *Catching a Wave* mirror a person's process of self-discovery and identification as a feminist. We used this configuration deliberately: because backlash rhetoric and our own complacency have inured many of us to inequalities that persist around us, we wanted to show our readers how to wake up to these injustices and begin to do something to redress them. The consciousness-raising format provides a model of the transformations involved in coming to feminist consciousness: becoming aware of inequalities, identifying our own part in them, and then taking steps to change them. As the structuring principle of the book, this consciousness-raising model will, we think, provide a tool both for changing people's minds about feminism and for changing the world.

Perhaps more than other books, *Catching a Wave* questions and critiques the third wave. Because they were early texts in the field, *Listen Up, To Be Real,* and *Third Wave Agenda* sought to claim a place for young feminism. Now that the third wave is a decade old, it is time to take stock and think about its theoretical contributions. We argue that the third wave has less to do with a neat generational divide than with a cultural context: the third wave consists of those of us who have developed our sense of identity in a world shaped by technology, global capitalism, multiple models of sexuality, changing national demographics, and declining economic vitality. Third wavers often come to feminist consciousness through the academy, an academy shaped by feminism, poststructuralism, and postmodernism. The essays in *Catching a Wave* refine our understanding of the third wave by examining the terrain on which third wave ideals play out, interrogating perceived differences between the second and third waves, and suggesting new ideological battles that feminism's next generation should undertake. Though the book is grounded in the realities of the life of a young feminist in the twenty-first century, we are ultimately more interested in reclaiming feminism as a much-needed force for social change, as our subtitle suggests, than in making a case for the third wave in particular.

THE SECOND AND THIRD WAVES: CONFLICT OR COMMUNITY?

Although claiming the presence of the third wave has been an exuberant act for young feminists, it has been seen by many in the second wave as profoundly alienating, an act of amputation. This perception is not entirely inaccurate; many third wave feminists perceive the second wave as a movement to which they don't want to belong, and they are not quiet about these feelings. According to many third wavers, second wave feminism is repressive and restrictive, and this is one reason that the third wave has had to break away and formulate new ways of being feminist. As Rebecca Walker explains in the introduction to *To Be Real:*

> For many of us it seems that to be a feminist in the way that we have seen or understood feminism is to conform to an identity and way of living that doesn't allow for individuality, complexity, or less than perfect personal histories. We fear that the identity will dictate and regulate our lives, instantaneously pitting us against someone, forcing us to choose inflexible and unchanging sides, female against male, black against white, oppressed against oppressor, good against bad.[28]

Walker goes on to describe a feminism that is "simply another impossible contrivance of perfect womanhood."[29] Walker's characterization of the second wave rehearses the story told by Katie Roiphe in *The Morning After* (1993) that second wave feminists hate sex and perpetuate Victorian sexual ideals. In these stories, second wave feminists are cold figures with an agenda more than a personality; they seem somewhat like the often-invoked "feminazis."

Descriptions like Walker's and Roiphe's are echoed at feminist and women's studies conferences, in third wave books, on feminist listservs, and even in popular media. In all these venues, the relationship between the second and third waves of feminism is characterized as confrontational and uncooperative, even hostile. This emphasis on intergenerational conflict has certainly captured the media's attention: typically, the media describe one generation as the victim and the other as the perpetrator, with frequent role reversals, depending on the cultural climate. Though there's no denying that this makes a good story, it's really just the latest incarnation of the feminist catfight. For example, an episode of *Oprah* in 2002 featured younger and older feminists in conversation. Instead of using this hour to educate Oprah's 6 million viewers about violence against women, pay equity, and the myriad other issues on which feminists of both generations collaborate, the show depicted family dysfunction and culminated in the younger feminists obsequiously thanking the older ones. This staging of conflict and reconciliation ultimately works to dissipate feminist energies and to trivialize the real work being done in the movement.

Instead of focusing on the alleged conflict between the generations, we see many strands of continuity between the second and third waves.[30] After all, the goals set by the second wave have not yet been accomplished, and thus the current generation of feminists is—and should be—working on many of the same issues as the second wave, often alongside older feminists. Indeed, in "Please—Stop Thinking about Tomorrow: Building a Feminist Movement on College Campuses for *Today*," Sarah Boonin describes not just her frustration with the antagonism she sees between older and younger feminists but also the intergenerational collaboration between the second wave Feminist Majority Foundation and third wave campus leaders. Boonin's essay shows that, while some third wave writers may depict older feminism as puritanical, repressive, and homogeneous, such a picture is a distortion that relies on a reductive rendering of an incredibly varied social movement. The second wave feminists we've met and worked with— women such as Robin Morgan, Gloria Steinem, Susan Douglas, and Katha Pollitt, as well as our own personal mentors—aren't strict disciplinarians monitoring our feminism for its allegiance to their agenda. They aren't puritanical figures who shy from anything sexy or fun, either. Although there are conflicts between the generations—second wavers may see third wavers as more concerned with image than with material realities, and younger feminists may see older feminists as essentializing gender and unconcerned with diversity—there is far more continuity than discord between the two waves.

Nonetheless, there are certainly some differences. One way that the third wave distinguishes itself from the second wave is through its emphasis on paradox, conflict, multiplicity, and messiness. This generation's feminism is often informed by postmodern, poststructuralist theories of identity; as a result, we are able to see the constructed nature of identity as well as the ways in which gender may be a performance that can be manipulated and politically altered as it is performed. Because this theoretical framework calls into question the very idea of a unified self, it allows for a playful incorporation of performed identities, even when they contradict one another. This contradiction and multiplicity of identities plays itself out especially in third wavers' love/hate relationship with the media and pop culture. For instance, in

"Do the Ladies Run This . . . ? Some Thoughts on Hip-Hop Feminism,"
Gwendolyn D. Pough describes her problematic relationship to hip-
hop: as a feminist, she deplores its sexism, but as a music lover, she enjoys its soul and rhythm. Another kind of multiplicity important to the
third wave has less to do with performance and more to do with reality: third wavers themselves are multiracial, multi-ethnic, and multi-
issued.

Although we see efforts to embrace diversity as a valid and important
theoretical contribution, we are troubled by the ease with which scholars, writers, and activists lay claim to multiplicity in third wave discourse. That is, sometimes it seems as if everything and everyone can
fit within the third wave—it doesn't matter what they actually think,
do, or believe. We call this the "feminist free-for-all": under this rubric,
feminism doesn't involve a set of core beliefs that one shares or goals
that one works for, but instead involves claiming beliefs and ideas one
day and discarding them the next, as they go in and out of fashion or
as they become personally or intellectually difficult to sustain. This is
the worst interpretation of bell hooks's edict that "feminism is for everybody": it implies that anybody can be a feminist, regardless of her
or his actions.[31]

The seduction of the "feminist free-for-all" is evident in much third
wave writing. For instance, in an essay in the perceptive and hard-
hitting collection *Jane Sexes It Up* (2002), a book that explores third
wave feminism and heterosexuality, Merri Lisa Johnson challenges
some views of the feminist theorist bell hooks. In an earlier essay
(1984), hooks argued that lifestyle choices must not undercut feminist
politics. To that end, she asserted that feminists concerned with eradicating violence against women must not perpetuate violent models of
sexuality in their own lives; in particular, hooks demanded that feminists relearn desire so that they would not be turned on by hypermasculine, oppressive men. Although Johnson agrees with hooks's
goal of ending violence against women, she takes issue with hooks's
agenda. Almost as if she is echoing Rebecca Walker's complaint about
the difficulty of conforming to a rigid second wave identity, Johnson
notes hooks's "old-school feminist style" and suggests that her demand
is "daunting in the discipline it would require." She goes on to say, "I

won't do it. I am not that feminist, not that kind of feminist."[32] Rather than exploring why hooks's ideas upset her, she simply backs away.

This moment in an otherwise-probing essay is emblematic of a key conflict between second and third wave feminists: many in the third wave—in their attempt to complicate and broaden feminism, in their attempt to bring postmodern and poststructuralist theoretical concepts to bear on feminist theory and praxis—run the risk of abandoning feminist politics. In other words, Johnson seems to be just on the verge of saying, "I don't want to change my desires because it's just too hard." And the unspoken assumption behind this statement is that "feminism's not supposed to be that hard." It's one thing to examine hooks's demand and conclude that it isn't theoretically sound; it's another to reject it because it would demand too much work from us.

Granted, there are many ways of going about changing the world, and one of the theoretical contributions of third wave feminism is the notion that politics isn't that simple—and neither are identities, desires, or the intersections of our internal and external landscapes. Johnson's interrogation of the congruence between feminist identity and performed desire represents a theoretical contribution of the third wave; Johnson questions whether one's desires need to conform to one's politics. We think that the third wave impulse to challenge certain perceptions of what feminism is or how it should be performed is valid, as is the impulse to make feminism as inviting as possible to a broad range of people. However, we contend that this invitation to feminism must be politically rigorous; rather than emptying feminism of its political content, we must embrace feminism's potential to transform our lives and our world. And if someone's challenge to feminism simply rests on the difficulty feminist ideology poses, then she runs the risk of making feminism nothing but a posture.

Unfortunately, the feminist free-for-all is what many people—particularly older feminists—think of as the third wave. And it is one face of this generation. But it's reductive to see this as the only image of the third wave. As many third wavers realize, it's fine to engage with the world in a playful, individualistic way, but for that engagement to be informed by feminism, it has to take into account the power relations surrounding gender, race, class, and sexual orientation. We live in a society undergirded by racism and sexism and propelled by capitalism; in such a culture, we are all shaped by the operation of invisible systems of power and privilege. A feminist perspective acknowledges this reality and seeks to change it.

Ultimately, to be effective, feminism must embrace action, even when action calls us to make difficult choices. As bell hooks asserts, "Feminist movement to end sexist oppression actively engages participants in revolutionary struggle. Struggle is rarely safe or pleasurable."[33] In this era of consumerism and instant gratification, we don't hear much about committing ourselves to a difficult struggle, and yet this must be the guiding philosophy of feminist consciousness in the twenty-first century. In "Becoming the Third Wave," Rebecca Walker acknowledges this imperative, explaining: "I realize that I must undergo a transformation if I am truly committed to women's empowerment. My involvement must reach beyond my own voice in discussion, beyond voting, beyond reading feminist theory. My anger and awareness must translate into tangible action. . . . To be a feminist is to integrate an ideology of equality and female empowerment into the very fiber of my life."[34] Here, Walker demands that she embody a radicalized feminist consciousness; she calls upon herself to stop merely talking about women's issues and to live her life in a way that is not only intellectually engaged but also activist. Every action she takes needs to align with this political ideology, she argues, so that her inner consciousness and her outer behavior are seamlessly integrated. As Merri Lisa Johnson suggests, the kinds of commitment hooks and Walker articulate are "daunting in the discipline [they] . . . require," but this level of political commitment—or at least a striving toward it—is necessary for feminism to continue as a viable movement. We do not claim to be the inventors of this call; it is a legacy of the second wave that feminists of the next generation must be willing to embrace. Although a third wave commitment to political struggle may look different—it may focus on cultural productions and individual identity, for instance—this engagement with personal and political transformation remains the core of both waves of feminism.

Contemporary feminist activism reveals not only a commitment to political struggle but also the creative energy inherent in such action. For example, the Street Harassment Project, based in New York City, insists that the streets are public space and must be safe for all women. Its activism includes handing a card to a catcaller. One side of the card says, "Hey, guys! Wanna get laid?" The other side says, "Then stop harassing women!!!" Another group, the National Asian Women's Health Organization (NAWHO), focuses on health equity for Asian women and their families. Founded in 1993 in San Francisco, NAWHO has promoted the role of Asian women as the "change agents" of their families, realizing that only through their education and empowerment will appropriate health care reach the Asian American community. Although it is not a project or organization, the annual Southern Girls Convention, held at college campuses around the South, brings young feminists together for informal collaboration and discussion on topics ranging from do-it-yourself health care to fighting hate crimes. These examples of feminist organizing are significant because they reveal an engagement in transformational activism. We don't mean to suggest that these groups have reinvented the activist wheel; indeed, the tactics and goals of these groups bear a strong resemblance to those of second wave groups. The point, though, is that much creativity and many insights are possible when people commit to changing their world. At its best, the third wave embodies the rage and the joy of feminism. By taking much that is good from the second wave, listening to critiques of earlier feminism's lack of diversity, and responding to a changing world, the third wave has the potential to be the second wave's better self.

Yet, if there are so many connections, if the third wave borrows second wave activist strategies and operates from the same belief that feminism is a transformational politics, is the third wave actually an independent entity—a movement with its own identity? Although we and our authors use the "wave" terminology to describe feminism, mainly because it provides a sense of solidarity and identity for young feminists, we recognize that this rhetoric is problematic.[35] Talking about a third wave may divide older and younger feminists because it implies that the second wave is over and done with. It is clear to us that this is not the case. This kind of definitional mapping of the third wave strikes us as reductive and risks essentializing—and, indeed, creating—differences between generations of feminists. This clear, distinct naming and defining is certainly an easy move to make; at the beginning of this project, we unproblematically assumed that *Catching a*

Wave was a book about the third wave. Now we see that, although this is a book about the third wave, what we mean by that is very different.

CONSCIOUSNESS-RAISING AND *CATCHING A WAVE*

At a recent lecture, the second wave feminist activist Robin Morgan discussed the involvement of young people in feminism. In particular, she addressed the idea that older feminists should "pass the torch" to the next generation. Morgan chided younger feminists to "get your own damned torch. I'm still using mine. And we need all the light we can get." Although Morgan's unwillingness to have the older generation give up its torch and pass it on to the younger folks is valid, our concern is that many young people don't know how to pick up their own torch. They lack the models, the sense of community, and the sense of their own power. The consciousness-raising model that *Catching a Wave* employs shows how to gain the knowledge and the power. Consciousness-raising groups and the model these groups employed were incredibly effective in the 1960s and 1970s, providing not only a feminist awakening but also a means to bridge the personal and the political. Many essay collections rely on thematic organization; the essays in *Catching a Wave,* however, are arranged to take a reader through the stages of consciousness raising. The essays ask the reader not to become an expert on the content but to begin to see the world from a feminist perspective.

The first step in claiming feminism is to recognize that sexism exists and that feminism is therefore still necessary. The book begins with "Needing Feminism," a section that demonstrates that, in spite of the strides made by second wave feminism, traditional structures of oppression continue to maintain power. The essays in this section point out the inequalities that persist in the news media, popular culture, and literature. In "The 'Big Lie': False Feminist Death Syndrome, Profit, and the Media," Jennifer L. Pozner draws readers' attention to the political power of the media: "By determining who gets to speak and who is excluded from this ongoing conversation, as well as which issues are discussed and how they are framed, the media have the power to maintain the status quo or challenge the dominant order." Further, Pozner asserts that the corporate-controlled mainstream media not only distort public understanding of feminism but also present a view of the world that obscures and perpetuates real inequalities. Susannah B. Mintz's "In a Word, *Baywatch*" examines representations of women on some of the most popular television shows today. Mintz notes that, even when these programs proclaim that they are breaking new ground by dismantling sexist stereotypes, they depict women as vacuous, silenced, or sexual objects. She writes that "those very shows that present women as comfortably and securely 'liberated' are often the blithest perpetrators of stereotyped attitudes about gender." The larger media structures examined in Pozner's and Mintz's essays not only affect our public world but also shape the self-images and the choices available to people—especially adolescent girls. In the final essay in the section, "Reviving Lolita; or, Because Junior High Is Still Hell," Alyssa Harad notes that "girls still find themselves, in a thousand large and small ways, forced to choose between pursuing their sexual desire and pursuing the power that comes from being at ease with their human selves." Harad's essay critiques society's sexualization of girls and theorizes ways of understanding female sexual desire. Together, the essays in this section argue persuasively that patriarchal and racist structures dominate our public rhetoric and our private understandings of ourselves.

The ability to recognize injustice is only the first part of consciousness-raising. Essays in "Coming to Feminism" address the process of beginning to identify oneself as feminist, a process made more difficult by the pervasive antifeminist rhetoric of our backlash culture. As essays in this section note, overcoming this hostile climate becomes easier with the help of feminist mentoring. Nancy Gruver, the founder of *New Moon: The Magazine for Girls and Their Dreams*, argues that, although girls have a natural sense of outrage at the world's injustices, the process of socialization into womanhood teaches them to swallow their feminist voices. In "'That's Not Fair!' Nurturing Girls' Natural Feminism," Gruver asserts that, "to change girls' mistaken ideas about feminism and to join with them in a common pursuit of justice," older women, including those in college, "must challenge [their] own assumptions, exercise new muscles, and change [their] own behavior." Exchanging ideas between older and younger women is likewise the subject of "Voices and Visions: A Mother and Daughter Discuss Coming to Feminism and Being Feminist." In this dialogue, Roxanne Harde and Erin Harde grapple with Roxanne's second wave feminist identification and Erin's reluctance to label herself a feminist. By sharing the experiences that have brought them to feminism, this mother and daughter model the kind of cross-generational conversation that Gruver feels is necessary. In the final essay of the section, Sarah Boonin discusses feminist mentorship not only at a personal level but also at an institutional one. In "Please—Stop Thinking about Tomorrow: Building a Feminist Movement on College Campuses for *Today*," Boonin describes her efforts to bring more students into the work of the Feminist Majority Foundation. The key to those efforts, she asserts, is recognizing young people as co-leaders. According to the pieces in this section, coming to feminism means taking our insights and experiences seriously. Although a feminist mentor can help in this process, ultimately it is most important for each one of us to develop the ability to interrogate the world and our place in it and to identify the role feminism can play in changing it.

Even after we have come to feminism, we are challenged by backlash images that demonize feminism as threatening, deviant, and irrelevant. To counter these images, the essays in "Recognizing Feminism" argue that, once we identify ourselves as feminists, we begin to notice a range of feminist activities in seemingly unlikely places. In "Who's the Next Gloria? The Quest for the Third Wave Superleader," Jennifer Baumgardner and Amy Richards disclose the prevalent tendency on the part of media and foundations to bemoan the lack of young leadership. Baumgardner and Richards offer a new paradigm of young feminist leadership, one that values women's grassroots activism and organizing. Based on this new model, they see feminist leadership everywhere. Similarly, Michele Byers identifies feminist action and engagement in a popular television show. Her essay, *"Buffy the Vampire Slayer:* The Next Generation of Television," asserts that "it is hard not to recognize [the show] as articulating a vision of feminism, albeit one that is primarily white and middle class." Although *Buffy*'s feminism has its limitations—in particular, it replicates white privilege and idealized body types—the show's vision of female power asks us to think of heroism in terms of a female leader. The final essay of the section moves us from a consideration of Buffy's powerful white body to an examination of the feminist empowerment of Arab and Arab American women's lives. Given the many stereotypes that inform mainstream perceptions in the United States, such an analysis might seem counterintuitive; however, as Susan Muaddi Darraj argues, feminism is organic to the lives of Arab women. In "Third Wave, Third World Feminism(s): The Evolution of Arab American Feminism," Darraj asserts that third wave feminism needs to bring together first world and third world women. Only when this interaction takes place, she argues, can the real work of making better feminist movement begin. Because the essays in this section address a wide range of topics, they illustrate that far from being an irrelevant or outdated ideology, feminism is a vibrant, living, far-reaching movement. The pieces not only enable us to recognize a history of women's action but also allow us to develop new tools and language to perform feminism in areas as disparate as grassroots organizing, popular culture, and cross-cultural communication.

One of the strengths of feminism is its self-awareness and self-criticism. Because of feminists' willingness to identify and rectify the shortfalls of feminism, feminist theory is continually revitalized. The essays in "Redefining Feminism" illustrate ways in which young feminists are examining and critiquing feminism. Astrid Henry's "Feminism's Family Problem: Feminist Generations and the Mother-Daughter Trope" describes the somewhat problematic characterization of the relationship between second and third wave feminism as a mother-daughter relationship. She warns, "a cohesive generational unit is itself always a fiction. . . . Even as we use the often-productive concept of generations, we must be wary of the ways in which it provides a reductive image of relationships between women, feminisms, and historical periods." Henry's essay offers a framework for assessing other third wave critiques of the second wave. The other two essays in the section offer specific redefinitions of feminism. Gwendolyn D. Pough's "Do the Ladies Run This . . . ? Some Thoughts on Hip-Hop Feminism" contends that feminism needs to make use of hip-hop discourse in order to counter sexist and materialistic messages currently being sent to young women and men of color. In "The Transfeminist Manifesto," Emi Koyama redefines feminism by demanding the inclusion of transgendered, transsexual, and intersex people, a group that has been ignored or has been viewed with suspicion by mainstream white feminists. Koyama asserts that "transfeminism is primarily a movement by and for trans women who view their liberation to be intrinsically linked to the liberation of all women and beyond." Together, these pieces demonstrate that new voices can change feminist discourse and practice. By launching and responding to critiques, young feminists, in particular, play a crucial role in shaping feminism into a more diverse and effective social force.

The final stage in consciousness-raising involves activism: taking a feminist awareness and using it to effect change in the larger world. While essays throughout *Catching a Wave* have offered glimpses of activism, the pieces in "Doing Feminism" provide more sustained models for young feminist activism. In "Hearing the Daughter Voice: The *Bat Kol* as Rrrabbi Grrrl," Alana Suskin asserts that a feminist perspective can help return Judaism to its activist roots. Suskin explains, "[f]eminism taught me that to do God's will means to listen to people's pain, but then to take action to change society so that people do not have to adjust to injustice." Just as Suskin describes working within and against the patriarchal structure of Judaism, Mimi Schippers's "Rocking the Gender Order" analyzes the ways alternative hard rockers critique the hypermasculinized world of rock music even as they participate in it. The musicians Schippers interviews use their performance as a way to redefine what it means to be a rocker; as a result, their performance is their feminist activism. The artist/activist Kristina Sheryl Wong works in a medium that is much newer than the rock concert: through her mock mail-order bride/fake porn Web site, Wong has created a new feminist space, one that has, in effect, revolutionized activism. As Wong explains in "Pranks and Fake Porn: Doing Feminism My Way," her site is subversive because it targets both those who are uninterested in Asian issues and those who are surfing for Asian porn and thus participating in the commodification and exploitation of Asian women. The essays in this section reveal that activist work can take some unconventional forms; we see that young feminists' activism is not just passionate, creative, and cool but also effective and inspired—in fact, it is so effective precisely because of the passion behind it.

These activist projects reveal what the other essays in *Catching a Wave* confirm: many of us aren't waiting anymore. We aren't waiting for someone else to correct the injustices and inequalities that we see around us. We are taking action, claiming feminism as our own, and using our political commitments to take responsibility for the world we live in and want to improve. We are forming communities and working collectively because the second wave concept of collective action is an imperative today. While we can't say when social structures will change, we believe that they will, especially if we work together. We won't have to wait forever.

NOTES

1. Susan Estrich, *Sex and Power* (New York: Riverhead Books, 2000), 72.

2. Ibid., 28.

3. The list that follows is inspired by the one in the introduction to Susan Faludi's *Backlash* (New York: Anchor, 1991).

4. National Committee on Pay Equity, "Little Progress on Closing Wage Gap in 2000" in "Pay Equity Fact Sheets," http://www.feminist.com/fairpay/f_wagegap.htm (May 15, 2002).

5. Equality 2020 GAO Report, "Women in Management," http://www.equality2020.org/women.pdf (May 15, 2002).

6. Molly Manchenton, "Feeling the Heat," *Eagle-Tribune,* March 17, 2002, http://www.eagletribune.com/news/stories/20020317/BU_001.htm (May 15, 2002).

7. Shawn Meghan Burn, *Women across Cultures: A Global Perspective* (Mountain View, Calif.: Mayfield, 2000), 13.

8. Amnesty International, *Interact: A Quarterly Bulletin on Women's Human Rights,* spring 2000, http://amnestyusa.org/women/21_century.html (May 15, 2002).

9. "Working First but Working Poor: The Need for Education and Training Following Welfare Reform," Executive Summary, Institute for Women's Policy Research and the NOW Legal Defense and Education Fund, September 2001, http://www.iwpr.org/pdf/workpr.pdf (May 15, 2002). For a discussion of women's work post–welfare reform, see Barbara Ehrenreich's *Nickel and Dimed: On (Not) Getting by in America* (New York: Metropolitan, 2001).

10. World Health Organization, "Violence against Women Information Pack," http://www.who.int/frh-whd/VAW/infopack/English/VAW_infopack.htm (May 15, 2002).

11. "Violence against Women Statistics," http://www.vday.org/index2.cfm?ArticleID=522 (May 15, 2002).

12. World Health Organization, "Violence against Women Information Pack."

13. Betty Rogers, "Bitter Harvest," *Ms.,* October/November 1999, 45–53.

14. United Nations Population Fund, "Trafficking in Human Misery," http://www.unfpa.org/gender/trafficking.htm (May 15, 2002).

15. Alan Guttmacher Institute, "Facts in Brief, Induced Abortion," http://www.agi-usa.org/pubs/fb_induced_abortion.html (May 15, 2002).

16. Jennifer L. Pozner, "Viagra: A Tale of Two Pills," http://www.fwhc.org/viagra.htm (May 15, 2002).

17. Ellen Bravo, *The Job-Family Challenge: A 9 to 5 Guide* (New York: Wiley, 1995); Burn, *Women across Cultures,* 113–15.

18. Barbara Smith, "Racism and Women's Studies," in *All the Women Are White, All the Blacks Are Men, But Some of Us Are Brave,* ed. G. Hull, P. Scott, and B. Smith (New York: Feminist Press, 1982).

19. Sheila Ruth, "Feminist Activism: Historical Context," in *Issues in Feminism,* 4th ed., ed. Sheila Ruth (Mountain View, Calif.: Mayfield, 1997), 487.

20. Leslie Heywood and Jennifer Drake, *Third Wave Agenda* (Minneapolis: University of Minnesota Press, 1997), 8.

21. Jennifer Baumgardner and Amy Richards, *Manifesta: Young Women, Feminism, and the Future* (New York: Farrar, Straus and Giroux, 2000), 17.

22. We thank Alyssa Harad for sharing this insight with us.

23. Barbara Findlen, *Listen Up: Voices from the Next Feminist Generation,* 2d ed. (Seattle: Seal, 2001), xv.

24. *Hypatia: A Journal of Feminist Philosophy* devoted a special issue to third wave feminism in 1997. Articles in this issue tried to define the third wave, positioning it in relation to the second wave, postmodernism, and postfeminism.

25. Heywood and Drake, *Third Wave Agenda,* 3.

26. In addition, Heywood and Drake let their subjectivity mark the boundaries of the third wave, defining this wave as coterminous with "Generation X," and marking out years in which third wavers were born (1963–1974), a move that would seem to ignore many of the young women and men who came of age in the 1990s or who may be coming to feminism now.

27. We do not mean to suggest that the books we've named are the only ones on third wave feminism. A number of other texts address the issues faced by young feminists, including Nan Bauer Maglin and Donna Perry's *"Bad Girls"/ "Good Girls": Women, Sex, and Power in the Nineties* (1996) and Anna Bondoc and Meg Daly's *Letters of Intent* (1999). Other third wave titles explore topics such as the body, sexuality, and motherhood; notable among these are Ophira Edut's *Adiós, Barbie: Young Women Write about Body Image and Identity* (1998), Ariel Gore and Bee Lavender's *Breeder: Real-Life Stories from the New Generation of Mothers* (2001), Merri Lisa Johnson's *Jane Sexes It Up: True Confessions of Feminist Desire* (2002), and Paula Kamen's *Her Way: Young Women Remake the Sexual Revolution* (2002). Although the third wave has had a relatively brief history, this body of work indicates that this field is vital and thriving, with new texts appearing all the time.

28. Rebecca Walker, *To Be Real: Telling the Truth and Changing the Face of Feminism* (New York: Anchor, 1995), xxxiii.

29. Ibid.

30. We are in agreement with Drake and Heywood on this point.

31. bell hooks, *Feminism Is for Everybody: Passionate Politics* (Boston: South End Press, 2000).

32. bell hooks, *Feminist Theory: From Margin to Center* (Boston: South End Press, 1984); Merri Lisa Johnson, "Pearl Necklace: The Politics of Masturbation Fantasies," in *Jane Sexes It Up: True Confessions of Feminist Desire,* ed. Merri Lisa Johnson (New York: Four Walls Eight Windows, 2002), 318, 320.

33. hooks, *Feminist Theory,* 28.

34. Rebecca Walker, "Becoming the Third Wave," *Ms.,* January/February 1992, 41.

35. As Robin Morgan notes, the "wave" terminology describes only a U.S. context and fails to account for the generations of women before the nineteenth century who fought for their own liberation and empowerment. Speaking of the suffragists and abolitionists as the first wave makes invisible the generations of women before them.

PART ONE

Needing Feminism

JENNIFER L. POZNER

The "Big Lie": False Feminist Death Syndrome, Profit, and the Media

Hello, my name is Jennifer, and I'm an FFDS survivor.

Don't be shocked; my condition is more common than you might think. This pernicious media-borne virus, technically known as *False Feminist Death Syndrome* (FFDS), has popped up in print and over the airwaves on and off for decades, poisoning public opinion against the "F-word" (feminism) and contaminating our collective understanding of the history, ideology, and goals of the women's movement. Third wavers negotiate their lives, their work, and their activism in a climate mediated by strains of FFDS, whose symptoms include what I call the "Passing Fad Fantasy," the "Premature Obituary," and the "Postfeminist Fiction."

From the first days of the women's movement, the mainstream media have done their utmost to stunt feminism's growth. Headlines have been both trivializing—like the *New York Times*'s 1972 wish-it-were-so story, "Is Women's Lib a Passing Fad?"—and fatalistic, like "Feminism: A Lost Cause?," published by *Vogue* eleven years later.[1] As early as 1965, a defensive *Harper's* essay charged that women "do not feel sorry for themselves—and wish their self-appointed champions would find something else to fret about," while a 1967 *McCall's* columnist offered this bit of helpful advice: "Husbands, praise your wives! And marvel at how quickly they stop complaining about discrimination."[2] While hundreds of thousands of women flocked to the newly formed *Ms.* magazine to read Gloria Steinem, Angela Davis, Alice Walker, and others wax prolific on abortion, rape, poverty, marriage, lesbianism,

31

and affirmative action, anchorman Harry Reasoner, who originated *60 Minutes* with Mike Wallace, bet that the groundbreaking publication would "run out of things to say" within six months.[3]

Such swipes at the sisterhood were sadly typical, with journalists branding women's rights activists silly nitwits or strident separatists, prudish harpies or promiscuous harlots. In 1971, an *Esquire* writer described women's lib as "a hair-raising emotional orgy of hatred" led by "neurotic, inadequate women" who are "not normal" but rather "freaks . . . incapable of coming to terms with their own natures as females."[4] Careers are still being made on such fodder: right-wing bigot Rush Limbaugh dominated talk radio in the '90s by railing against "feminazis" and calling the National Organization for Women (NOW) a "terrorist organization."[5] By the late 1990s, networks from NBC to PBS and newspapers from the *Pittsburgh Post-Gazette* to *USA Today* were portraying feminists as "hateful, hysterical demagogues" waging unjust "sex wars"—in particular a "war on boys" that was heralding a "gender Armageddon" for modern men.[6]

In tandem with this dismissive and derogatory coverage, feminists have endured another persistent strain of FFDS: the premature obituary. The mainstream media have prepared untimely eulogies for feminism at laughably regular intervals.[7] Even *Harper's* ran "A Requiem for the Women's Movement" in 1976, the same year that the Supreme Court ruled that states could not require women to get spousal or parental consent for abortions, and NOW Legal Defense and Education Fund charged forty states with violating federal requirements for ending sex bias in education.[8] In 1988, the *New York Times Magazine* gloated about "When Feminism Failed," despite evidence that it was alive and well: polls conducted not long before this dismal declaration showed that 68 percent of the electorate favored affirmative action laws, 75 percent wanted to pass the Equal Rights Amendment, and 84 percent approved of pay equity measures.[9]

A 1990 *Newsweek* column titled "The Failure of Feminism" claimed that feminism had "backfired against women" and blamed the women's movement—not the wage gap, the glass ceiling, or deadbeat dads—for the feminization of poverty. Other media outlets charged that "Feminists Have Killed Feminism," as the *Los Angeles Times* averred in 1992. According to author Sally Quinn, "feminism . . . is dead" because its leaders were "hypocrites" who had "outlasted [their] usefulness." The "sad part," Quinn wrote in mock concern, is that average women feel feminism "doesn't represent them or their problems," because they believe feminists are "anti-male, anti-child, anti-family, anti-feminine."[10] (Gee . . . wonder where those stereotypes came from?)

No outlet has attempted to light feminism's funeral pyre as often as *Time* magazine. In a controversial 1998 cover story headlined "Is Feminism Dead?," reporter Ginia Bellafante claimed that while the once-powerful women's revolution of the 1960s and 1970s "was steeped in research and obsessed with social change," late-1990s "feminism has devolved into the silly," producing only "the narcissistic ramblings of a few new media-anointed spokeswomen."[11] Bellafante's evidence for this claim came in the frail form of Fox's "Ally McBeal," an underdressed, neurotic waif lawyer played by Calista Flockhart, a Hollywood caricature *Time* absurdly implied had succeeded real-life activist foremothers Susan B. Anthony, Betty Friedan, and Gloria Steinem as the feminist "it" girl for the new millennium.

According to *Time*'s woe-is-us premise, the 1970s women's movement *meant something*, but modern feminist art, literature, and activism are, to quote Bellafante, just "a whole lot of stylish fluff." Why? Because contemporary pop culture is overrun with "images of grown single women as frazzled, self-absorbed girls" like Ally or the Spice Girls, self-indulgent drivel like *Bridget Jones's Diary* (1998) and regressive, poorly researched polemics like Katie Roiphe's *The Morning After* (1993) and Camille Paglia's *Sexual Personae* (1990) have replaced intellectually challenging works such as Kate Millet's transformative *Sexual Politics* (1970).

Such crocodile tears . . . and such a crock. Though hyped by corporate media as "feminist" commentators, Roiphe and Paglia—who built their careers claiming date rape is a myth concocted by shrill, weak-minded women—are hardly Kate Millet's counterparts. *Bridget Jones* may be the literary equivalent of cotton candy, but a book isn't a feminist text merely by virtue of having a female author. Without question, *Ally McBeal* was one of the most misogynistic wastes of celluloid ever to hit the boob tube, but what did Bellafante expect from Fox, the net-work of *Married, with Children* and *Cops?* And as for the shallow, sim-pering, Spandex-clad Spice Girls, no amount of candy-coated "girl power" packaging can convince me that "zig-a-zig-ha" was Spice short-hand for "subvert the dominant paradigm."

Clearly, the mainstream media—not the women's movement—her-alded these mass-marketed, pop-culture prima donnas as postfeminist poster girls. Equating the movement with the media is ludicrous. Since when have feminists (or even women, who are only 10 percent of exec-utives and 12 percent of board members of Fortune 1000 media com-panies)[12] controlled the products of male-dominated Hollywood? Or the content of journalism, for that matter? Even in middle manage-ment, only one-third of the newsroom supervisors for daily news-papers are female, and women of color hold just 3 percent of those positions.[13]

Had *Time* been truly interested in contemporary feminist literature, Bellafante could have profiled bell hooks, Urvashi Vaid, Lisa Miya-Jervis, Amy Richards, Laura Flanders, Farai Chideya, or other writers who, though marginalized in the mainstream media, bring critical, progressive perspectives to the alternative press and publishing worlds. Instead, *Time's* hit-piece glossed over the young feminist 'zine scene, ignored independent feminist publications like *Sojourner: The Women's Forum, Bitch: Feminist Response to Pop Culture, Hues, New Moon,* and *Teen Voices,* and dismissed girls' antiviolence writings as a "preoccupation with sexual abuse and self-help."[14] Bellafante complained that main-stream music was vapid but wrote off bold, Riot Grrrl culture as "bratty," overlooking fiercely independent and passionate feminist punk, rock, and folk artists such as Ani DiFranco, Le Tigre, and 7 Year Bitch. Instead of claiming that compelling feminist activism no longer exists, *Time* could have profiled provocative and hilarious street-theater groups like the Lesbian Avengers or political art groups like the Guerilla Girls.

But these are the stories *Time* won't tell, so real feminists were erased from the picture, and not just in the magazine's content. Coinci-dentally, just as *Time* was firing off its latest anti-feminist salvo, the magazine was also firing its only regular feminist voice, the essayist and editor Barbara Ehrenreich. Hypocritical? Sure, but pretty damned predictable. Despite Bellafante's nostalgia for the strident days of yore, are we supposed to believe that *Time* longed for a twenty-first century return to Kate Millet's '70s militance? Please. Not if we remember that, back in 1970, the first thing *Time* told readers about Millet's manifesto was her former professor's opinion that "Reading the book is like sitting with your testicles in a nutcracker." "He should know," the magazine concurred.[15]

Another virulent strain of FFDS is the disingenuous, hand-wringing news feature wondering why more young women don't identify themselves as feminists. One popular answer is that activism is no longer needed because "the feminist movement appears to be a victim of its own success," as the *Florida Sun-Sentinel* put it in an April 2002 story headlined "Women's Issues Face a Tough Sell." Another theory, posed in yet another *Time* cover story, is that young women are skittish because "hairy legs haunt the feminist movement, as do images of being strident and lesbian."[16]

Of course, the media's role in creating such "haunting" images has gone virtually unexplored, as has their campaign to discredit and erase young feminists from the political landscape. News outlets would have us believe we're living in "the golden age of post-feminism—Wonderbras, not burning bras—an age in which the right to sexual equality in all fields is taken for granted," as the London *Independent* wrote in 1995.[17] This cloak of invisibility dates back twenty years, to a 1982 *New York Times Magazine* article headlined "Voices from the Post-Feminist Generation." The author, *Times Book Review* editor Susan Bolotin, overloaded her story with antagonistic quotes from young women who called feminism "an exclusively radical, separatist, bitter movement." Then, when she "heard feminists described not as women who were helping other women to achieve economic equality but as icy monsters, as women who had 'let themselves go physically,' who had 'no sense of style,'" she claimed to be distressed. "Who had done this amazing public-relations job?" Bolotin asked.[18]

Maybe Bolotin didn't read her own newspaper. From the suffrage movement to the third wave, corporate media spin doctors have labeled feminism unladylike, unnecessary, and—above all—unwanted.

Yet while these media-manufactured stereotypes stigmatized feminists, they failed to stem the tide of progress. Over the last thirty-five years, women have engaged in grassroots street protests and inside-the-Beltway politics; their efforts, combined with legal activism, won *Roe v. Wade* as well as class-action lawsuits against sexual harassment and brought about the passage of educational equity legislation, including Title IX, among other things. The feminist agenda broadened beyond demands that resonated strongly with white, middle-class housewives (e.g., the right to equal pay for work outside the home) to issues addressing the interconnections between oppressions based on gender, race, and class. The expanded agenda included such issues as federal funding for reproductive health care for low-income women, opposing forced sterilization of Latina and Native American women, combating domestic violence in immigrant communities, and improving labor conditions for blue-collar women.

Sounds pretty lively for a bunch of corpses, eh? Indeed, postfeminism is a fiction. Far from the media spotlight, girls and young women are undertaking exciting, creative, and uncompromising activism every day. Some are fighting to stop sexual assault and protect reproductive freedom in campus feminist groups, while others are combating abuses of female workers, immigrants, and prisoners in organizations like Refuse & Resist, Students Against Sweatshops, and United for a Fair Economy. Women across the country are challenging corporate media censorship by taking up the reins in the IndyMedia.org movement. Trained in nonviolent civil disobedience by groups like Ruckus Society, they're engaging in large-scale protests against such targets as the antidemocratic World Trade Organization and International Monetary Fund, drawing international attention to corporate corruption, international poverty, environmental degradation, police brutality, and global human rights abuses. And on high school and college campuses all across the country, independent bands of bad-assed "Radical Cheerleaders" are wearing mismatched uniforms, shaking ratty pom-poms, and chanting about everything from NAFTA to nuclear proliferation, belting out anthems like "Riot, Don't Diet!" with lyrics like "We're sexy, we're cute, we're radical to boot! We're angry, we're tough, and we have *had enough!*"[19]

Now that—and not the cutesy, compliant chicks on the corporate-dominated music scene—is *real* "girl power."

HOW WE KNOW WHAT WE KNOW:
MEDIA AND HEGEMONY

Control of the media is the single most important issue of our time, with the possible exception of the corruptive influence of corporate money in politics. Our most common organ of socialization, the corporate-controlled media shape and inform our collective ideas about people, politics, and public policy. Young and old, urban and rural, working class and wealthy, we all rely on mass media to provide the information we need to function as active members of a democracy. As the mouthpiece of the "white supremacist capitalist patriarchy" discussed by feminist theorists such as bell hooks, the corporate-dominated mass media are the key to why our fast-moving culture is so slow to change, stereotypes are so persistent, and the power structure is so entrenched.

Pop culture images help us determine what to wear, whom to date, whom to vote for, how we see ourselves, and how we relate to racial, sexual, socioeconomic, and religious "others." Journalism directly links and affects every individual issue on the sociopolitical continuum—from rape to racism, international poverty to civil liberties, hate crimes to war crimes—in a national debate. By determining who gets to speak and who is excluded from this ongoing conversation, as well as which issues are discussed and how they are framed, the media have the power to maintain the status quo or challenge the dominant order. Only a well-informed and vocal public can foment cultural and political revolution. Without accurate, nonbiased news coverage and challenging, creative cultural expression, it is virtually impossible to move public opinion significantly on women's and human rights issues, to activate (or even reach) the citizenry, and to create lasting social change.

But as discussed earlier, women's rights advocates and allies have been demonized, pathologized, and eulogized by media for decades. This resistance to feminism can be felt in coverage of topics editors narrowly define as "women's issues" (e.g., rape, abortion, child care), where stereotypes are invoked and perpetuated. Women are most often depicted as victims, and victim-blaming is still prevalent. A 1993 *Newsweek* column about anti-rape activists on campus was headlined "Stop Whining!"[20] When dozens of women were publicly sexually assaulted in New York's Central Park in the summer of 2000, *Dateline NBC* asked, "What responsibility, if any, did the women have for what happened that day in the park?"[21]

When issues fall outside journalists' "pink ghetto," yet implicitly affect women's survival (for example, economics, global trade, war), gender is rarely used as a lens for analysis.[22] This obscures the fact that injustice for any disenfranchised population is, by its nature, a feminist concern. Along with an overreliance on widely quoted views of Wall Street and White House reps, the misrepresentation and marginalization of feminist voices from broad public debate leads to a skewed vision of politics and public life, with serious consequences for social policy. For example, well before September 11, conclusions based on irresponsible and inaccurate coverage of the anticorporate globalization movement had been cited by law enforcement to justify police violence, civil liberties violations, and counterintelligence programs targeting young women and men working for global justice. Though the vast majority of protesters have been peaceful, well-informed, and articulate, the mainstream U.S. media have attacked them as "violent," ignorant "extremists," as "crazies" and "kooks," and even as anti-American "terrorists." Obsessed with trumped-up tales of destructive anarchist thugs, news outlets have all but ignored the substantive arguments of anticorporate globalization activists: in February 2002, ABC's *Nightline* canceled a planned segment on the World Economic Forum protests in New York because, the producers explained, there "wasn't enough violence" to make the events newsworthy.[23]

By promoting sexist notions about "women's issues" while largely ignoring the consequences of broad social inequities for women, the mainstream media hide the connections between gender oppression and the subordinate status of all disenfranchised groups, and help to fragment a coalitional movement for social justice. And on an immediate level, misrepresentations by the media have taken a serious toll on our country's legislative agenda, as some of the following examples illustrate.

War Coverage: Where Are the Women? Let's call it "The Case of the Missing Gender Gap." Following September 11, the mass media across the United States presented a picture of a flag-waving, Rambo-embracing populace in which "women's voices are resonating across the country and doing away—for the first time in recent history—with the gender gap on many military issues," as a front-page article in the *Christian Science Monitor* claimed.[24] Headlines of poll-based stories like the *Washington Post*'s "Public Unyielding in War against Terror; 9 in 10 Back Robust Military Response" gave the misleading impression that Americans were "unswerving" in their "demand for a full-scale response," an image Bush administration officials seized on to broaden the war effort in Afghanistan and to push through dangerous rollbacks of civil liberties like the USA Patriot Act.[25] But "the public" is not monolithic, and such numbers didn't compute. Looking more closely, the 9-in-10 statistic cited in the headline referred to Bush's approval rating alone; buried at the end of the *Post*'s story was the acknowledgment that women's "hesitancy . . . may turn into more hardened opposition as a military action proceeds." Women "were significantly less likely to support a long and costly war"; in fact, although 44 percent of women (according to the poll reported by the *Post*) would support a broad military effort, "48 percent said they wanted a limited strike or no military action at all." These numbers, which clearly contradicted the media's image of a unified, bloodthirsty public, were ignored by almost every leading news outlet.

While our "patriotic" news corps covered polls selectively, coverage of women and war was often opportunistic. Broadcast outlets seized on the restrictive *burqa* forced on Afghan women as a symbol of the Taliban's cruelty and a reason the regime should be vanquished; they ran triumphant visuals of women removing their coverings upon the Taliban's ouster, yet devoted scant attention to the history of extreme violence and rape committed against Afghan women by the U.S.-endorsed Northern Alliance. Nor did the networks' favorite pundits—current and former government officials who presented war and civil liberties rollbacks as necessary and inevitable—see fit to mention that prior to September 11, the United States had largely ignored efforts by the Feminist Majority and RAWA (Revolutionary Association of the Women of Afghanistan) to end what they called gender apartheid under the Taliban.[26] Feminist and progressive dissenters who dared give the question "Why do they hate us?" an answer more substantial than the ubiquitous "because we love freedom" (say, by criticizing American foreign policy) were immediately branded as traitors. And as soon as Bush no longer needed to use brutalized Afghan women as propaganda for our bombing regimen, the continued oppression and near-invisibility of women in Afghanistan's new, U.S.-approved government faded from the U.S. news cycle.[27]

Women are one-half the population in this country, so why were our more moderate views eclipsed in the critical debate about terrorism and war? A college-style drinking game might offer some clues: Play along! Grab a few friends and your remote, flip between network news broadcasts, and pour a drink every time a female expert is interviewed. I promise you'll end up parched—and peeved. Start with the influential, agenda-setting Sunday morning talk shows of ABC, NBC, CBS, CNN, and Fox, where women were a measly 11 percent of all guests for a year and a half prior to—and just 9 percent for six weeks following—September 11.[28] Women fare no better in print: men wrote a whopping 92 percent of all bylined op-ed pieces published by the *New York Times, Washington Post,* and *USA Today* in the month after the terrorist attacks.[29]

With women so underrepresented as media commentators, is it any surprise the public didn't learn that almost half of us wanted limited *or no* military action? Likewise, the appalling scarcity of women's voices in media has had serious ramifications for journalistic and legislative responses, not only to terrorism and war but also to important social issues.

Global Trade: Silencing the Real Experts Ninety percent of sweatshop workers in the world are women and girls, yet editors rarely frame global economics as a "women's issue." Instead, world trade stories are told from the perspective of transnational corporations and not from that of the female workers who suffer labor and human rights abuses daily in overseas and domestic sweatshops.[30] Business features breathlessly report on rising NASDAQ numbers, but fail to mention when those profits are made via union-busting or using prison or child labor. Merger announcements quote enthusiastic PR wonks who insist that bigger equals better, ignoring or downplaying the dangerous economic impact massive layoffs and corporate welfare incentives have on individual workers and on local economies. Meanwhile, government officials quoted in these stories are typically reluctant to bite the corporate hands that feed their electoral war chests. The mainstream media protect the financial interests of their advertisers and parent companies, while denying the rest of us access to information that might make us question our personal consumer decisions or collectively oppose corporate dominance.

When real globalization experts—the women of color who are paid pennies to make our Gap baby-Ts and DKNY dresses—are interviewed, the media often add insult to injury. Take, for example, a *60 Minutes* segment on the garment industry aired in December 1994. The segment featured twelve Chinese seamstresses from Oakland, California, who were in the midst of a nasty battle for unpaid wages with manufacturer Jessica McClintock. CBS approached the workers for interviews, which the network wanted to film without the protection of blurred images or vocal disguises. The immigrant women agonized about whether to reveal their identities on camera; to do so could mean getting fired or blacklisted, author Miriam Ching Yoon Louie noted in a May 2002 article in *Sojourner*.[31] "The producers argued that the women could tell their story most effectively if they showed their faces and spoke directly to the American public," Louie wrote, so the workers agreed to take the risk. When the segment eventually aired, *60 Minutes* included visuals of the workers describing how the sweatshop boss had threatened them, restricted bathroom use, and posted signs ordering "No loud talking." The public never learned of these abuses, however, since CBS never translated the women's comments. Displaying the Chinese seamstresses only as victims behind a voiceover from correspondent Morley Safer, the network effectively reinforced the sweatshop's policy of silence for immigrant women.

Welfare and Poor Mothers Punitive welfare reform policies were enacted in the mid-1990s only after years of biased reporting and editorializing that had depicted poor women on public assistance—especially young mothers of color—as "public enemy No. 1."[32] Taking their cue from characters like conservative radio host Ken Hamblin, many U.S. media outlets branded poor women as promiscuous, irresponsible, immoral, unintelligent "broodmares" cranking out babies for checks. (No similar criticisms were leveled against the adult men who impregnate most teen mothers.) What these "greedy welfare queens" deserved, we heard repeatedly, was not government aid that "pamper(ed) the poor" but a good, hearty dose of public humiliation for their "sins."[33] In a December 1994 diatribe headlined "The Name of the Game Is Shame," *Newsweek*'s Jonathan Alter insisted that "every threat to the fabric of this country—from poverty to crime to homelessness—is connected to out-of-wedlock teen pregnancy."[34] Time and again, the mass media pinned society's supposed downfall on young women: "Beyond the drugs and the gunfire lies what is perhaps the most shocking of social pathologies: rates of out-of-wedlock births," *USA Today* raved in December 1993.[35] Even the mild-mannered Ann Landers published numerous letters in the early 1990s from readers describing young mothers on welfare as "lazy slobs" and "moochers" for whom "forced birth control is the only solution."[36]

News coverage of the plight of poor women ran counter to reality. Contrary to media myths scapegoating young black and Latina mothers, before the passage of welfare reform, the average woman on public assistance was white, had fewer than three kids, and stayed on public assistance for only two years, often while escaping domestic violence—and only 6 percent of mothers who received Aid for Dependent Children (AFDC) in the mid-1990s were younger than twenty.[37] After years of similarly skewed reports, public opinion moved rightward, and the social safety net was gravely damaged for all women and children.[38]

Reproductive Rights as Political Football On July 3, 1990, a *Los Angeles Times* story headlined "Can Women Reporters Write Objectively on Abortion Issue?" offered frank insight into the mainstream media mindset.[39] Perhaps the *Times* was befuddled by the tendency of many female reporters to cover abortion as if it might matter to women. Like coverage of many social issues, reproductive rights news is usually reported as a political football. Proposed policy changes on everything from parental consent laws to foreign aid for family planning are generally examined from the standpoint of inside-the-Beltway politics (for example, "How will Congressman X's stance on abortion affect his standing with voters?"), rather than how the proposed changes might affect women and girls who require reproductive health services.[40]

At the same time, the right wing's decades-long semantic war over abortion has often gone unchallenged in the U.S. media and has thus succeeded in manipulating public opinion. Since mainstream media outlets rarely correct conservative disinformation campaigns, most people don't know that "partial birth abortion" (the grotesque-sounding term used repeatedly in news reports without quotation marks) is not an official medical term for any known procedure or that the phrase was created by the anti-abortion lobby as a political ploy to weaken *Roe v. Wade*. The same holds true for journalists' indiscriminate use of terms like "feticide," "infanticide," and "fetal protection."[41] Similarly, the U.S. media have failed to expose conservative "crisis pregnancy centers" where, under the guise of "counseling," anti-choice activists scare women with inaccurate information about "Post-Abortion Stress Syndrome," another political construct that is not recognized by leading psychological or medical associations.[42] Most shocking, many media outlets have been loathe to label shootings, bombings, death threats, and other politically motivated forms of violence against women's health clinics and abortion providers as "terrorism."[43] Only after September 11, when newscasters received letters that claimed to be laced with anthrax, did the mainstream media finally report that anti-choice terrorists have subjected reproductive health advocates and providers to a regular campaign of anthrax threats for many years, with more than five hundred such letters arriving post–September 11.[44] By excluding real women from debates about reproductive health, and by refusing to call anti-abortion terrorism by its rightful name, the mass media in this country deprive the public of the information

needed to develop informed opinions about abortion and other repro-
ductive-freedom issues.

THE MEDIA'S "BIG LIE": PROFIT, NOT PUBLIC INTEREST

To boost circulation, *USA Today*'s founder, Al Neuharth, once instructed his editorial staff to "run a picture of a nice, clean-cut, all-
American girl," and be sure to "get her tits above the fold."[45] This crass
combination of sexism and commercialism offers insight into the priorities that drive corporate media production. Feminists and other cultural critics often prefer to focus on sexism and racism in the content
of news, advertising, and pop culture. Although these are of vital im-
port, our analysis must move beyond media products to the big picture. That is to say, before we can challenge media misogyny and
achieve effective reform, we must understand not just that media content *is* biased, but *why* it is. To understand why feminist and public interest voices are eclipsed, we need to look at the way the American media system is structured. The problem includes the gender and racial
breakdown of the people who sit in the executive suites but goes beyond it, to ownership and control of corporate media. These structural
issues (including advertising and media consolidation) invariably compromise what we are given to read, watch, and hear.[46]

Today, the vast majority of newspapers, magazines, and network, cable, and on-line news and entertainment outlets in this country are
owned by just ten multinational corporations: AOL Time Warner, Disney, General Electric, News Corporation, Viacom, Vivendi, Sony,
Bertelsmann, AT&T, and Liberty Media. These media monopolies control not only the scope and content of public debate but also U.S. record labels, radio stations, theaters, TV and movie production companies, publishing houses, Internet and cable distribution chains,
telecom and Internet companies, and advertising billboards—not to
mention sports teams, stadiums, theme parks, and myriad other hold-
ings.[47] For instance, besides owning NBC and (with Microsoft) MSNBC,
General Electric is also invested in the financial services, insurance,
medical technology, aircraft engine production, and nuclear and weapons manufacturing industries. (GE isn't the only weapons manufacturer that has controlled a major news network: before being gobbled

up by the media giant Viacom, CBS was owned by the nuclear energy colossus Westinghouse.) This presents serious journalistic conflicts of interest: when companies that own two of the most powerful weapons producers—GE and Westinghouse—also own two of the Big Three news networks, what are the chances that serious or sustained criticisms of the military-industrial complex will make it to the nightly news? Is it any surprise that news outlets whose parent companies reap hundreds of millions in government subsidies are quick to attack poor mothers' need for food stamps, but slow to critique corporate welfare?

The financial bottom line looms large for "the media cartel," so dubbed by Mark Crispin Miller, director of PROMO (Project On Media Ownership). Beyond lulling us into a politically ignorant, apathetic, hyperconsumerist stupor, these companies could not care less about informing or entertaining us: their only goal is profit. The key to profits is advertising, which generates more than $70 billion annually for print and broadcast companies. "The network is paying affiliates to carry network commercials, not programs. What we are is a distribution system for Proctor & Gamble," an ABC insider once explained.[48] This profit-based model jeopardizes editorial integrity and contributes to the sidelining of controversial subjects. Consider the instructions Proctor & Gamble once gave to *Ms.*: none of its ads were to be placed in *any issue* of the magazine that included any material on gun control, abortion, cults, or criticisms of religion, and the editors were to be "cautious" about covering sex or drugs, even for educational purposes.[49] Demands like these are as common as they are brazen. When such stipulations are made by even one major sponsor, editors who rely on ad revenue are often forced to eliminate "offensive" material. "Make no mistake: The primary purpose of mass media is to sell audiences to advertisers. *We* are the product," ad critic Jean Kilbourne explains.[50]

That's the media's dirty little secret: we—and not news or entertainment content—are what's being sold in vast quantities by the media, and in this transaction some of us are worth more than others. Media economics revolves around audience demographics—often around racism as much as ratings, as FAIR's (Fairness and Accuracy in Reporting) Janine Jackson notes: "The WB's *Felicity* draws similar numbers of 18- to 49-year-olds as the net's two highest-rated black series, *The Steve*

Harvey Show and *The Jamie Foxx Show*. But last season, *Felicity* commanded more than twice as much money per 30-second commercial than either show ($80,000, vs. less than $40,000)."[51] Networks accommodate advertisers' biases by providing programming that is tailored to, and will subsequently deliver, the lucrative demographics they covet—in particular, eighteen- to thirty-four-year-old white men with lots of disposable income: *The Man Show* viewers and *Maxim* readers. The rest of us are out of luck.

This pandering to advertisers, regardless of (and sometimes despite) consumers' wishes, exposes the media's Big Lie: that programming fails or thrives based on free market dictates. We're constantly told that sensationalistic, sexist, and stupefying media fodder exist because "That's what the public wants." This is the rationalization for every bottom-feeding offering, from dumbed-down newsmagazines to sexed-up "reality TV" to *Jerry Springer*. When we're ready to cover our ears before hearing "Hit Me Baby, One More Time" yet again, we're told that *we* asked for this endless supply of mind-numbingly boring, carbon-copy corporate crooners.

What a fallacy! When media prioritize profit over the public interest, our desire for artistic, creative cultural content that challenges and expands our worldview—and the democratic need for independent journalism to serve as the watchdog over political power—is beside the point. News and entertainment divisions are increasingly headed by white, male businessmen with no experience in journalism or the arts, but with a mandate to maximize their shareholders' investments. To that end, consolidation is king. Media oligopolies and "duopolies" constantly seek to merge with other behemoths in a quest to monopolize the market, inevitably drowning out competitive voices, crushing smaller players (often the few media outlets that are female- or minority-owned), and jeopardizing diversity both within content and behind the scenes in the industry, with little interference from the business-friendly FCC.

Massive layoffs accompany every new media merger; those reporters who remain in downsized newsrooms are treated like factory workers, ordered to produce two and three times as many stories in half the time, with greatly reduced budgets. Journalism suffers when media owners treat news like any other product to be manufactured, like soda or sneakers or tampons. Reporters are less able to do in-depth research or long-term investigations, so complicated stories are covered superficially or not at all; and less time for fact-checking means that inaccuracies abound. Not given leeway to interview diverse expert voices, journalists rely instead on the same mostly white, mostly male sources in their Rolodexes.[52] Pressed for cash, newsrooms find it difficult to hire translators for interviewees, to authorize travel to check out leads, or to report from the scene firsthand; pressed for time, editors and reporters are more prone to run slick, prepackaged PR materials from corporations and conservative think tanks as news items.[53]

Sometimes the quest for profits even results in direct censorship of news that is critical of corporate practices. In 1997, when investigative reporters Jane Akre and Steve Wilson refused to "doctor" an exposé about health risks associated with rGBH, a hormone developed to boost dairy cow output, Fox News responded to pressure from Monsanto, the producer of the hormone, by firing the journalists and killing their story. "We paid $3 billion for these television stations. We will decide what the news is. The news is what we tell you it is," a Fox station manager said.[54] More frequently, self-censorship means that certain stories aren't produced in the first place. In many corporate newsrooms, women and people of color who regularly pitch pieces about discrimination find themselves stuck with the career-halting label "troublemaker," while journalists wishing to investigate corporate excess understand that this will not suit the financial priorities of their higher-ups. "No one here wants to piss off the bosses," unnamed ABC News insiders told the *New Yorker* in August 2000; a *20/20* producer dropped a piece on executive compensation because "no one wanted to draw attention to the extraordinarily rich pay package of Disney's chairman, Michael Eisner."[55]

Indeed, few people embody media greed as much as Mickey Mouse's main man. Capitalizing on the country's grief after September 11, the ABC News owner told the *Los Angeles Times* that he had a plan that would help Americans "get back to normal" and boost his bottom line, all at the same time: "We're going to use our own media companies to make sure the word gets out that it's a good idea to have a good time after a period of mourning—to come to our parks, movies and buy 'Snow White' on DVD," Eisner said.[56]

In the media biz, that's what's called "synergy." Synergy is the buzz-word for the process by which media conglomerates consolidate, buy up cross-holdings in broadcast, print, and online outlets, and then use these outlets as platforms to promote one another's products relent-lessly, thereby boosting viewership, readership, and market reach for advertisers. All the big media players do it, but Eisner's a practiced pro. After Disney purchased a 5 percent stake in Pets.com in 1999, the on-line pet supply retailer turned up at least twenty-nine times on ABC News, according to a Nexis news database search. The site's mascot, a wisecracking sock-puppet dog, was "interviewed" on *Good Morning America, Nightline,* and *World News Now,* which ran clips of Pets.com commercials and puff pieces instructing viewers to buy the puppet for their kids. *Good Morning America* anchor Charles Gibson even asked the puppet if it was "ready to go to Disney World." You ain't seen nothing 'til you've seen a Serious Newsman addressing questions to a sock on a chair with a puppeteer's hand up his butt (the puppet's butt, that is). Erasing the line between news, entertainment, and commerce, syn-ergy turns sock puppets into "news" and newscasters into corporate puppets.[57]

Synergy is responsible for the appearance of overwhelming yet spon-taneous popular interest in a certain subject—when in fact, that popu-larity has been carefully constructed via corporate branding and multiplatform media attention. One of the clearest examples of this is Eden's Crush, a marketing-scheme-turned-TV-show-turned-girl-group created to cash in on the power of the AOL Time Warner empire. Dur-ing the winter of 2001, hundreds of girls competed to become Pop Stars in a show of the same name that aired on the WB network. Girls at home were encouraged to identify with the hundreds of Spice Girl wanna-bes as the contenders for the group were whittled down to five finalists over several prime-time episodes. "You can't buy that kind of advertising," *Pop Stars* producer David Foster told the *St. Petersburg Times,*[58] without acknowledging that the entire series itself was one long ad. Because of the guaranteed, built-in fan base that was sure to result from hours of "editorial" exposure on network television, Warner's London/Sire Records signed a contract before the band had a name—or even singers. Not until the songs were written, the show placed in the TV lineup, and the pre- and post-production plans made were the artists plugged in, like an afterthought. Once selected, Eden's Crush appeared on WB-affiliate news stations in New York and Chicago, guest-starred on the WB's *Sabrina, the Teenage Witch* and the infotainment show *Extra* (syndicated by Warner Brothers), and conducted an AOL on-line chat. Eden's Crush's first single, which could be bought at record stores as well as downloaded on AOL, sold 219,000 copies in its first few weeks on the charts. Whether the girls in the group had any talent was irrelevant.

If that isn't disturbing enough, let's return to our case study of FFDS and *Time* magazine. In an on-line debate about their "Is Feminism Dead?" attack, feminist author Phyllis Chesler asked *Time*'s Ginia Bellafante why she "didn't . . . take on the media" instead of blaming the women's movement for its own misrepresentations in pop culture. Bellafante's curt answer spoke volumes: "My next job won't be at Time Warner, and then I'll rip the media to shreds."[59] Like most working journalists, Bellafante knew where her paycheck was coming from, and she knew that antifeminism sells at her magazine. Now part of the AOL communications cartel, *Time*, long the purveyor of False Feminist Death Syndrome, has multiple platforms through which to spread its sexist gospel.

We are at a crucial moment. Ownership (and thus control) of the media is already concentrated, to the public's detriment, yet the deregulatory structure favored by the media industry and its favorite nonwatchdog, the Federal Communications Commission chair Michael Powell, would pave the way for the tightest convergence of media power ever seen in this country. This concentration of con-trol over media access threatens to sideline and subvert feminist voices more thoroughly than ever. We have two choices—we can sit back and wait until all our news is filtered through the lens of MSNBCNNBCBS ABCFOXAOLWB, Inc., or we can work for progressive feminist media reform.

DON'T BE DEPRESSED—BE DEMANDING

Imagine what American politics might look like if the hundreds of campus feminist groups fighting for women's empowerment and justice incorporated media activism as an intrinsic part of their work.

What would happen if progressive and liberal women's organizations used media as effectively as conservatives do, articulating their own messages to the public and debunking right-wing myths? What if journalists sought out women and people of color as experts for news stories as often as they do PR flaks and White House insiders? And what if the media considered a broad range of human rights issues newsworthy?

That's my vision for Women in Media & News (WIMN), a new non-profit I'm forming to educate women about structural media biases, to train them to challenge both sexist content and official media policy, and to promote their voices to journalists seeking sources.[60] The goal is to help facilitate a more media-critical and media-savvy feminist community, one that will be better able to articulate and further our efforts on behalf of social justice, and one which will bring an analysis of women's rights to the forefront of the media democracy movement. Like many others in this movement, I do this work because I believe that for those who care about women's and human rights, media access is a matter of survival.

In this new era of corporate consolidation, feminists need to get back to our roots. In the 1930s, Eleanor Roosevelt would speak only to female reporters at her press conferences, forcing newspapers to employ women journalists. Second wavers made media reform an integral part of the movement: they threatened legal action to revoke the licenses of TV and radio stations that discriminated against women, monitored FCC policy, fought to integrate the National Press Club, and held sit-ins and teach-ins at editors' offices to demand an end to sexist reporting, advertising, and entertainment. Throughout the 1970s, leading newspapers, magazines, and TV networks had to be sued before they would stop discriminating against women in hiring and promotion; feminist columnist Anna Quindlen began her decade-long run on the *New York Times* op-ed page as a result of one of those class-action lawsuits, and she proceeded to write about gender, race, class, and sexuality issues as if they mattered.[61]

It's time for us to make the media a top priority feminist issue again. Media conglomerates are not magnanimous; like the rich, white men who run them, they will not change their priorities without a fight. For feminism to advance in the twenty-first century, we need to give them that fight—and we have many tactical and practical options through which to engage the mass media. We can read and support critical, noncommercial, pro-feminist information sources that challenge dominant news and entertainment messages: sources such as *Sojourner, Extra!, Bitch,* CommonDreams.org, WomensEnews.org, and radio shows like Amy Goodman's *Democracy Now!,* Laura Flanders's *Working Assets Radio,* FAIR's *CounterSpin,* and *FIRE (Feminist International Radio Endeavor).*[62] We can embrace the motto "Don't like the media? Be the media!" by learning to create alternatives, with guidance from do-it-yourself, pro-feminist projects, including IndyMedia.org, Dyke TV, Paper Tiger TV, and others.[63] We can attend media training sessions and utilize strategy materials from groups like WIMN, We Interrupt This Message, Media Education Foundation, and MediaChannel.org, which will teach us how to critique and deconstruct media spin, build relationships with reporters, and launch effective media campaigns. And we can (and must) increase our numbers in the media democracy movement, where groups like the Women's Institute for Freedom of the Press, FAIR, the Center for Digital Democracy, Prometheus Radio, Media Tank, and others are working for structural change based on the belief that what the media produce should be made for people, not profit.[64]

Most important, instead of getting depressed when confronted with derogatory reports in the media, we can get demanding. We can lobby our leaders, submit public comments to the FCC, and write letters to editors calling for media companies to be held accountable to the public. We can support independent, noncorporate artists, musicians, and journalists. We can pressure news producers to interview female experts and public interest advocates, and contact local outlets when women are ignored, distorted, or covered in opportunistic ways. We can conduct studies debunking bias in media reports, and then hold press conferences, release reports, and demand meetings with editorial boards to discuss ways they can improve.

And every time we stumble upon a case of FFDS, we can call the corporate media to task. We can ask for a retraction, and maybe a series of follow-up stories exploring the broadbased, multiplatform, multicultural feminist work they've been ignoring and insulting for years. We can tell them, to paraphrase Mark Twain, that the rumors of our demise have been greatly exaggerated and that women deserve—and demand—better from the media.

NOTES

1. Cited in Toni Carabillo et al., *Feminist Chronicles: 1953–1993*, http://www.feminist.org/research/chronicles/chronicle.html (May 18, 2002).

2. Ibid.

3. Reasoner's quote cited on Pacifica Radio's *Democracy Now!*, December 11, 2001.

4. Cited in Paula Kamen, *Feminist Fatale: Voices from the "Twentysomething" Generation Explore the Future of the "Women's Movement"* (New York: Donald I. Fine, 1991).

5. Cited in Steve Rendall, Jim Naureckas, and Jeff Cohen, *The Way Things Aren't: Rush Limbaugh's Reign of Error* (New York: New Press, 1995).

6. Laura Vanderkam, "Cupid Combat Rages on Campus," *USA Today*, February 14, 2002; Norah Vincent, "For a New Era, a New Feminism," *Pittsburgh Post-Gazette*, September 19, 1999.

7. The media's tendency to try to pigeonhole feminism as past its prime (what I think of as the "have we killed it yet?" phenomenon) has been widely discussed by feminist writers. For an interesting exploration in the context of third wave feminism, see Kamen, *Feminist Fatale;* for exhaustive documentation of this practice and its broad effect, see Susan Faludi, *Backlash: The Undeclared War against American Women* (New York: Crown, 1991).

8. Cited in Carabillo et al., *Feminist Chronicles: 1953–1993.*

9. Mary Ann Dolan, "When Feminism Failed," *New York Times Magazine,* June 26, 1998; Times-Mirror/Gallup and New York Times/CBS News surveys cited in Carabillo et al., *Feminist Chronicles: 1953–1993,* and Faludi, *Backlash.*

10. Key Ebeling, "The Failure of Feminism," *Newsweek,* November 19, 1990; Sally Quinn, "Feminists Have Killed Feminism," *Los Angeles Times,* January 23, 1992.

11. Ginia Bellafante, "Feminism: It's All about Me!" *Time,* June 29, 1998; Jennifer L. Pozner, "False Feminist Death Syndrome and Feminist Resurrection," *Sojourner,* August 1998; Jennifer L. Pozner, "And the Category Is . . . 'Simpering Wimps for 1,000,'" *Sojourner,* September 1998.

12. Jennifer L. Pozner, "Power Shortage for Media Women: Studies Document Absence from Influential Roles," *Extra!,* July/August 2001; Jennifer L. Pozner, "Women Have *Not* Taken Over the News," *Extra!,* January/February 2000.

13. American Society of Newspaper Editors 2001 Newsroom Census, http://www.asne.org/kiosk/diversity/2001Survey/2001CensusReport.htm (May 18, 2002).

14. Bellafante, "Feminism: It's All about Me!"

15. "Who's Come a Long Way, Baby?" *Time,* August 21, 1970.

16. Victor Greto, "Women's Issues Face a Tough Sell," *Florida Sun-Sentinel,* April 4, 2002; Claudia Wallis, "Onward, Women!" *Time,* December 4, 1989.

17. Genevieve Fox, "Goodbye to All That . . . ," *London Independent,* October 31, 1995.

18. Susan Bolotin, "Voices from the Post-Feminist Generation," *New York Times Magazine,* October 17, 1982.

19. Information about young women's activism in these varied fields can be found on-line at http://www.refuseandresist.org/altindex.html; http://www.usasnet.org; http://www.ruckus.org; http://www.feministcampus.org; http://www.now.org/issues/young; http://www.kwru.org; http://www.ufenet.org; http://www.billionairesforbushorgore.com; http://www.indymedia.org; and http://www.geocities.com/radicalcheerleaders/cheers.htm (May 18, 2002).

20. Mary Matalin, "Stop Whining!" *Newsweek,* October 25, 1993.

21. *FAIR Action Alert: Dateline NBC Exploits Central Park Victims,* http://www.fair.org/activism/dateline-central-park.html (June 23, 2000); "New York Police Department Was Slow to Act," *Dateline NBC,* June 20, 2000.

22. Laura Flanders, *Real Majority, Media Minority: The Cost of Sidelining Women in Reporting* (Monroe, Maine: Common Courage Press, 2000).

23. Phil Skaller, "ABC *Nightline* Cancels Special on Group Preparing to Protest World Economic Forum," http://nyc.indymedia.org/front.php3?article_id?18995&group=webcast (May 18, 2002).

24. Alexandra Marks, "In This War, American Women Shed Role as 'Doves,'" *Christian Science Monitor,* November 6, 2001.

25. Dana Milbank and Richard Morin, "Public Unyielding in War against Terror," *Washington Post,* September 29, 2001; Jennifer L. Pozner, "Casualty of War: The U.S. Press Corps Wimps Out," *Ms.,* December 2001/January 2002.

26. See the Feminist Majority's "Gender Apartheid in Afghanistan" campaign at http://www.feminist.org/afghan/facts.html and the Revolutionary Association of the Women of Afghanistan at http://www.rawa.org and http://www.sojourner.org (May 18, 2002) for a variety of articles, both current and historical, on the conditions of women in Afghanistan, as well as on Afghan women's resistance to oppression.

27. Laura Flanders, "It's Not Just the Veil: Media Need to Look Deeper at Women's Role in Afghanistan," *Extra!,* January/February 2002; Laura Flanders, "The Press and the Patriarchy: Understatement Marks Coverage of the Taliban's Gender Apartheid," *Extra!,* November/December 2000.

28. "Who's Talking: An Analysis of Sunday Morning Talk Shows," White House Project, December 2001, http://www.thewhitehouseproject.org/forums.html (May 18, 2002).

29. These statistics on women op-ed writers come from a survey I conducted

for the media-watch group Fairness & Accuracy In Reporting (FAIR), where I formerly served as Women's Desk director. Survey analysis appears in *Extra!*, November/December 2001.

30. See Feminists against Sweatshops, http://www.feminist.org/other/sweatshops/sweatshops.html (May 18, 2002), and UNITE (Union of Needletrades, Industrial and Textile Employees, AFL-CIO, CLC) Stop Sweatshops campaign, http://www.uniteunion.org/sweatshops/whatis/whatis.html (May 18, 2002).

31. Miriam Ching Yoon Louie, "Sweatshop Workers Are Warriors; Organizing for All Women Workers' Rights," *Sojourner*, May 2002.

32. Diane Sawyer, *PrimeTime Live*, February 16, 1995, quoted in Laura Flanders and Janine Jackson, "Public Enemy Number One? Media's Welfare Debate Is a War on Poor Women," *Extra!*, March/April 1995.

33. Mensah Dean, "Ken Hamblin Is Quite Happy to Be a Radio Shock Jock on the Right Side," *Washington Times*, November 13, 1996.

34. Jonathan Alter, "The Name of the Game Is Shame," *Newsweek*, December 12, 1994.

35. William M. Welch, "Age-Old Debate on Morality Takes New Life," *USA Today*, December 14, 1993.

36. Ann Landers, "Resentment Explodes over Welfare Abuse," *Chicago Tribune*, September 3, 1991.

37. For an extensive American Psychological Association report debunking myths about women on welfare, see http://www.apa.org/pi/wpo/welftowork.html (May 18, 2002). For a FAIR report on media coverage of welfare, see *Extra!*, March/April 1995.

38. Barbara Ehrenreich, *Nickel and Dimed: On (Not) Getting By in America* (New York: Metropolitan Books, 2001).

39. David Shaw, "Can Women Reporters Write Objectively on Abortion Issue?" *Los Angeles Times*, July 3, 1990; Tiffany Devitt, "Abortion Coverage Leaves Women out of the Picture," *Extra!*, Special Issue on Women, 1992.

40. Jennifer L. Pozner, "Self-Gagged on Gag Rule: Coverage of Family-Planning Restrictions Inaccurate, Incomplete," *Extra!*, May/June 2001; Jennifer L. Pozner, "Media Ignores Gag Rule's Harm to Free Speech," *Women's Enews*, http://www. womensenews.org/article.cfm/dyn/aid/558/context/archive (May 18, 2002).

41. Miranda Kennedy, "Partial Truth Abortion Coverage: Media Adopt Rhetoric of 'Fetal Rights,'" *Extra!*, March/April 2000.

42. Cynthia Cooper, "Abortion under Attack," *Ms.*, August/September 2001.

43. "'Terrorists' Attack Ski Lodges, Not Doctors," *Extra! Update*, December 1998; Laura Flanders, "Far-Right Militias and Anti-Abortion Violence: When Will Media See the Connection?" *Extra!*, July/August 1995.

44. Francis X. Clines, "A 'Small Wonder' of a Life Brings One Woman the American Dream," *New York Times*, January 4, 2001.

45. Peter C. Newman, "The Best and the Worst of 1987," *MacLeans,* December 21, 1987.

46. Robert W. McChesney, *Rich Media, Poor Democracy: Communications Politics in Dubious Times* (Urbana: University of Illinois Press, 1999); John Nichols and Robert W. McChesney, *It's the Media, Stupid* (New York: Seven Stories Press, 2000); Edward S. Herman and Noam Chomsky, *Manufacturing Consent: The Political Economy of Mass Media* (New York: Pantheon Books, 1998); Norman Solomon and Jeff Cohen, *Wizards of Media Oz: Behind the Curtain of Mainstream News* (Monroe, Maine: Common Courage Press, 1997); Jeff Cohen and Norman Solomon, *Through the Media Looking Glass: Decoding Bias and Blather in the News* (Monroe, Maine: Common Courage Press, 1995).

47. Mark Crispin Miller, "What's Wrong with This Picture?" *Nation,* January 7, 2002; "Who Owns What," *Columbia Journalism Review,* http://www.cjr.org/owners (May 18, 2002); Ben H. Bagdikian, *The Media Monopoly: With a New Preface on the Internet and Telecommunications Cartels* (Boston: Beacon, 2000).

48. Cited in Jean Kilbourne, *Can't Buy My Love: How Advertising Changes the Way We Think and Feel* (original title, *Deadly Persuasion: Why Women and Girls Must Fight the Addictive Power of Advertising;* New York: Free Press, 1999).

49. The Proctor & Gamble example is one of many like it cited in Gloria Steinem, "Sex, Lies, and Advertising," *Ms.,* July/August 1990.

50. Kilbourne, *Can't Buy My Love.*

51. Janine Jackson, "Anything but Racism: Media Make Excuses for 'Whitewashed' TV Lineup," *Extra!,* January/February 2000.

52. Women constitute just 18 percent of news sources (including articles and photographs) in the world, according to World Association for Christian Communication, *Who Makes the News? Global Media Monitoring Project 2000,* which can be downloaded from http://www.mediachannel.org/atissue/womensmedia (October 30, 2002).

53. The right-wing funded Independent Women's Forum has mastered this sort of media manipulation, preparing slick PR materials in which they package erroneous data about women and politics as facts. Last year they made headlines claiming that American women now earn equal pay for equal work—a totally inaccurate statement. Nevertheless, reporters (some overworked, others lazy, and others simply sexist) used these prepackaged IWF materials as the basis for a spate of stories contending that feminists are lying about the "myth" of income inequality. See http://www.iwf.org (May 18, 2002).

54. "We Paid $3 Billion for These Stations. We'll Decide What the News Is," *Extra! Update,* June 1998.

55. ABC insiders quoted in the FAIR report "Fear & Favor 2000: How Power Shapes the News," http://www.fair.org/ff2000.html (May 18, 2002).

56. James Bates and Richard Verrier, "Disney Says It's on Way to Recovery," *Los Angeles Times,* September 22, 2001.

57. "Party Review from the Night of 100 Stars," ABC News, *Good Morning America,* March 27, 2000.

58. Eric Deggans, "Is This Any Way to Make Music?" *St. Petersburg Times,* April 13, 2001; Brian Lowry, "Television: New Faces of Synergy 2001," *Los Angeles Times,* March 11, 2001.

59. Time/Yahoo Chat Transcript from June 25, 1998, http://www.time.com/time/community/transcripts/chattr062598.html (May 18, 2002).

60. As this essay goes to press, WIMN is not yet on-line; by the time you read this essay, it is likely that WIMN's Web site will be available by typing the words "Women in Media & News" into an Internet search engine. Because WIMN is being formed to aid feminists and others interested in learning to become media literate and media active, the group will welcome comments, questions, and inquiries from students, activists, and reporters.

61. Carabillo et al., *Feminist Chronicles: 1953–1993;* Pozner, "Missing in Action: Whatever Happened to the Gender Gap?" *Women's Review of Books,* February 2002; Barbara Rick, "She Says: Women in News," PBS, December 19, 2001, and the Washington Press Club Foundation's "Women in Journalism" Oral History Project, http://npc.press.org/wpforal/ohhome.htm (May 18, 2002).

62. http://www.sojourner.org; www.fair.org/extra; www.bitchmagazine.com; www.democracynow.org; www.workingforchange.com/radio/index.cfm/; www.fair.org/counterspin/; www.fire.or.cr/indexeng.htm (May 18, 2002).

63. http://www.indymedia.org; www.dyketv.org; www.papertiger.org (May 18, 2002).

64. http://www.interrupt.org; www.mediaed.org; www.mediachannel.org; www.wifp.org; www.democraticmedia.org; www.prometheusradio.org; and www.mediatank.org (May 18, 2002).

SUSANNAH B. MINTZ

In a Word, *Baywatch*

▬ ▬This essay explores the contradictory representation of women on television, particularly the way in which a single program can at once challenge and underwrite traditional attitudes toward gender. While financial and technological advances may seem to afford women ever-broader choices—not only of careers and lifestyles but also of ways to define female identity itself—TV nonetheless perpetuates a reductive counternarrative about what it means to be a woman in contemporary American culture. On one level, current programming has responded to the real influx of women in jobs traditionally held by men, as well as to the increased political and economic presence of ethnic minorities, people with disabilities, and gay women. It's easy to be persuaded that sexism is a relic of a bygone era when the fictional world of TV features so many self-actualized women: toughened cops, lawyers, and judges; paramedics and physicians; single and sexually active women; divorced women and working moms; women of color and lesbians. Women on TV are well educated, professionally ambitious, and they claim top billing in any number of prime-time dramas on network TV. Yet, as I will argue here, the fact that television now includes configurations of gender, race, class, disability, and sexuality that would have been utterly foreign to the world of Carol Brady or Mary Tyler Moore does not necessarily indicate that complicated social issues are being treated particularly seriously. Nor does it mean that any fundamental change has occurred in the baseline conservative ideology prevalent on network TV.

To the contrary, the deeply ambivalent representation of women by popular media serves to perpetuate—even as it may also seem to resist—conventional values. Indeed, those very shows that present women as comfortably and securely "liberated" are often the blithest perpetrators of stereotyped attitudes about gender. In what follows, I will outline several common narrative and structural tactics that work to reinforce a limited vision of acceptable female identity or behavior, subordinating women who stand outside the boundaries of the normative position. Many mainstream TV shows present audiences with ethnically diverse, communal workplaces in which women seem to enjoy positions of authority or equality with their male colleagues, yet alongside such guilt-assuaging fantasies lie traditional expectations about subjectivity that destabilize portrayals of women as intellectual, economic, or professional peers. An informal tally of plots from popular crime shows, for example, reveals that violence against women continues to be fetishized. Such programs tend to fuse cultural myths about women, conflating their image both as helpless innocents in need of "special" protection and as threateningly sexualized objects (on these shows, women who are victims of violent crime are bandied about between the perpetrators, the police, and the opposing lawyers in a macabre mimicry of patriarchal marriage rituals).[1] Television also depicts women in bifurcated roles of temptress and nurturer. Women's professional status is frequently mediated by overt efforts to "beautify" or maternalize them, or both. Further, the typical female character on TV is white, financially secure, healthy, and heterosexual. African American women who are cast in positions of power and social cachet have only a negligible impact on an episode's plot. Working women rarely figure at the forefront of the most popular shows. Women with disabilities or with "abnormal" bodies are often shown making unconventional choices, as if to further stigmatize physical differences. Contemporary popular television reinforces the idea that women are less intelligent and less authoritative than men, and more focused on their relationships, their looks, and other people's feelings.

In effect, much current programming overlays the putative achievement of second wave feminist goals—such as equal employment and education opportunities, better access to health care and child care, and a recognition of women as legitimate and vocal agents in the public sphere—with the postfeminism popularized by Naomi Wolf, Katie Roiphe, and Rene Denfeld.[2] Associated with hostility toward what they deem "victim" feminism and by an emphasis on the individualistic rewards of "the boys' world of sex and capital" (as Carolyn Scrisio and Deborah L. Siegel have argued),[3] these postfeminist writers put forward an image of American women as the fully empowered legatees of older feminists' struggles for economic self-sufficiency and psychological, sexual independence. In so doing, they simplify complex intersections of race, class, sexual orientation, and embodiment that not only differentiate some women's lives and identities from others', but also render the notion of equal access to money and power utopian in the most reductive sense.[4] In persistently representing women as professionally successful, sexually expressive, able to make their own "choices"—but also white, upper middle-class, heterosexual, youthful, and able-bodied—popular television perpetuates those elisions that problematize so-called "power" feminism. While the preponderance of women represented as smart and capable is meant to prove TV's "feminist" leanings,[5] marking its transcendence of the sexism that drove *Charlie's Angels* or *Three's Company*, television nonetheless demonstrates the way in which misogyny can go underground, asserting its force through less visible—and therefore more difficult to combat—avenues. This makes television an enormously effective tool with which to sustain patriarchal ideology.

RUNWAY MODELS AND MOMS: THE TWO FACES OF FEMALE LAWYERS

Consider the paradigm typified by three white, female, assistant district attorneys: *Law & Order*'s erstwhile Abbie Carmichael, Helen Gamble from *The Practice*, and Alexandra Cabot on *Law & Order: SVU* (Special Victims' Unit). Each of these women is professionally successful, assertive, and outspoken, not afraid to wield her knowledge of the law and her verbal eloquence as potent armaments in legal battles with men. These are women with voices, women who don't seem to suffer insecurities about their gendered identity. They are also—by contemporary standards of beauty—remarkably, even improbably, alluring. Abbie (Angie Harmon) and Helen (Lara Flynn Boyle) are especially thin; their bodies and features are hard and angular. They accentuate their femaleness through clothing and make-up. Alexandra (Stephanie March) dresses in outfits more appropriate for a cocktail party—sleeveless black dresses, for instance—than for stressful disputes over child homicide or domestic abuse. Helen favors tight miniskirts and high heels that show her legs to advantage, and she wears high-gloss lipstick that draws attention to her mouth for erotic, rather than rhetorical, appeal. All of these characters speak in soft, husky tones.[6] Their penciled brows arc unnaturally over their eyes, conveying both scorn and surprise, a curiously flirtatious expression that encapsulates women's double-edged sexual appeal as objects at once domineering and penetrable.

How do we read women who exhibit the conventionally manly traits of intelligence and mental toughness—especially the cunning and the gritty, take-no-prisoners aggressiveness we associate with lawyers? To the degree that female lawyers are problematic trespassers into the domains of men, especially in the romanticized world of TV dramas, TV shows attempt to make such masculinized women less threatening by overtly eroticizing them, exaggerating a conventional style of femininity. Prime-time's lady lawyers soften their intellectual edge with lip gloss and form-fitting outfits that confirm something soothingly basic about them: they are still available to, even actively seeking, male desire. To compensate for the role-reversal—in effect, to ensure that women haven't become men just because they have become lawyers—TV portrayals of professional women reassert two traditional poles of Western culture's myth of essential femininity: woman as sex object and woman as mother.

The latter strategy is exemplified by series like *Law & Order: SVU*, *Family Law*, and *Judging Amy*, each of which tends to champion the rights of children. *Family Law* and *Judging Amy* feature female lawyers and judges who specialize in "family law," and the main characters' own experiences as mothers and daughters are prominent components of both series. Although these shows do seem concerned with exploring the difficulties of divorce and single mothering, they also depend for much of their appeal on cultural stereotypes of women as naturally caring and empathetic, highly attuned to interpersonal dynamics. By making women the special guardians of children and the family, TV allows professional women to "leave home" literally, but not figuratively, in the new context of their jobs. In this way, women are insistently redomesticated, a narrative and structural move that assuages audience anxiety about the fact that women have crossed the boundaries of domesticity to work alongside men whose positions they continually threaten to assume. On one level TV offers a realistic depiction of women's entrance into the public sphere, yet on another, it manages to insinuate that they haven't moved very far from the domestic sphere at all. If the old saw had it that brains and beauty couldn't coexist in a woman, that a working woman would inevitably neglect her responsibilities—or worse, destroy her "real" identity, that is as a mother —contemporary TV has simply conflated the various antitheses. Women may be smart, it tells us, but they must also be either gorgeous or motherly (or both). Women are still women (and therefore *not* men).

(JURIS)PRUDENCE: PROTECTING THE INTERESTS OF THE DOMINANT FEW

If we look more closely at *The Practice, Law & Order,* and *ER,* we can observe how narrowly popular television conceives of what's beautiful, successful, or even possible for women. The normative female character in each of these shows is Anglo-European, upper middle-class, heterosexual, and able-bodied. The characters in *The Practice* act out especially marked hierarchies of gender, class, and race. Between assistant D.A. Helen Gamble and lawyers Lindsay Dole and Ellenor Frutt, women do dominate many of the story lines. But notice the way in which the show allocates power among the ranks. Bobby Donnell (Dylan McDermott) stands at the center of the firm and the head of the series. It is *his* practice, and he is the one to whose decision-making control all the other members of the firm, if at times reluctantly, defer. He is flanked by pretty women: both Helen and Lindsay are former girlfriends, and Lindsay is now his wife.[7]

Moreover, *The Practice* implicitly denigrates the firm's two most obviously "other" women, Ellenor Frutt (Camryn Manheim) and Rebecca Washington (Lisa Gay Hamilton). For instance, the overweight Ellenor once dated George Vogelman, a psychopath who toted around the decapitated head of his victim in a black doctor's bag and disguised himself as a nun before attacking first Lindsay and then Ellenor with a gleaming butcher's knife. In the development of these events over several episodes, Ellenor lamented her susceptibility to deceit by violent males, making it clear that she understood that her vulnerability had everything to do with a sense of being unattractive to "normal" men—men like Bobby, for example, whom the other white women were already sharing. Such a confession was built into the script in order to assure us that the show fully recognized the association it was making between Ellenor's weight—the sign of her failure to be appealing to attractive men—and social deviance. We were meant to feel sorry for Ellenor, as well as to admire the series' implicit awareness of the "problem" faced by heavy women in a world obsessed by thinness. All the while, however, *The Practice* quite uncritically perpetuated the notion that women whose bodies or behavior do not conform to the norm should expect (that is, deserve) no better than to be courted by homicidal maniacs. Though it may be true that romantic troubles afflict many women who are, like Ellenor, otherwise fiercely independent and self-confident, this particular story line reduced the enormous complexity of such questions to something cartoonishly, even grotesquely unsubtle.

The 2000–01 season of *The Practice* began with both Lindsay and Ellenor announcing their pregnancies. But it was Ellenor, already marked as having an "abnormal" female body—at once excessively fleshy and insufficiently "feminine"—who was determined to parent alone. Ellenor's gutsiness was, in one way, deemed admirable, her willingness to be a single mother yet another example of her strength and courage. Yet, it was also a further sign of her difference, her inability to meet standard expectations of womanly behavior. How is it that Ellenor's intelligence, appearance, and bravery do not add up to a convincing exploration of the limitations of patriarchal definitions of "family"? How does the show manage to manipulate our disdain for the notion of single mothering, even as it seems to exhort us to share Ellenor's happiness? It has another character object. When Jimmy Berluti (Michael Badalucco), the firm's spokesman for overly simplified, good-hearted, working-class morals, accuses Ellenor of selfishly jeopardizing the welfare of her child by choosing to have it without "a father," his message is purely punitive. Far from voicing any clearly articulated position about the role men could or ought to take in rearing children, Jimmy's complaint stems from an openly personal anxiety about losing male privilege in the face of women's psychological and economic independence. By embedding a critique of Ellenor into the script itself, *The Practice* absolves itself of responsibility for its own dissemination of conservative rhetoric. Later, in response to Ellenor's anger at his surveillance of her, Jimmy has recourse to that same paternalistic ideology, defending himself on the grounds that his no-holds-barred moralizing is an expression of familial affection. Substituting "feeling" for critical inquiry, Jimmy claims that judging each other is just what people in big families "do." Such a notion, however, merely enables the perpetuation of a conservative status quo under the guise of liberal inclusivity. In a world where the mythic bonds of family wrap securely around divergent perspectives, a man like Jimmy is not challenged to rethink the biases of his moral perspective.

Ultimately, *The Practice* doesn't uphold its premise that Ellenor's choice is just one other among many possible versions of family and mothering. The structural juxtaposition between Ellenor's pregnancy and Lindsay's, compounded by the fact that Ellenor is already marked as having a "freakish" female body, redoubles the stigma of her pregnancy. Ellenor's sexuality has been demonized by her involvement with George Vogelman, which is itself connected to the "problem" of her weight; it's hard not to hear Lindsay's assurance that Ellenor's friends will eventually accept the idea of her having a baby as code for the less tasteful image of an obese woman having sex. By failing to grant Ellenor any kind of "normal" erotic relationship (such as the one Lindsay enjoys), *The Practice* portrays Ellenor's out-of-wedlock pregnancy as the logical outcome of her undesirability on one hand and her own (unconventional?) desires on the other. Lindsay's pregnancy is both the result of, and now safely contained within, the bounds of lawful, loving, marital sex; Ellenor's pregnancy is mysterious, unauthorized, and, by dint of the way in which the show has already presented her size as a disability, one more sign of her culturally determined difference. That *The Practice* so resolutely piles up instances of difference in the figure of Ellenor suggests an inability to fully unearth or up-end a fundamentally traditional perspective.

It is the pronounced marginality of Rebecca Washington (Lisa Gay

Hamilton), however, that most clearly testifies to *The Practice*'s failure to think critically about its representation of diversity. As if in unapologetic imitation of black women's double cultural invisibility, Rebecca is the least prominent of the show's primary lawyers. Rebecca is often literally in the background of scenes shot in the law office. As a junior member of the firm, she is more often a conveyor of information to others than an active participant in the firm's cases. During a staff meeting in one episode, members of the firm eagerly ask to assist Lindsay on a serial-killer case; Bobby grants the second-chair position to Jimmy. As the scene shifts, we hear Rebecca cry, "That's not fair!" With pointed irony, the phrase encapsulates the way in which all the other lawyers are busier and more powerful than Rebecca. Bobby's act of choosing Jimmy reinforces both the dominance of white characters and the priority of men over women, yet at no point does the script correct for this "unfairness." Rebecca fares worse on *The Practice* than do Eugene Young (the black male lawyer also frequently cast as onlooker) or Ellenor. As if to dramatize this point, Rebecca's face no longer appears on screen at the moment of her saying "That's not fair." Detached from her body, the outcry seems intended to have "universal" meaning—both Eugene and Ellenor could just as well have voiced the same objection. But by disembodying Rebecca's complaint, the camera work and video editing also obscure its origin in the specific situation of a black woman. And without further comment, the script draws the lines of allegiance around Bobby and Jimmy, the firm's two white men.

LAW AND THE PHALLIC ORDER

The Practice depicts African American women in roles of putative authority that have the paradoxical effect of reasserting an essential ineffectuality. This is equally evident on *Law & Order,* which strips away the power that its sole black female character appears to have by consistently subordinating her either to more prominent white women or to male characters. As a police lieutenant, Anita Van Buren (S. Epatha Merkerson) supervises the show's male detective duo, Lennie Briscoe (Jerry Orbach) and Ed Green (Jesse L. Martin). There's no question that lieutenant ranks above detective; Van Buren has institutional power over the men in her squad, which she expresses almost entirely by giving them instructions during the early stages of a case. I call these "stating the obvious" moments, because her advice is often on the order of suggesting that the detectives check DMV records when a victim turns up in an abandoned car (though there are also moments when she sets her clumsy detectives straight). Whereas the most recent cohorts of assistant D.A. Jack McCoy (Sam Waterston) have been white women whose intelligence, if not their participation during trial, matches his, Van Buren plays no significant crime-solving role that would signify her intellectual equality with her male detectives. One might argue that this dynamic merely reflects the reality that a lieutenant's connection to a case is indeed more managerial than hands-on. Yet Lieutenant Van Buren's authority seems merely titular, her function mediatory and contingent; she is primarily a conduit linking the binary pair of police and lawyers and rarely does anything on her own to forward the evolution or resolution of the case. While all the other primary characters actively track down clues and think up strategy, Van Buren remains static—a prop rather than an agent. Worse, to the degree that the lieutenant's actions serve to assist her male subordinates on the one hand and the white lawyers on the other, she seems more handmaiden than head-honcho.

By casting a black woman as police lieutenant or depicting the struggles of working-class men against men of status and privilege, *Law & Order* encourages its audience to identify with its good intentions. Nonetheless, embedded at its core are problematic configurations of gender, race, and power that reproduce age-old assumptions about women. The show's tendency to stimulate our compassion for men, for example—even when, and perhaps especially when, those men admit to colluding against the achievement of "justice" for female victims—works to underwrite the concerns of a patriarchal system. In a story during the 2000–01 season, Briscoe and Green reopen a twenty-year-old case—an unsolved rape and murder perpetrated by an ambassador's son, whose powerful father pulls strings to protect the ne'er-do-well from indictment. The trial initially goes badly for the prosecutors; the bereaved mother endures the proceedings with a pained expression; and Lieutenant Van Buren seems in danger of further reprimands from her supervisor for a surplus of open cases. In the eleventh hour, however, the lead detective on the original case, now retired, admits on the stand that he was coerced into withholding vital evidence that would have led investigators to the ambassador's son. His motive for succumbing to the pressure? A coveted promotion, which in turn earned him the pride of his elderly father, who was in a nursing home at that time. The case is salvaged for the district attorneys by the change of heart of this retired policeman. The introduction of this second father-son couple fully shifts our attention away from the episode's other parent-child pair, the dead woman and her mother. Moreover, we now have a new set of victims—not only the wounded ego of the retired detective who is caught up in guilt and crisis of conscience, but also his late father, who (we realize) was duped into unjustified pride for his son's accomplishments.

This juxtaposition of narrative elements is quite revealing. The episode concerns the abuse of power; we are meant to sympathize with the retired cop, to recognize the conflict between his desires to win his father's affection and to maintain ethical integrity. But in another way, this tale—in which the individual eager for institutional and parental approval of his sham accomplishments ends up trapped in his own deceit—reproduces the patriarchal structure it is ostensibly unpacking. Women haunt the periphery of this episode. Their problems merely get collapsed, however, into the patriarchal dance of men who compete with, domineer, and ultimately redeem each other. In the final scene, Lennie assures his older pal that what he did was, if not exactly "right," at least understandable, and the last shot in the episode frames these two warriors of crimes committed on both sides of the blue wall. It is a potent visual, but it also manages to exclude the two women who were the original focus of the episode: Lieutenant Van Buren, whose "failure" to close enough cases sets this one back in motion, and the woman whose death led to an illustration of patriarchal power, even as it ultimately leads to the scene of male bonding that closes the episode. Confession is followed by at least partial absolution: if we are shown the ways in which our longing for paternal approbation (or conversely, our resistance to it, as in the case of the ambassador's son) can make us compromise our values, we are also encouraged to recognize the essential legitimacy of this urge for parental approval. As Lennie adopts the role of father-confessor, knowingly excusing his old friend's actions in a wave of sentimentality for a flawed hero-mentor, the retired detective insinuates himself—as son, father, and police officer—into the forefront of our sympathetic response to the show. And in the process, three aggrieved women—the daughter, the mother, and the lieutenant—are utterly elided from our view. An episode that looks like a sensitive critique of class privilege and patriarchal power ends up re-entrenching the monolithic singularity of the father.

EMERGENCY ROOM: RESCUING AN IMPERILED CENTER

ER also capitalizes on a veneer of demographic diversity that hides a more uncritical acceptance of normative identities. The ensemble that makes up the cast has always included a fairly even mix of men and women, and over the years, women have moved into positions of greater authority and visibility. Drs. Kerry Weaver, Elizabeth Corday, Susan Lewis, and Jing-Mei Chen are integral to the success of both the fictional E.R. and the TV program as well; like their counterparts in the courtroom, they are confident, intelligent, independent women whose medical moxie and professional ambition match the men's. By focusing our attention primarily on doctors, however, the show creates a breach between the dominant characters (most of whom are white) and the supporting cast (most of whom—the nurses and technicians—are not). Indeed, white, upper middle-class, heterosexual experience is situated at the very core of the E.R. The marriage of Doctors Mark Greene (Anthony Edwards) and Elizabeth Corday (Alex Kingston), for example, puts an end to a string of bad pairings for Mark, first with his wife, a prickly lawyer who put her career ambitions above his; then with Latina nurse Chuny; and finally with an emotionally unstable desk clerk. The choice of fellow physician Elizabeth as Mark's second wife allows the show to sidestep thorny questions about whose needs take priority—husband's or wife's, working father's or working mother's. Following the departure of Doctors Peter Benton (Eriq La Salle) and Cleo Finch (Michael Michele), white couples' liaisons dominate the landscape: Carter (Noah Wyle) and Abby (Maura Tierney), Carter and Susan (Sherry Stringfield), Luka (Goran Visnjic) and Abby. *ER* sends the message that other types of relationships—particularly ones that cross class and race boundaries, such as Mark and Chuny's, or Peter's brief affair with Elizabeth—constitute a discomfiting, and ultimately ill-fated, deviation.

Consider the evolution of Laura Innes's character, Kerry Weaver. As one of *ER*'s two characters with a disability (the other was Peter's son, who is deaf), Kerry is in a unique position to demystify cultural stereotypes about physical difference, and the show has in fact handled Kerry's disability with remarkable seriousness. Disability is freighted with cultural meaning: for some, the broken body functions as both what David Mitchell calls "a metaphor of social collapse" and a sign of personal moral or ethical failure.[8] When Kerry first joined the E.R., she was presented as shrewd and unfeeling, overly invested in rules and regulations. This made her success problematic; she was an ugly indication of how feminism has "crippled" femininity, perverting women's natural capacity for healing and nurturance. Over time, however, Kerry's personality has modulated toward a balance of insisting on protocols and genuinely caring for her staff and patients. The fact that her need for a crutch has never been explained integrates her disability as simply one among many aspects of her character, rather than reducing the crutch to a symbol of one stigmatizing trait: on only a few occasions has the subject become explicit, and Kerry has always refused to explain. To an extent, then, Kerry's disability is represented as just one other form of corporeal reality. As her character has become less unidimensional, so too has her physical handicap become more than—or perhaps, just something more mundane than—a sign for the crabbed bitchiness associated with female authority or control.

Yet the problem with Kerry's character is that, much like Ellenor on *The Practice,* she is made to occupy too many positions of otherness. As the chief of emergency medicine, Kerry wields more power than any of the other major female characters; she is also the most stereotypically masculinized. One might argue that an abrasive resistance to being swept up in the personal problems of one's underlings is an inevitable by-product of success in the competitive world of medicine; using this interpretation, she is a "power" feminist. But we have only to compare Kerry to Mark to see that power need not be wholly associated with stern aloofness. If Mark starts out as the unthreatening, "sensitive," slightly dorky, balding man offered up as patriarchy's response to feminism (the appeal of which is proven by his getting the most brilliant and beautiful girl), Kerry's limp and crutch end up seeming inseparable from her strength of will and control, her command over people, money, and knowledge within the domain of the E.R.—which are also bound up with the fact she seems isolated and lonely. Indeed, the writers of the show can't seem to figure out how to accord Kerry a satisfying love life; like Ellenor, Kerry is situated, by virtue of physical difference, at the outskirts of romantic "success." In one brief, tantalizing moment a few years ago, Kerry leapt into the arms of an African man who wandered into the emergency room just as the episode was ending; he never reappeared. Later, she fell for a sleazy doctor-cum-businessman who manipulated her to gain advantage with hospital administrators. Most recently, she has come out as a lesbian, yet neither of her two affairs thus far have led to a sustained relationship. By thus linking atypical lifestyles or identity formations with the figure already designated as "other" by virtue of physical dysfunction, *ER* fails to take both disability and gay or interracial relationships completely seriously. Network television favors such piling on of marginalizing characteristics, which has the effect of telescoping those characteristics as if they are functions or symptoms of a kind of internal, holistic wrongness. While engaging with tough social questions on one level, these shows also reinforce the beliefs of the dominant culture through the double encoding of difference—disability with lesbianism, obesity with single mothering, and so on.[9]

The character of Cleo Finch (now departed from *ER*) serves a purpose similar to that of Lieutenant Van Buren on *Law & Order.* Cleo was clearly meant to be seen as independent and assertive, yet her typical mode on the show was stern, bitter, and resentful. In one episode, Cleo referred to the fact that her mother was white, which was meant to account for her prickly defensiveness about instances of discrimination in the hospital. Again, a whole set of complicated issues was evoked— including both the status of African Americans in medicine and the subtler question of how race is defined, according to what sort of taxonomy. Yet to present her as a one-dimensional angry woman is not to address those questions in a thoughtful way, but rather to flatten her character to the singular and supposedly stable "fact" of race. Few episodes spotlighted Cleo; she was rarely portrayed as medically savvy; and although nearly every other main character has had a plot line devoted to his or her personal life, Cleo's relationship with Peter was consistently overshadowed by the romantic lives of the white couples. She remained unidimensional; like Lieutenant Van Buren in *Law & Order* and Rebecca in *The Practice,* Cleo took a backseat to the more prominent characters and their dramatic existences, serving a kind of backup function in the emergency room. And like the others, Cleo was both a sign of guilty oppression and a token of liberal tolerance: as a "half"-black woman in power who keeps bringing up race, she could assuage the writers' guilt about the dominance of white characters on the show; nonetheless, by situating her in the background of the narrative time and again, the *mise-en-scène* became Cleo's *mise-en-abyme* of suppression.

CLIPPED WINGS:
THE GROUNDING OF WOMEN IN POLITICS

It is on NBC's hit show *The West Wing* that misogyny rears its head most flagrantly and most insidiously. This dreamscape of American politics is like the *ER* of Capitol Hill—hip, smart, good-looking thirty-somethings stride along White House corridors with lots of swooping camera work and clipped repartee. *The West Wing* practically exhorts us to pledge allegiance, with its righteous rhetoric and well-timed upswells of violin music. The question is, to what sort of worldview would we be offering our loyalty? I want to focus here not so much on *The West Wing*'s representation of a Democratic president (a sanitized John F. Kennedy or Bill Clinton) as on the way in which that liberal platform makes the show's depiction of gender so deeply problematic. In an episode called "Galileo," first broadcast in November 2000, various story lines combined to present the two primary female characters—Press Secretary C.J. Cregg (Allison Janney) and secretary Donna Moss (Janel Moloney)—as childish, vaguely incompetent, and self-doubting. In contrast, all of the men exhibited sharp wit, keen political insight, and at times brash self-assurance. This gendered distinction seems especially apparent in the last two seasons, and it represents a conspicuous shift from the depiction of women during the program's first season.

When the episode begins, C.J. is preparing President Bartlet (Martin

Sheen) for a televised classroom, scheduled to coincide with the landing of the spacecraft *Galileo 5* on Mars. In their brief exchange, the president complains that C.J. is not enunciating *"Galileo 5"* "correctly"—that is, with a child's passion and wonder: "You didn't say it right," he says. She responds, "I said it fine." And he demands: "Say it again." It is as if C.J. were indeed an uncoordinated child who requires paternal coaching. Moments later, we see Deputy Communications Director Sam Seaborn (Rob Lowe) ad-libbing a speech for the president; rousing music cues us to pay attention, just as C.J. and the president are themselves riveted on Sam's display of extemporaneous eloquence. The performance is impressive (if unlikely), and its purpose in the narrative made clear when Bartlet taps C.J. on the arm and whispers, *"He said it right."* C.J. sighs—she's been upstaged by a man, gotten it "wrong."

In the next scene, C.J. and Communications Director Toby Ziegler (Richard Schiff) disagree about whether a quote in a midwestern paper that the president doesn't like green beans will be picked up by the national press. Toby worries that it will become news; C.J. insists that it won't. Her legitimacy as the media liaison is implicitly on the line here: it's part of C.J.'s job to ward off potential public relations snags for the administration and to foresee the ways in which even seemingly insignificant events can initiate much more complex political situations. Each time she declares that the green beans bit is inconsequential, therefore, C.J. indicts herself as professionally incapable. In this case, the president's legume preference extends all the way to Oregon, where snap bean farming is big money—and where Bartlet won the electorate by only a small margin. But it is Toby, not C.J., who immediately grasps the political implications of the story, and he assumes an attitude of smug superiority: certain that C.J. is wrong, he has only to wait for her to realize it. "See me in three hours," he says, and she does, admitting that she *was* wrong (again): "So it took me two hours and twenty minutes longer to figure it out than it took you. Doesn't make you smarter than I am." Toby replies, "Of course not." Moments later, however, we hear C.J. protest, this time in response to a crack from Sam, "Hey, that is like the fourth time I've been called dumb today."

The running theme in all of this is that while C.J. tries frantically to bone up on everything, men are literal know-it-alls (President Bartlet is a Nobel Prize–winner in economics, and his exaggerated stores of knowledge are showcased persistently). The question of C.J.'s aptitude for a position that requires a good deal of political know-how has been a component of her characterization from the beginning of the series. It is not at all uncommon for her to make such ironically self-deprecating remarks as, "Don't ask C.J. She doesn't know anything," or "Excuse me. I need to go look like an idiot." I would argue, however, that the "Galileo" episode crossed a threshold from irony to a far more disturbing disregard for women that explicitly exalts men at women's expense. In this episode, C.J. is anticipated, outdone, corrected, chided, and bossed about by every man in the show, from the president himself down to the president's personal aide, Charlie Young (Dule Hill). Worse yet, there is no scene in which she is able to recoup her dignity or intelligence against the tide of male condescension. What differentiates the portrayal of women and men on *The West Wing* is precisely this—while the male characters also roundly and constantly mock each other, they have already convinced us of their brilliance by being able to debate policy, rattle off statistics, point out the flaws in opposing political views, and so forth. In contrast, C.J. merely transports that knowledge from one site to another. Much like Lieutenant Van Buren, Rebecca Washington, and Cleo Finch, C.J. plays a mediatory role. While (white) men make laws, debate policy, and generally determine the fate of the nation, C.J. reacts to and transmits their needs, ideas, words, and actions to others.

Things go from bad to worse for C.J. in "Galileo." Toward the end of the episode, Charlie admits to C.J. that he was the one who leaked Bartlet's dislike of green beans to a food writer. C.J. attempts to explain to Charlie the delicacy of this apparently innocuous incident—and to recover, in effect, her professional stature:

> "Did you leave any wriggle room?"
> "Wriggle room? What the hell, C.J., he doesn't like green beans."
> (C.J. explains about the farmers and the votes.)
> "C.J.—"
> "This is a serious thing now!"

"Well, I'm sorry I mouthed off to the reporter, but you're out of your mind."

"No, I'm—"

"Education's a serious thing. Crime, jobs, national security. In eighteen months I've been to Oregon four times, and not a single person I've met there has been stupid."

"Everybody's stupid in an election year, Charlie."

"No, everybody gets treated stupid in an election year, C.J."

Phrases like "What the hell, C.J." and "you're out of your mind," Charlie's repeated resistance to her arguments, his interrupting her, even his use of C.J.'s name, all suggest a mild dressing-down more than a dialogue between equals. Charlie, a smart but inexperienced aide in his twenties, is guilty of having set in motion a situation "serious" enough to get prominent White House staffers worried about its repercussions. Yet he speaks to C.J. with all the authority of an insider who knows the terrain better than she, rejecting her every assessment of events. He even invokes an age-old association between women and madness. C.J. starts the episode getting riled up like an agitated teenager in the face of Toby's unflappable superiority, and she ends it an overreacting, "hysterical" woman, "out of her mind."

If C.J.'s problem is that she lags behind her male colleagues, always on the verge of a mild bungle, Donna's is that she is too eager, and not properly cognizant of her own ignorance. Conversations with her boss, Deputy Chief of Staff Josh Lyman (Bradley Whitford), make brutally obvious the hierarchy subtending their relationship—he is the wise-cracking teacher, friendly but also capable of sardonic digs; she is the bright but flighty pupil, sincere and ultimately not to be taken seriously. Josh humors Donna but does not really listen to her, instructing rather than engaging with her. In turn, Donna's bubbly non sequiturs seem to prove that at a certain point she will not be able to keep up with Josh's experience or intellect; he (or some other man of the show, such as the president), will swoop in to save her. Donna is a character with whom the average viewer can readily identify; she represents the kind of generalized, unspecific, and slightly misguided knowledge about politics that many Americans have. At the same time, it's clear we're meant to be impressed with Josh, and to feel comforted that such reasonable, well-versed individuals are at the country's helm. But Josh's good qualities are articulated at the expense of Donna, who ends up seeming daffy and uninformed rather than politically curious or committed to a legitimate cause. And to the extent that we do in fact identify with Donna, we must also experience the brunt of her naïveté.

C.J. and Donna strive to play ball with men who are forever one step ahead of them. C.J., whose position brings her into contact with a wide range of people, seems especially drained by men's conflicting messages and concerns. In "Galileo," she repeatedly recapitulates the ideas of others, and just as often finds herself rebuffed. She can't seem to do right, no matter how much effort she expends ventriloquizing what she hears. She begins the episode convinced—and not without reason—that her male colleagues do not respect her abilities or her intelligence, and she closes it with a proclamation that resolutely returns her to a sexualized body, seeming only to further undermine her intellectual and professional credibility. Referring to a dispute she had earlier in the show with a former boyfriend, C.J. announces to Sam, Josh, Toby, and President Bartlet that she is "good in bed." Although it may be fair to congratulate C.J. for owning her own sexual desire, her advertisement of being a skillful lover—and her choice of venue, the Oval Office—suggests not so much a modern or feminist acceptance of women's active sexuality than an attempt to resist patriarchal disregard by proving her successful participation in the heterosexual economy. Recognition of her skill in bed is the only approbation C.J. receives in this episode, and she insists upon it with as much defiant pride as she had previously insisted on having had good SAT scores. (As was true for Ellenor and Kerry, C.J.'s sexual appeal and prowess are essentially in question here, while those of Helen Gamble never are.) *The West Wing* denies its women any sort of realistic combination of sexual expression and intellectual activity; indeed, it subordinates the latter to the former, equating a woman's self-worth with her attractiveness to men (compare Josh and Sam, whose dalliances and flirtations with all manner of beautiful women are integrated into their characterizations as deft and canny politicos). Far from self-actualized sexual expression, C.J.'s comment makes her seem ridiculous and immature, while her sophisticated male counterparts dart her sidelong embarrassed looks.

The West Wing compounds its gender politics with an accompanying, if more subtly deployed, complicity in hierarchies of race. In several episodes bridging the 1999 and 2000 seasons, a racist militia group targeted Charlie, who is black, because of his romantic relationship with the president's daughter, Zoey Bartlet. During an assassination attempt, both Josh and Bartlet (but neither Charlie nor Zoey) were shot. Rather than follow Charlie through this traumatic ordeal, however, the show focused on the emotions of the less vulnerable white men. In a particularly disturbing scene, Toby described feeling sickened by what the skinheads had done, by having witnessed a near-"lynching" of their beloved Charlie. In a manner similar to *Law & Order*'s habit of layering subplots about men on top of cases involving dead women, *The West Wing* made use of Charlie—and the whole history of slavery and lynching behind him—to soothe the consciences of white men (those within the narrative as well as the writers of the narrative). We were encouraged to empathize with Toby's distress, to sympathize with Josh and Bartlet as victims, while Charlie and Zoey disappeared from the radar. This sequence of episodes was intended to prove to us that the locus of power in the fictional United States of *The West Wing* merits our admiration and our trust: these are men who really care, men who champion the cause of pluralism and struggle to combat racist and intolerant behavior. What gets obscured in this swagger of oppressor guilt, however, is the series' own normative assumptions. We are still looking at white men, seeing the world from *their* perspectives. Theirs is the prevailing consciousness of the show, and they have swelled to appropriate every subject position—dominance and victimhood alike.

The West Wing has brought racism to the forefront, where it can appear to be "solved" in slick story lines about the president's daughter's love for a black man or outrage at the conformity violently enforced by groups like the Aryan Nation. Yet in the meantime, the show's own marginalization of women carries on unchecked. Does Charlie's interaction with C.J. suggest that the writers are recuperating him—retrieving him from invisibility—at the expense of the woman? More to the point, the fact that *The West Wing* hasn't staged an elaborate "apology" for sexism, in the way that it has for a variety of other social injustices, indicates that it doesn't perceive women to be unequal. Feminism, some might protest, has "worked"; why keep harping on women's problems? (References to "lipstick feminism"—as when White House legal counsel Ainsley Hayes [Emily Procter] noisily defends her right to enjoy compliments from men on how she looks and then demands that someone "get [her] a muffin" [2002]—merely trivialize the divergent and complex varieties of contemporary feminism.) Yet TV programs like *The West Wing* are active purveyors of what Craig Davidson once referred to as "casual prejudice."[10] Discussing homophobia, Davidson writes that the most "problematic" offenders are people "who claim to have nothing against gays—or even to support them—but who nevertheless think, speak, and behave in ways that rely on and reinforce anti-gay attitudes," and he goes on to suggest that while "fag-bashing" is acceptable humor on TV, "similar black-, Jew-, or women-bashing routine[s]" would be unthinkable.[11] Nonetheless, a distinct, if subtle, form of "women-bashing" *is* taking place on *The West Wing.* It's possible, if uncritical, to bracket hostile, patronizing references to women ("rancid piece of meat," "I didn't know you'd be so beautiful") when the speakers of such remarks are already encoded in a program as scoundrels or pathological killers. But the fab five on *The West Wing* are supposed to be the good guys. When women encounter systematic belittling from liberal men who espouse the virtues of civil rights—men who defend interracial relationships, argue for gay marriage, lobby for drug company donations to AIDS victims in Africa, back gun control, fall in love with deaf women, and support Hispanic judges for the U.S. Supreme Court—then we are witnessing something more pernicious, the incredible tenacity of patriarchal ideology. The white men on *The West Wing* may seem to be fighting the good fight, but not once have they critiqued their own implication in hierarchies of gender, race, and power.

CODA

The advent first of cable television and then of the Internet has ensured a type of entertainment for every predilection and personality, literally thousands of electronic venues whereby to satisfy one's desires and to see oneself represented. Yet network television seems to have responded to the proliferation of choices by offering not its own expanded range of styles, identities, and narratives but rather an endless repetition of the same—renewed series, spin-offs, clones, and programs that recapitulate tired tropes of gender, race, class, sexual orientation, and so forth. And millions of households are tuned in to these televised conduct manuals every week. The three *Law & Orders, The West Wing,* and *ER* regularly rank in the top twenty on the Nielsen list. Who's watching? Prime-time advertising is geared toward audiences with substantial discretionary income, especially women; investment brokerages, cars, electronics, and beauty and child care products predominate. During a recent episode of *The Practice,* ads for three separate films—all love stories featuring popular, hunky actors—crowded the commercial breaks. In effect, there is not much difference between the programs and the advertising. Both present highly idealized versions of "reality" in which upper middle-class white women either pursue—or implicitly fail because they haven't pursued—the basic narrative we recognize from fairy tales. The underlying messages of TV have not changed that much since Samantha Stevens was enchanting her way in and out of bourgeois female subjectivity, despite the strategies for reinventing ourselves that postmodernism and technology alike seem to hold out.

When third wave feminists demand not "power" as it is narrowly defined by fundamentally patriarchal and capitalist standards but rather the cultural legitimacy of their multiple identities—transgender, bisexual, interracial, straight, religious, married, maternal, queer, "crippled," and so forth—they indicate the extent to which television has yet to grapple with the serious debates taking place within feminism or with its own conservative leanings. The improved status of women generally may be measurable in terms of economic autonomy, access to health care and reproductive freedom, political activity, presence in professional and managerial occupations, educational levels, and so on. Yet a focus on "opportunities," on what women can *do,* may nonetheless overlook or even obscure more thorny questions about what women *are,* as well as questions about how the popular media work more to restrict than to enlarge women's imaginative possibilities. Television's incessant repetition of reductive images of women—as sexually objectified or "marriage material," as "incomplete" without heterosexual romantic fulfillment, as dumb, flaky, vulnerable, insignificant, or "other"—has a psychological impact on women that is not necessarily reflected in whether they vote, go to college, or own a business. The bottom line of television programming is corporate profitability; as long as the networks, the cable stations, and the Internet are controlled by megaconglomerate interests, one can expect only the most homogenized values to be represented, ones that underwrite, however disguised the mechanism may be, the ideology of white, male power.

NOTES

1. The weekly display of raped or murdered female bodies often includes detailed conversations with doctors or coroners whose clinical anatomization reduces those bodies to their wounded genitalia. One episode of *The Practice,* for instance, centered on the serial killing of nine women, who were variously referred to as "dissected carcass[es]," bodies subjected to "dismemberment," and "bloody mutilations." The use of graphic description, while serving the thematic purpose of villainizing criminals and establishing the terms of the legal battles, also produces a more unconscious effect, forcing us to imaginatively witness (to reenact, in a sense) the murders themselves. The prevalence of plots involving dead female bodies performs a familiar objectification of women, reiterating common assumptions about women being at once vulnerable to men and threateningly sexual, and reifying the acceptability, even the pleasure, of gender-oriented violence. Yet in a more complicated way, it is the very women who are portrayed as empowered and independent—the legal and medical professionals—who frequently serve television's less egalitarian messages.

2. See Naomi Wolf, *Fire with Fire: The New Female Power and How It Will Change the Twenty-First Century* (New York: Random House, 1993); Katie Roiphe, *The Morning After: Sex, Fear, and Feminism on Campus* (New York: Little, Brown, 1993); and Rene Denfeld, *The New Victorians: A Young Woman's Challenge to the Old Feminist Order* (New York: Warner Books, 1995).

3. Carolyn Sorisio, "A Tale of Two Feminisms: Power and Victimization in Contemporary Feminist Debate," in *Third Wave Agenda: Being Feminist, Doing Feminism,* ed. Leslie Heywood and Jennifer Drake (Minneapolis: University of Minnesota Press, 1997), 134–49, 143. See also Deborah L. Siegel's cogent critique of Wolf, Roiphe, et al. in "Reading Between the Waves: Feminist Historiography in a 'Postfeminist' Moment," in the same volume, 55–82.

4. In this sense, these third wave writers merely reproduce, in their critique of second wave feminism, what women of color have said about white, middle-class, heterosexual, academic feminism of the 1970s and 1980s—that it ignores the material experiences of working-class women and women of color.

5. For an excellent discussion of television's response to the feminist and antiracist movements of the 1970s, see Kirsten Marthe Lentz's article "Quality versus Relevance: Feminism, Race, and the Politics of the Sign in 1970s Television," *Camera Obscura* 15, no. 1 (2000): 45–93.

6. I would add to this list Jill Hennessey from *Crossing Jordan,* whom I like to call "coroner-Barbie." With super-glossed lips, Abercrombie and Fitch outfits, and a Monroe-style beauty mark, Dr. Jordan Cavanaugh is a caricature of the overlap of sexual enjoyment and economic solvency taken for third wave feminist "success." Another recent but short-lived addition to the lineup was *Philly*'s Kim Delaney, originally from *NYPD Blue,* who played lawyer and single mother Kathleen McGuire. Like many of her counterparts, Kathleen favored low-cut blouses, spiky heels, and any opportunity to reveal some upper thigh. More significantly, all of *Philly*'s primary characters were white.

7. It is unsurprising that Bobby eventually chose to marry not Helen, the spike-heeled dominatrix hinted at by Lara Flynn Boyle, but Lindsay, the farm-fresh, girl-next-door that Kelli Williams more convincingly pulls off. On *Law & Order,* this role is occupied by new assistant district attorney Serena Southerlyn (Elisabeth Rohm), who replaced the hard-edged Abbie Carmichael. The official *Law & Order* Web site (http://www.nbc.com/law_&_order/index.html [May 15, 2002]) describes Southerlyn as "brilliant and aggressively ambitious." But in clingy turtlenecks and bouncy ponytails, she more often resembles a co-ed than a D.A. She is clearly subordinate to Jack McCoy, whom she repeatedly thanks, and the fact that Jack always tries the cases means that each episode of the show culminates with his rhetorical prowess and authority, not hers.

8. David Mitchell, "Modernist Freaks and Postmodern Geeks," in *The Disability Studies Reader,* ed. Lennard J. Davis (New York: Routledge, 1997), 348–65.

9. Like *The Practice, ER* also featured a single mother, Dr. Jing-Mei Chen (played by Ming-Na, one of prime-time TV's only major Asian American actresses). Because the father of Chen's baby was African American, and *not* a doctor, this liaison was clearly marked as alternative and unlikely to last. Unlike Ellenor, Chen decided to give her baby up for adoption. But Chen's pregnancy was also juxtaposed to that of a "normal" couple, Mark and Elizabeth. Chen is at once diminished because of her race (she does not represent Western culture's idealized female body, though she could be considered "exotic," as an Asian woman) and is privileged by her socioeconomic status as a doctor. On both counts, the representation of her condition recapitulates familiar biases. For one thing, most single mothers in the United States do not earn high salaries as doctors and lawyers. At the same time, both *The Practice* and *ER* treat getting pregnant out of wedlock as something only "other" women do. *ER* has something of a penchant for "bad" mothers: Carter's mother, guilt-ridden and distant; Abby's mother, a manic-depressive played brilliantly by Sally Field; Elizabeth's mother, self-involved and icy; and, years ago, Mark's first wife, the ambitious lawyer.

10. Craig Davidson, "Can We End Media Bias against Gays?" in *American Cul-*

ture and the Media: Reading, Writing, Thinking, ed. Anne Cassebaum and Rosemary Haskell (Boston: Houghton Mifflin, 1997), 152–58.

11. Note the preponderance of female secretaries on the show, women whose bosses are forever barking out their names or (paternalistically) soothing them—Ginger, Margaret, Kathy, Carol, and Donna.

Reviving Lolita; or, Because Junior High Is Still Hell

JUNIOR HIGH HELL—DEDICATION AND INTRODUCTION

If, like me, you think junior high is a cruel experiment designed by sex-hating robots who have never been hunted down by a ferocious pack of fourteen-year-old girls; never had to keep a secret; never lost a best friend; never longed to be part of a ferocious pack of fourteen-year-old girls; never walked down the hallway buzzing with hormones, excitement, and fear, baffled by desire (or by its absence!); never been stared at by men or women twice your age; never stared back; never wondered how everyone could just keep going on, going to class, eating lunch, going home, sleeping, while all this (and so much more) was going on—well, then, this essay is for you.

If you enjoyed junior high (or "middle school") and have no idea what I'm talking about, then this essay is also for you. Maybe you can help out the rest of us.

This essay was inspired by "The Rhetoric of Sexy Girls," a writing class I taught in 1998 at the University of Texas at Austin. In that class, my students and I worked to define a rhetoric—by which we meant a collection of metaphors, arguments, and plot lines—that framed young girls as erotic objects. We began with Lolita, an archetypal sexy girl who first came to America in the 1950s. We then went on to meet a series of very different sexy girls created by women who had been girls of Lolita's age in the 1950s and had written about what that had been like, or what they wished it could have been like. Their work was, in many ways, made possible by the call for women's testimony and stories about women's lives that was issued by the social and political movement of the 1970s, also known as women's liberation or the women's movement. In retrospect, this movement is now sometimes called second wave feminism.[1] Many of the students in my writing class found the stories told by these feminist authors startlingly familiar. They were surprised, and a little shocked, to remember that the stories were set in a time before they were born—surely, they said, the characters and their lives should have seemed more distant. We ended the class by reading stories that were currently being told by girls in books, in handmade self-distributed 'zines, and on personal home pages on the World Wide Web. We found their connections to the stories set in the 1950s undeniable.

The point of this essay is to answer one of the questions posed by this book: why is feminism still relevant for young women? The short answer my students gave to me was simple: junior high is still hell. Adolescent struggles over gender and sexual identity—what a girl is and how to be one, whom to desire, and how to be desirable—had, it seemed to them, changed very little at their emotional core, in spite of the tremendous social and political changes wrought by feminism in the last thirty years. The Lolita fantasy, a fantasy authored by and for men, exerts its fascinating, pervasive influence more than ever on our youth-obsessed culture, still setting the standard for feminine sexuality and femininity itself. Hemmed in by the limitations of this fantasy, girls still find themselves, in a thousand large and small ways, forced to choose between pursuing their sexual desire and pursuing the power that comes from being at ease with their human selves. Feminism is present and available for young women today, but it must be learned, in the passage from adolescence to adulthood, by following much the same pattern that previous generations of women discovered for themselves.

On a hot June day in Austin, two years after I taught "Sexy Girls," I faced an angry group of junior high girls, of many different races and social classes, who clarified for me the reasons why adolescence will always be feminism's final frontier. The girls had, with some prodding from me, been writing stories about their lives. We had been talking about their fears, the things that made them feel helpless. The girls were loudly agreeing, in spite of the great diversity of their life experiences, that labels—categories to which they were assigned by others and from which they could not escape, save through transfer to another school or equally radical action—were the thing that had the greatest and most negative effect on their lives. What they feared most, the girls insisted, was not the power of men or boys or teachers or parents or criminals, but the power of other girls, who invented and enforced the labels.

I suggested that we make a "top ten" list of their most dreaded labels. In a tie for number one on their list: "slut" and "bitch/feminist." Bitch/feminist, I queried? They're the same thing, the girls explained. Bitches got angry a lot, bossed people around, and thought they were better and stronger than other people, especially boys. So did feminists. These, then, were the girls' greatest fears: to be seen as having too much desire, too much anger, too much power—and to be cast out of the circle of "normal girls" for these sins.

These fears are depressingly familiar to anyone who knows about the women's movement. Behind them lurk a series of equally familiar, though unspoken, assumptions that oppose power and desire and are driven by the need to be desirable to, but protected from the desire of, men and boys. In the commonplace formula, a slut is "easy" and relatively powerless. She doesn't, or can't, say no to those who pursue her. A bitch is powerful but sexless and undesirable—to men and boys, at least. This means the only way to be a bitch/feminist and sexual is to be a lesbian, a possibility so frightening to the girls that they wouldn't even mention it until I did so. Homophobia combines with the narrow options for expressing heterosexual desire to pit girls against one another, competing, controlling, and labeling someone else's flaws so their own won't be noticed.

One way to counter these beliefs is to offer the corrective of feminist theory, which provides the analytical tools to undo these assumptions. Another is to offer the corrective of the history of feminism, which reveals feminists and feminism as a wildly varied people and political movement. Although feminism is still defined as a social and political movement that works to improve the lives of women and to analyze their circumstances, at the opening of the twenty-first century no sound-bite version of "what feminists think" or "what a feminist is" exists. Indeed, only those who wish to vilify or ignore feminism would dare to offer such a thing.

Yet the women who made and continue to make feminist history did not, by and large, come to believe in the relevance of feminism to their lives because they felt reassured by the varied agendas from which they could choose if they "joined up." Feminism is as much a change of heart and vision as it is any particular political affiliation. It is a waking up, a coming into consciousness. In order to gain a feminist consciousness, women (and girls) must admit to connections between their individual lives, the lives of other women, and larger political and social structures. But more than that, they must *feel*, at least once, the truth of these connections: *That's me. I know what that feels like. Yes. That's how it works.*

For that, we need stories.

Many of the women whose work we read in "The Rhetoric of Sexy Girls"—authors such as Dorothy Allison, Joan Nestle, and Audre Lorde—were women who fought actively *within* the second wave of the women's movement for the primacy of, and the importance of expressing, many different kinds of female desire. As a result, they were at times cast out of the circle of "normal feminists" themselves, in fights that were as passionate and as painful as any that happen in junior high.[2] Young women who identify themselves as third wave feminists are sometimes surprised by this history. In the preface to her anthology of essays on third wave feminist sexuality, *Jane Sexes It Up* (2002), Merri Lisa Johnson writes that Carol Vance's anthology of the 1982 Barnard Sexuality Conference, *Pleasure and Danger* (1984), "would have been the template for the essays in *Jane Sexes It Up*—if we'd ever heard of it. But revolutionary ideas about sexual politics are consistently misrepresented or simply 'disappeared' in most narratives of U.S. history."[3]

Because I think Johnson is right, I have focused this essay on the work of an earlier generation of feminists. History may be elusive, but these stories still stand—a gorgeous, open, sexy secret available to anyone who is beginning to find the tightrope of traditional femininity too narrow to walk.

REVIVING LOLITA

Who is Lolita, anyway? Why would we want to revive her, and what does that have to do with junior high (and with feminism)?

In the beginning, Lolita was the title character of Vladimir Nabokov's *Lolita* (1955). She is twelve years old when the novel begins. When it ends, she is seventeen, married, pregnant, and doomed to die in childbirth. She doesn't call herself Lolita, and neither does her mother or any of her friends. She calls herself Dolores Haze, Dolly, or Lo. It is Humbert Humbert, the professorial, sophisticated, self-deluding, snobbish European, who calls her Lolita. *Lolita*, the book, is many things—a travelogue, a detective story, a romance, a comedy, a language game, and one of the funniest, most lyrically tragic, and most celebrated of modern novels. At bottom, however, *Lolita* is a long monologue by its narrator, Humbert Humbert, who recounts from a prison cell the story of his life as a pedophile. He relates how at age thirty-seven he moved to America, fell in love with the twelve-year-old Lolita, married her mother in order to be near her, and then, after her mother's bizarre accidental death, became Lolita's sole guardian and lover/jailor/father for a few years until she successfully ran away, or was kidnapped, depending on how you look at it.

At the end of *Lolita*, in spite of, or because of, Humbert's obsession, we know far more about Humbert Humbert than we do about Dolores Haze. Even Humbert admits this—it is the source of his greatest despair. But if we don't learn much about Dolores Haze, we do learn a fair amount about the part-girl, part-fantasy named Lolita. Primarily, we know that she is a preternaturally sexy girl, a "daemonic nymphet," as Humbert calls her. Lolita is the archetype of a special category of girl who seduces without knowing it, who works her charms unconsciously, even unwillingly, who attracts without necessarily being, in any of the most obvious ways, attractive. Though she may be an ordinary, vulgar, or even literally dirty girl (Humbert often complains about Lolita's bad personal hygiene as well as her common tastes), she is possessed by, or contains within herself, an erotic demon who will haunt her only between the ages of ten and seventeen or so. This demon can be detected only by men who are at least ten years her senior. Although her powers may be great, they depend wholly on recognition by that type of man. Lolita herself has little chance at manipulating these powers for her own purposes.

Nabokov's Lolita is a compound of Dolores Haze and Humbert Humbert's literary and sexual fantasy-making machine, but there are many, many other, less complex Lolitas. Humbert repeatedly reminds us that Lolita has many precursors in history, ancient and otherwise, especially among the ranks of literary muses.[4] In spite of the genius of many of her inventors, the Lolitaesque "sexy girl" is easily recognized by the literary clichés that follow inevitably in her wake. She is a fresh, dewy flower or a just-ripening fruit (*fruits verts,* Humbert calls his nymphets), a delicate thing to be consumed quickly before it fades, spoils, or rots. She is a fawn, kitten, colt, or any other young animal that needs to be tamed, trained, and protected. She is a spooky, liminal being, hovering not simply between childhood and womanhood, but between this world and the next: Humbert's daemons, or the folktale's legendary virgins, with their bewitching powers. She is a (virgin) forest or country (as in "virgin shores") to be conquered. She is, in short, quintessentially *female,* as defined in the most traditional and confining and never-quite-completely-human way possible. As such, she sets the standard not only for girls but also for women.

Since the success of Nabokov's novel, "Lolita" has grown into a vague and generally applicable brand name, the way "Xerox" has come to mean "copy" or "Kleenex" to mean tissue. Now, any underage girl whose sexiness is a compound of childish prettiness and erotic potential and who appeals to, or is attached to, older men, can be a Lolita. Thus, when sixteen-year-old tennis player Anna Kournikova burst onto the media scene with long blonde locks and a boyfriend nearly twice her age, she was dubbed "the tennis Lolita."[5] In the fantasy world of the popular media, Lolita moves further away from a girl and becomes a *style.* To find the latest word in "Lolita-appeal," visit your local record store (you can start with the cover of Britney Spears's first album), or check your local TV and movie listings. To prime yourself, try watching *American Beauty,* or *The Man Who Wasn't There,* or whatever Lolita-type movie has come out most recently while you are reading this. Or you can simply flip through a men's or women's fashion magazine or catalog and count the number of women posed as innocently erotic girls, and the number of girls posed as sexually knowing women.

Nonetheless, the photographs, the fiction, and the movies are all just the visible markers of a fantasy that easily interposes itself between a real body—a real girl—and whoever is looking at that body, including the girl herself. It's my guess, in fact, that you went to junior high with at least one Lolita. You remember her on the cheerleading team, don't you? She was so popular that no one really knew her; and then there were the rumors about that teacher. Or maybe she smoked cigarettes, cut school, and wore too much make-up. Intimidating, sexy in her silence, she spent her days waiting to be picked up by that older guy after school. Or maybe you met her at summer camp and found out later about that counselor.

Or maybe she was you.

Hamlet's spurned betrothed, Ophelia—perhaps most famous for her beautiful madness and subsequent suicide by drowning—is the title figure of *Reviving Ophelia* (1994), Mary Pipher's best-selling book on the crisis of female adolescence, though she scarcely appears in the book itself. Missing from the picture Pipher draws of mostly white, almost wholly heterosexual and middle-class adolescence, however, is the story of girls who are driven as much by complicated sexual desire and curiosity as by the need for love and acceptance. (Indeed, it is difficult to imagine such a book becoming popular with the parents of adolescent girls.) Pipher's important work did much to focus attention on the sudden dip in self-confidence and self-esteem that girls suffer when they hit puberty. So it is with all due respect to her that I suggest it is Lolita—an ordinary middle-class white girl transformed by the obsessive gaze of a middle-class, middle-aged white man into the essence of femininity—as much as mad Ophelia, who haunts the days of girls. Girls who are suddenly captured by powerful, silent rules about how to be a girl. Girls who have suddenly lost their right to simply be "people." Girls who grow up to be women who are still afraid of being bitches or sluts, or who have to adopt those labels as badges of pride in order to act on their desires. And who still watch each other warily, waiting for a mistake, a betrayal.

My class, "The Rhetoric of Sexy Girls," tackled the prospect of reviving Lolita in two fairly simple ways. First, the course was built around a few direct questions: What is a "sexy girl"? Who gets to decide? What are the repercussions for the girl and her judges? Second, as we explored the myth of Lolita and its implications, we moved as a class from the creation of Lolita to "Lolita Speaks" and "Lolita Writes Back," two units in which we examined the work of women and girls who responded to and complicated her mythic status. I gave the class its provocative title partly because it was accurate, partly to draw attention to the use of "girl" in the phrase "sexy girl," and partly (with my tongue firmly in my cheek) to see if I could get some men to take a course that was cross-listed as a women's studies class and that featured a syllabus in which Nabokov was the only male author.

It worked. I was, in fact, naïve about the power of the phrase "sexy girl." As soon as the course catalog came out, a male reporter from the local paper called me for an interview about the course solely on the basis of its title. I got plenty of raised eyebrows, winks, and nudges from my male colleagues, including those on the committee who approved the course. ("Not such a sexy title," wrote one in the margin of my proposal. "How about 'Girls! Girls! Girls!'?") When I checked the roster before the first class, it showed that twenty-two men and three women had registered for twenty-five available places.

The message was clear: sexy girls were a private dirty joke between heterosexual men. The absoluteness of this conclusion had overridden everything else about the course, including its status as a college class, its content, its departmental context as a rhetoric and women's studies class, and the fact that it was being taught by a woman. On the first day of class, I explained to the roomful of over fifty students who showed up to try to get in that they would spend most of the class looking through the eyes of young girls, and that we would be talking about sex, yes, but that that would include talking about difficult things like rape, sexual abuse, shame, and guilt as well as pleasure. I shared a cartoon and a quote from one of the 'zines we would be reading at the end of the class and we discussed them.

By the next class meeting, there were eleven men and twelve women in the class. Nearly all were white, middle- to upper-class, and hetero-sexual. Some students were there because they were interested in the material. Some were there because the class met at a convenient time. Some liked to read and write, but many did not. One or two had taken other women's studies classes; the majority had not, nor did they need to have. First and foremost, "Sexy Girls" was a composition course, and we spent most of our time learning how to read closely and write criti-cally. (And rewrite, and rewrite again.) We read no feminist theory. In-stead, we employed the simple feminist technique of bringing the women and girls in everything we read to the center of our discus-sions and analysis, a technique made necessary by the class's guiding questions.

We spent the first four weeks honing our reading skills on Nabokov's stunning prose. We began to see how he simultaneously invited us to revel in Humbert Humbert's voluptuous deceptions while leaving plenty of room for an alert reader to see through them. We saw, for ex-ample, how careful Nabokov is to show us that Humbert reviles every woman who might have helped Lolita—her mother, her teacher, her friends. And how each of these women, in her single-minded focus on training Lolita and herself how to get and keep a man, pushed Lolita further into her dilemma. We saw that Lolita was lonely and penniless.

But no matter how much we marveled at Nabokov's skill and discov-ered new complexities in the novel, our conversation about Lolita was essentially static. It boiled down to one question: was Lolita a slut, or was she a victim? Again and again, we returned to two "threshold" scenes in the novel. In the first scene, Lolita sits on Humbert's lap on the couch (he tells us) eating an apple, singing, and squirming while he gradually maneuvers himself into a (supposedly) covert orgasm. In the second, Humbert is alone with Lolita on the road and they have what appears to be consensual sex, after which Humbert has Lolita tell him about her previous sexual adventures, which include a brief les-bian affair before his arrival at the Haze household, as well as a "game" of sexual intercourse that she and a girlfriend had played with a boy at camp. What the students wanted to know about the first scene was: did Lolita know what was going on, or didn't she? What they wanted to know about the second scene was: if Lolita wasn't a virgin and she "did it" willingly with Humbert, then why should we feel sorry for her later? Hadn't she just gotten what she deserved? If she had stepped over the threshold willingly, Lolita's detractors argued, she was a slut. Lolita sympathizers pointed out evidence of Lolita's struggles in both scenes. They argued that Lolita could hardly have said no, given the amount of power Humbert had. They pointed to a later scene in which Humbert admits he "used more force than was strictly necessary" to have sex with Lolita.

We could produce evidence for both sides of the argument. But we had no language, no framework in which Lolita could have desired Humbert Humbert, played with sex, been thrilled by the power she could wield and the attention she received, and yet been utterly alone, powerless to leave her tormentor or even tell her story. Without Lolita's point of view, we had no sense of her desire as separate from Humbert's—she existed only in relation to him and his desires and remorse. The class was made up of smart, sophisticated students who were becoming better readers by the minute. Nonetheless, limited to condemning Lolita for her sexual knowledge or arguing that she was really an innocent victim, we found ourselves back in junior high, where the only options for describing the complexities of desire were bright, hard labels that marked easily separated categories: *is she a virgin, or is she a slut?*

Then we read Dorothy Allison. What Lolita lacked, in the resonant language of feminism, was a *voice:* not just a point of view, but the personhood—the physical and psychological presence—necessary to tell her own story and be heard. In the wry, stubborn voice of Bone, the girl narrator of Dorothy Allison's *Bastard Out of Carolina* (1992), we could hear clearly the complex mixture of knowledge and ignorance, fear and bravado, desire and curiosity that we had suspected but had been unable to trace in *Lolita.* The class soon fastened on a scene in Allison's book that seemed to speak directly back to the "couch scene" from Lolita—the scene about which we had spent so much time arguing. Like Humbert, Bone's stepfather, Daddy Glen, takes her onto his lap and uses the pretense of fatherly tenderness to bring himself to orgasm against her body. Like the scene from Lolita, this moment in *Bastard* marks the beginning of a series of sexual transgressions. Like Lolita, Bone says nothing about the incident. But unlike the reader of *Lolita,* the reader of *Bastard* can hear what Bone says in her head:

He started talking again, telling me Mama was going to be all right, that he loved me, that we were all going to be so happy. Happy. His hand was hard, the ridge of his wristbone pushing in and hurting me, I looked straight ahead through the windshield, too afraid to cry, or shake, or wiggle, too afraid to move at all. He kept saying, "It's gonna be all right." . . . I knew what it was under his hand. I'd seen my cousins naked, laughing, shaking their things and joking, but this was a mystery, scary and hard. . . . He was hurting me, hurting me![6]

Hearing Bone's voice didn't give us any definitive answers about what Lolita was thinking. In many ways the scenes were quite different: Lolita sat on her couch in a sunny, well-appointed room, while Bone crouched in the back of a car in a dark parking lot. Lolita's mother was safe at church, while Bone's mother fought for her life during a stillbirth. But the similarities between the scenes made it possible to imagine that Lolita's description of what happened to her would be quite different from Humbert's.

Even more important, the class began to see how Lolita might, like Bone, know something about sex ("I knew what it was under his hand") and still be baffled and frightened—even after the fact, by a particular sexual encounter ("But this was a mystery, scary and hard"). Too, though Allison makes it clear that Bone is hurt, she also refuses to let her be seen as a passive victim without a sexuality of her own. One student, who had started his paper before finishing the reading, came in complaining that his thesis had been overturned by the following passage, where Bone reflects on sex:

. . . It *was* mushy. Mama and Daddy Glen always hugging and rubbing on each other, but it was powerful too. Sex. Was that what Daddy Glen had been doing to me in the parking lot? Was it what I had started doing to myself whenever I was alone in the afternoons? I would imagine being tied up and put in a haystack while someone set the dry stale straw ablaze. I would picture it perfectly while rocking on my hand. The daydream was about struggling to get free while the fire burned hotter and closer. I am not sure if I came when the fire reached me or after I had imagined escaping it. But I came. I orgasmed on my hand to the dream of fire.[7]

My student explained he'd wanted to talk about how Bone was innocent, and how Glen had imposed his own desire on her, but now, here she was, coming into her own sexuality—because of? in spite of?—Glen's abuse. And though her fantasy seemed connected to the abuse, he couldn't decide whether it was a masochistic fantasy about being consumed, or an apocalyptic dream of being burned clean, or something else he hadn't thought about yet—so could he have an extension on that assignment?[8]

This kind of productive confusion grew as we met more girls with their own complex voices and very different lives. Meeting poor white country girls like Bone, and poor Jewish, black, and Mexican American city girls, we began to see Lolita's whiteness and her carefully detailed middle-class suburban existence as integral to her sexual history and to the particular male fantasies she battled. And like Bone, we began to wonder about our definition of sex itself: Was it the act of sexual intercourse? Or could it be the act of looking? Or the thrill of danger that comes with the looking and the wanting? Is being thrilled by the danger of sexual possibility the same thing as wanting sex? Does it make you guilty? What if you desire something that doesn't seem to have anything to do with "normal" sex at all, an object, or another little girl? What if the desire for power gets mixed up in unexpected ways with sexual desire?

We were forced into asking these and other questions by the sheer variety of sexualities we encountered. The desires explored by the authors we read defied any containment by labels or categories, the plot lines we expected broke up or made strange turns. In *Zami* (1982), Audre Lorde barely notes her girl narrator's loss of virginity to a boy who threatens to break her glasses if she doesn't let him "stick it in." But the day on which her narrator gets her first period and is allowed by her stern, somewhat distant Caribbean mother to celebrate by pounding spices for curry in her mother's mortar is described in loving, deeply erotic detail: it is the narrator's first real sexual experience. In *A Restricted Country* (1987), Joan Nestle recalls her girlhood as a sexual adventurer who falls in love with a married woman more than twice her age (by whom she is very gently turned down), and who lets a sad, aging, male ranch hand fondle her breasts, out of curiosity and a new-found sense that sex can be a way to show pity and kindness. In Joanna Russ's *The Female Man* (1975), precocious sixteen-year-old Laura Rose (who has wanted to be Genghis Khan since she was five) has a happy affair with a woman twice her age who has time-traveled from an alternate future Earth with no men. Their initial sexual en-counter is everything that Lolita's and Bone's are not: consensual, ar-ticulate, funny, even practical. And it's explicitly about sex and enjoy-ment rather than, as with Humbert, fantasy and romance.

As we moved on from stories written by an earlier generation to sto-ries by young women who were writing in self-published 'zines and on Web sites, we looked forward to a further expansion of our ideas about desire. But this was not quite what happened. The class was excited by the idea of self-publishing. The students saw and liked the way the mixed-media style of many of the 'zines reappropriated and satirized the infuriating, seductive images of femininity with which they had grown up. They loved discovering the international underground com-munity of 'zinesters, and they admired the bravery and irreverent hu-mor with which the authors wrote about their intimate lives, detailing stories of abuse, fantasy, and persistent desire. After learning to love the density and play of literary prose, however, many students were also impatient with the deliberately crude testimonial style of many of the 'zines they read. As one exasperated student put it, "Just because you leave in the typos doesn't mean it's profound!" They sensed a sur-prising *sameness* among the 'zines, in spite of the variety in their con-tent: a commitment to confession rather than reflection, to speaking out rather than striving for complexity.[9] Especially in the most readily available, most commercialized Web 'zines, it became clear to the class that self-publication was not a guarantee of radical invention.

Had we been ordinary 'zine readers, we would have been more likely to write letters than to have a class discussion. We also might have seen more clearly that what we had found among the 'zines was a commu-nity in the process of inventing itself through writing and exchange— not one, as with the novels and short stories we read, looking back on more than ten years of such invention. As an emerging community, the 'zine creators and contributors were bound to repeat some of the work of an earlier generation, not simply because that work has been hidden or repressed, but because the experience of discovering our own voices and stories sometimes has to be something we do for ourselves. The earlier generation of women's literature and activism had made testimony about the places where the personal meets the political seem like common sense. By forging ahead without waiting for perfection, the 'zine writers made this kind of self-discovery immediately possible. Many of the students who would never have thought about writing on their own eagerly began their own 'zines. Still, one of the recurring complaints in the 'zines we read as a class was the *lack* of a flesh-and-blood community of women: Junior high (or high school, or college, or work) is still hell, wrote many of the 'zine writers, but I'm trying to start something here. Won't you write me a letter?

It was in Toni Morrison's *Sula* (1973) that we first glimpsed the possibilities for community that are lost by women when they condemn one another as sexual outlaws. At twelve, Nel and Sula are best friends. As they walk hand in hand toward an ice cream parlor past rows of men loitering on Main Street, Morrison perfectly articulates their thrill at playing—and protecting each other from—the Lolita role:

> It was not really Edna Finch's ice cream that made them brave the stretch of those panther eyes. Years later their own eyes would glaze as they cupped their chins in remembrance of the inch-worm smiles, the squatting haunches, the track-rail legs straddling broken chairs. The cream-colored trousers marking with a mere seam the place where the mystery curled. Those smooth vanilla crotches invited them; those lemon-yellow gabardines beckoned to them.[10]

With their eyes cast down not out of modesty, but from lust and curiosity, Nel and Sula spy on the young men and mix up the creamy cloth that covers their sex with the ice cream flavors—lemon and vanilla—that are their ostensible childish goal. They remember the walk "years later." It's not just a childish pleasure but an adult one, a foundational memory upon which they have built their present desire, desires that include the possibility of barely articulated danger:

They moved toward the ice-cream parlor like tightrope walkers, as thrilled by the possibility of a slip as by the maintenance of tension and balance. The least sideways glance, the merest toe stub, could pitch them into those creamy haunches spread wide with welcome. Somewhere beneath all of that daintiness, chambered in all that neatness lay the thing that clotted their dreams.[11]

Sula slips—jumps, really—off that tightrope and becomes a sexual outlaw, independent and mockingly rebellious. Sula earns the fear and spite, first of the small, tightly knit black community, and eventually of Nel herself, after she sleeps with Nel's husband, Jude, who leaves Nel shortly thereafter. Nel stops speaking to Sula and tries to bury her grief over Jude's departure in the practice of a strict, virtuous life. But in the final lines of the novel, as she walks home from Sula's graveside, Nel realizes that the true sorrow of her life is the loss of Sula's friendship: "'All that time, all that time, I thought I was missing Jude.' And the loss pressed down on her chest and come up into her throat. 'We was girls together,' she said as though explaining something. 'O Lord, Sula,' she cried, 'girl, girl, girlgirlgirl.' It was a fine cry—loud and long—but it had no bottom and it had no top, just circles and circles of sorrow."[12]

In junior high I learned, as so many girls learn, to dislike and distrust women. They were bitchy, mean, gossiping hypocrites: my certainty about this made me equally certain that feminism had no relevance for me. It wasn't until I was a senior in college that I began to connect the oppression of women with my estrangement from the friends of my girlhood. Now, behind every woman's catty comment, I hear Nel's cry. The circles of its sorrow describe the emptiness of our lives without one another, the true price of women's refusal to fight against the rules that bind us. We should be fighting the rules, instead of each other.

EPILOGUE: AS LONG AS THE LIBRARY IS STILL OPEN

Though many of the students in the class came to feel anger over the way girls or women were treated, only a few of them wanted to claim the label "feminist" for themselves. After all, hadn't the point of the class been to challenge labels and categories? To clear the way for new inventions of self and world? But while it's true that labels can exclude people and delimit our definitions of ourselves and "others," labels also make it possible for us to find each other. In the age of AIDS, articulating the way pleasure and danger work themselves out in our daily lives is more than ever a matter of life and death. Conservative politicians can refuse to fund studies of teen sexuality and attempt to suppress the studies that have been done, but as long as the library is open, there will be stories that help us think outside the bounds of most of the worlds presented to us by the mainstream media. You may not be ready to declare yourself a feminist in a crowded room, to help organize a protest, to write your own manifesto. But if there should come a day when the ghosts of junior high are noisy in their closet, when the airbrushed images of Lolita's much-photographed descendants seem to press in on your own flesh, a feminist community will be waiting quietly for you, disguised as books on the library shelf. As Joanna Russ's narrator tells a despondent Laura Rose: "Turn away, girl; gird up your loins; go on reading."

NOTES

1. In this essay I treat "second wave" and "third wave" feminism primarily as generational terms since, as I discuss here and below, I think any progress is marked by repression and forgetting, especially around the issue of desire. The history of women of color also greatly complicates any simple second or third wave construction, and I regret not having the space to say more about the confluence of race and sex in this essay. The publication of *This Bridge Called My Back: Writings by Radical Women of Color* in 1981 and the Barnard Sexuality Conference (1982), which I discuss below, may be understood as the beginning of the third wave, but I find it more useful to frame them as evidence of the second wave's great complexity. Many of the women I discuss in this essay as being part of second wave feminism are still publishing vital writing—which is not to say that their politics haven't changed.

2. Primarily, I am speaking here of the fierce struggle at the 1982 Conference on Sexuality at Barnard College between the antipornography movement as personified by Women Against Pornography, founded by Andrea Dworkin, and the so-called "pro-sex feminists" at the conference who openly explored, among other things, lesbian desire, sado-masochistic sex play, prostitution, and teenage sex. Some antipornography activists, reputedly members of the WAP, called Barnard and employers of targeted pro-sex feminists and alerted them to the

presence of "perverts" who avowed practices that were harmful to women. Many of the targeted women lost their jobs or were otherwise stigmatized. Barnard seized some of the conference materials and nearly canceled the conference. For more about the scandal and its effects, see Carol Vance's "More Danger, More Pleasure: A Decade after the Barnard Sexuality Conference" in *Pleasure and Danger: Exploring Female Sexuality* (1984; rept., London: Pandora Press, 1992), and Dorothy Allison's "Public Silence, Private Terror" in *Skin: Talking about Sex, Class and Literature* (Ithaca, N.Y.: Firebrand Books, 1994). On the necessity of thinking through desire, a good place to begin is Audre Lorde's now-classic essay "The Uses of the Erotic," in *Sister Outsider* (Trumansburg, N.Y.: Crossing Press, 1984). Many of the pro-sex feminists who spoke at the conference have gone on to vibrant and varied careers as writers, activists, academics, and public intellectuals. Amber Hollibaugh's collection of essays and conversations, *My Dangerous Desires: A Queer Girl Dreaming Her Way Home* (Durham: Duke University Press, 2000), is an amazing record of one such career; it is a testament to the politically radical possibilities of fully recognizing the multiple ways desire moves us.

3. Merri Lisa Johnson, *Jane Sexes It Up* (New York: Four Walls Eight Windows, 2002), 3. It is interesting to note that Johnson cites Dorothy Allison's work, and specifically Bone's fantasies in *Bastard Out of Carolina* (like the fantasy I describe as puzzling my student later in this essay), as both an influence on her anthology and what led her to Vance's anthology.

4. Among the most famous of these are Edgar Allan Poe's young cousin, Annabel; Petrarch's Laura, who provided her admirer with the inspiration to invent a new genre, the sonnet sequence; and Dante's Beatrice, who (though she aged, married, and became a mother) remained forever for Dante the young girl he fell in love with at first sight. There are many more—male artists and writers seem particularly fond of dead young girls, who don't grow up. Ophelia is as good an example as any here; the paintings of her as a drowned girl are legion.

5. A brief search on the Internet will turn up hundreds of Anna sites with this tag. Two print sources include "Love Interest: Anna's Open," in *Newsweek,* September 8, 1997 (p. 51), and Mitch Albom's sports column, "Kournikova Is on Thin Ice Trying to Deny Love Match" (*San Diego Union-Tribune,* July 2, 1997).

6. Dorothy Allison, *Bastard Out of Carolina* (New York: Dutton, 1992), 47.

7. Ibid., 63.

8. Those familiar with the reception of Allison's novel will know that my student was not alone in his confusion. In one of the many echoes of the Barnard debate described above (see note 2), some members of the feminist community, already critical of Allison's defense of sado-masochistic sexuality, have read this passage as a straightforward eroticization of Bone's abuse and have decried Allison and the novel for treating the incident that way. Other readers, myself included, see this passage as integral to the portrayal of Bone's finely drawn character, and an important contribution to the struggles of abuse survivors to claim their own highly complicated sexuality.

9. A dedicated 'zine reader might rightly object, at this point, that we were reading the wrong 'zines. Indeed, we had only a small collection of about fifteen or so, plus the anthology of excerpts collected by Karen Green and Tristan Taormino, *A Girl's Guide to Taking Over the World: Writings from the Girl Zine Revolution* (New York: St. Martin's, 1997). The sense of sameness may also have been exacerbated by my focus on personal 'zines and on 'zines written by young women and adolescents. However, it is hard to dispute that, for economic as well as aesthetic reasons, 'zines often valorize the rough and reject the "slick" and polished as inauthentic. This aesthetic echoes that of early women's movement publications, which sought to document "real women's voices" and "real women's lives." See Dorothy Allison's essay "Believing in Literature" in *Skin* (pp. 165–81) for how this complicated her own literary efforts.

10. Toni Morrison, *Sula* (New York: Knopf, 1973), 50.

11. Ibid., 50–51.

12. Ibid., 174.

PART TWO

Coming to Feminism

"That's Not Fair!"
Nurturing Girls' Natural Feminism

Most girls, like most young women, don't call themselves feminists. And yet, I find that many girls are feminists. What causes the disconnect between what girls believe about themselves and the world and what they think feminism means? Does it even matter if girls don't see themselves as feminists? What do girls and boys have to gain by being feminists? And what do feminism and adult feminists have to gain by including girls? These are the questions I'll explore here, sharing both girls' experiences and my own.

Some girls who write to *New Moon: The Magazine for Girls and Their Dreams,* the feminist magazine that I founded and publish, identify themselves as feminists, but most don't.[1] They don't feel part of "the girls' movement," a popular term that appeared in the 1990s. The girls' movement is a liberation movement, part of the third wave of feminism; it wants to extend the benefits of the women's movement to girls, freeing them from oppression and expanding their opportunities. The same thing is true when I meet girls and talk with them about *New Moon.* They love the magazine and the way it stands up for girls, but they don't think of that as feminism.

I am concerned that girls do not feel part of the girls' movement, which is supposed to be all about them. Many people take this apparent disinterest as evidence that girls aren't feminists and that we are really in a postfeminist age, at least as far as girls are concerned. Adult feminists, like me and *New Moon*'s staff of college students and twenty-somethings, wonder if we should try to convince girls that they are part of the third wave. We worry about what will happen to feminism if girls don't feel part of it. Will it eventually dwindle away like an unused muscle?

To me, whether or not girls relate to feminism matters a lot. First, girls gain so much by being part of feminism. Feminism can help them weather the trials and self-doubts of adolescence by feeling connected to a supportive larger community; help them push for equal opportunity at school and in sports; help make them safer by reducing violence; help them achieve economic self-sufficiency as adults; inspire them with the achievements and lives of girls and women, past and present, around the world; help them shape a more just world; and help them see that their dreams are worth reaching for. With so much to be gained, it's distressing to think of girls missing these benefits.

On the other side of the coin, feminism needs girls' energy, savvy, idealism, and impatience to keep it growing and changing. Just as the third wave has brought the perspective of a younger generation of women to the movement, we need to welcome girls' insights and opinions. At the very least, I believe that older feminists (including those in their late teens and twenties) need to understand why girls don't call themselves feminists or feel engaged in the girls' movement. I'm going to explore what that's all about and especially how girls' relations with women affect their experience of and feelings about feminism. I will also examine what feminism can gain by including girls and allowing them to be powerful in the movement.

First, let me share some stories about girls and feminism. In the past ten years, as publisher of *New Moon,* I've worked directly with the Girl Editors of the magazine, girls who attended the U.N. Fourth World Conference on Women in Beijing (1995), and girls who wrote a "Girls Declaration of Sentiments" in Seneca Falls in 1998 (as part of the 150th anniversary of the original "Declaration of Sentiments"). I've worked with many feminist college interns, and I've also raised two daughters, now adults, who proudly call themselves feminists. However, most of my experience with girls comes through *New Moon.*

New Moon magazine, founded in 1992, is grounded in research on girls' development. The magazine is targeted at girls between the ages of eight and fourteen because research has identified these years as a time of major psychological transition for girls. The work of Carol Gilligan and others has shown that many girls lose a strong belief in the validity of their own experience as they enter adolescence. In *Meeting at the Crossroads* (1992), Lyn Mikel Brown and Carol Gilligan report on longitudinal research on the development of girls between the ages of seven and eighteen. They and other members of the Harvard Project on Women's Psychology and the Development of Girls sought to understand the process by which girls silence their voices and take their knowledge underground as they get older. Observing that most younger girls (up through age ten or so) bring all of their voice and all of themselves into their relationships, Brown and Gilligan saw a change that results in girls "forgetting" what they know, what they feel, what they need, and who they are as they reach adolescence.[2]

Brown and Gilligan say that one way adult women can help girls is by staying in relationship with them. To do this, women must listen to what girls know, especially their painful truths. We must also be truthful with girls. When we do these things, we create supportive relationships that girls can rely on. My goal for *New Moon* is both to help girls maintain their knowledge and keep their unique voices as they enter the psychological and emotional challenges of adolescence and to build the truthful relationships that connect girls and women as girls grow up. Most girls aged eight, nine, and ten feel comfortable in their bodies and in their selves, understanding the world from the vantage point of their own experience, still secure that they can both see the world clearly and maintain relationships with others.

As girls get older, however, several factors combine to put immense pressure on girls to question their knowledge, themselves, and their relationships. They begin to develop abstract thinking, which introduces the perspective of "other" to their self-perception. As Mary Pipher says in *Reviving Ophelia* (1994), girls struggle to reconcile the perceptions of others (the culture) with their self-perceptions. Often, self-perception loses, and girls surrender, at least outwardly, to the culture's definition of who they should be and how they should act. Many girls feel this is the only way to maintain the relationships that are important to them, both with peers and with adults.

The best way to help girls resist these pressures and emerge from adolescence as strong young women is for the adults in their lives to stay close to them, honor what girls know, and be their allies as they change and struggle to grow. That's what we set out to do with *New Moon* by putting the editorial power in the hands of the Girls Editorial Board. Starting with my eleven-year-old daughters and some of their friends, we brainstormed together what *New Moon* would be.

We decided that the magazine would contain writing and artwork by both girls and adults, but no advertising. Many high-quality children's magazines, like *Cricket* and *Cobblestone,* don't take advertising, and this choice was particularly appropriate for our mission. The girls felt strongly that advertising is a primary pipeline for communicating cultural values about the roles of women and girls, and our job was to challenge those roles, not perpetuate them. If we accepted advertising, advertisers would expect us, like other magazines that depend on ad revenue, to promote products such as fashion, makeup, and music in articles, not just in ads. Our decision to exclude ads proved wise, because it makes us accountable not to advertisers but to our subscribers, who support the magazine financially.

Each issue of *New Moon* has a theme. In addition, regular departments and features include:
- Letters from readers
- Profiles of "real" girls, not celebrities
- Herstory: Stories about girls and women from the past
- How Aggravating: Things that are unfair to girls
- Fiction and poetry whose main characters are female
- Global Village: Profiles of girls from outside the United States
- Comic strips with female characters
- Puzzles and Experiments
- Stories about women and their work
- Girls' Dreams
- Stories by older women about their girlhood

When we were first putting *New Moon* together, the only thing we couldn't seem to agree about was a name for the magazine. I wanted to call it *Artemis,* after the Greek goddess of the moon. To me, the moon's historical and metaphorical connection to women and women's power and cycles was an important image for this time of transition in girls' lives. The girls hadn't known about the symbolism but liked it. The name *Artemis*, however, was a different story! They hated it and argued actively and persuasively against it for six weeks before I let go and agreed that we should find a name they liked.

That was my first experience in simultaneously speaking my voice and listening to the girls' dissenting voices. It was hard to do, both for me and for them. None of us was accustomed to sharing the power of a decision as important as naming a magazine. I was used to essentially leaving decisions completely up to my daughters or making them completely on my own. The girls were used to making decisions collaboratively with other girls, usually of the same age, but not with girls of other ages and not with adults. (Age segregation is so pervasive in American culture—particularly in school—that most children spend nearly all their time with others almost exactly their age.) The girls had expected me to overrule them eventually and to make the name decision on my own.

This experience made me realize that adults and girls don't do much collaborating, even in the routines of daily life. I began to realize how shallow and superficial our relationships usually are. Aside from my daughters, other girls rarely get to see my true self, my struggles and problems, my doubts and disappointments. And I didn't actually try to see who these girls were, what struggles and problems they faced. This was true even though our house was a regular gathering place for my daughters and their friends. My daughters frequently had friends in the house playing and sleeping over, yet I realized that I hardly knew any of these girls. Even though I saw them and talked with them often, our conversations were brief and limited to the same couple of sentences: How was school? (fine), How were their parents? (fine), and What was new? (nothing). When we started working on *New Moon* together, girls (including my daughters) and I had to develop a new kind of relationship. (This is still true for every adult who joins *New Moon*, even the college students who are only a few years older than our Girl Editors.)

In addition to learning how to produce a magazine, we had to learn how to listen to each other, keep our own voices, be true to ourselves, and stay in relationship at the same time. These are the things that

Gilligan and other researchers say that girls do naturally before adolescence and then stop doing when pressured by the culture—including adult women—to be grown up. Maintaining a relationship in the face of misunderstanding and disagreement is a very complex thing to do. Things are always changing in the group activity of producing the magazine. The girls are all changing, both in the magazine group and in the rest of their lives, as are the adults. It dawned on me that together we were learning how to stay connected, during the girls' transition to womanhood, through working on the magazine together. Having the real work of the magazine to focus on enables us to act out the meaning of staying connected, of speaking and being heard, and of listening.

Women and girls speaking together, listening to and hearing each other is a naturally feminist activity. Yet, when we started *New Moon,* I didn't think that girls could be feminists, since they were only girls. Somewhat condescendingly, I thought it was my role to introduce girls to feminism and to show them how it could help them. Now, ten years later, I'm happy to report that I've learned that girls definitely are feminists, even though they may not think of themselves that way. And I've discovered how much adult feminists can learn from girls, even from girls who don't call themselves feminists.

What makes me think that girls are feminists even if they don't realize it? Webster's *Collegiate Dictionary* defines feminism as "the theory of the political, economic, and social equality of the sexes," and a feminist as one who believes in that theory. That definition of "feminist" describes every girl I've ever met! I've yet to know a girl who doesn't believe that everyone, including her, should have equal rights. To girls, equal rights are a matter of justice, pure and simple. Girls believe in justice for everyone, which is why they can be so passionate about environmental protection, animal rights, and fixing social ills.

Before adolescence, girls are to justice what canaries are to miners: a very sensitive early-warning system. Girls have a well-developed sensitivity to the unfair treatment of any relatively powerless group. They have less cultural power than women do, but they still believe in their own knowledge, based in their actual experiences. This combination of clear vision and powerlessness can enable girls to see injustice more clearly than women do. This ability can be a great boon to feminism, if we are willing to listen to what girls know and willing to invest our energy in fighting for justice along with them.

Girls' passionate belief in justice makes them natural feminists. So how can women help girls to recognize their own feminism and to use the power that can be generated by joining their quest for justice with others'? And, most important, how can we break down the barriers we construct between girls and ourselves that undermine our desire to invite them into feminism? In order to change girls' mistaken ideas about feminism and to join with them in a common pursuit of justice, we must challenge our own assumptions, exercise new muscles, and change our own behavior.

To start, we must listen to girls. When girls are younger, they let us know when they see something that's unfair. Anyone who spends much time around girls younger than twelve hears the words, "That's not fair!" a lot. It's a feeling that's easy for adults to dismiss or tune out. The reality is that life isn't fair. Women know this, and we often think it's our obligation to share such wisdom with "whining" girls. We tell them that complaining about things doesn't help and that they're just going to have to accept the fact of unfairness. Sometimes we tell them to "lighten up" and not take themselves so seriously. That's what happened to Hannah (a *New Moon* reader) when she wrote to a popular girls' magazine:

> I used to get a magazine called *Girls Life*. In the past year I have noticed more and more sexism creeping into its pages. I tried to ignore it. But I couldn't ignore something in one of my last issues. I wrote the editors about my disappointment in them for writing that particular article. In return I got a very aggravating letter back saying that I should (not in these particular words) "loosen up." That did it. I canceled my subscription and asked for a refund. I give it to you, even though it is a very small contribution, so you may continue to make a better world for girls.

When we respond to girls' complaints by minimizing their importance, we're missing a great opportunity to strengthen girls' natural feminism. Hannah's response shows what can happen when a girl trusts her own knowledge and takes action based on that knowledge.

This is the essence of what makes younger girls natural feminists. They believe in the reality of their own experience, and they expect to be treated with respect and fairness.

But research has shown that girls often lose such strong belief in the validity of their own experience as they get older. As that happens, they also lose both the sense that they are entitled to justice and their connection to the goals of feminism.

Hannah is unusual for an older girl, in that she both understood *Girls Life*'s response to be disrespectful and still had enough confidence in her own knowledge of reality to decide that the problem lay with the magazine and not with her feelings. By taking the action she took, Hannah both strengthened her sense of who she is in the world and spoke up for her personal need for justice. It was very important for her to be able to share her outrage. She exercised her "justice muscle" and expected to receive cheers from the sidelines. By writing to *New Moon*, she got the cheers she deserved.

Unfortunately, many girls in and on the cusp of adolescence don't do what Hannah did. Instead, when they complain about unfairness, they succumb to blatantly self-defensive adult responses. Practically a reflex, our rote responses (such as "Loosen up," "Don't take yourself so seriously," "It's not that big a deal," and "You can't do anything about it") blind us to the importance and opportunity contained in a girl's recognition of unfairness. That recognition not only can open the door to conscious feminism for a girl but also can reopen the door to conscious feminism for the adult women who know her.

We have to ask ourselves why what happens too often instead is that the door to conscious feminism is shut in a girl's face by women who turn a deaf ear to her complaints. As girls get older, they become used to having their complaints met with adult indifference or implicit suggestions that girls resign themselves to the way things are. This is a subtle way to teach girls that their view of reality is not shared by others; this encourages girls to doubt their knowledge of reality. In Hannah's case, it would have been much easier for her to ignore the sexism she saw in *Girls Life*, minimizing its importance to her and her feelings of anger. Then she wouldn't have taken the risk of putting her version of reality down on paper, sending it in to the magazine (which espouses "Girl Power"), and receiving a response, almost certainly written by a woman, which essentially told her to disregard her own thoughts and feelings.

If you open your eyes, you will observe how many times in a day girls get this kind of message—one that urges them to discount or abandon their feelings—from the women around them: these women can be their mothers, grandmothers, older sisters, friends, and teachers. Imagine how much courage it takes for girls to keep asserting their experience of reality to people who are telling them, either subtly (by lack of response) or blatantly, that they just don't understand "real" reality. Now we can begin to see how girls start losing their feeling of entitlement to justice as they get older. And as they lose their expectation of justice, they lose their natural feminism.

Girls are very sensitive to any unspoken message being conveyed; they often adjust their behavior to the unvoiced expectations or needs of the more powerful person interacting with them. Often, that "more powerful person" is a woman who is unaware of how much power she wields in the situation. And unfortunately, without even realizing it, we sometimes use our greater power to tell girls that their concerns are unimportant and petty.

This happened with a national girls' conference that included several *New Moon* editors on its Girls Steering Committee. Planning took place over many months and involved deep discussion of every facet of the conference. The Girls Steering Committee planned one session that would be closed to the press in order to create a safer environment for girls who might disclose painful things there. When the session started, several reporters and camerapeople were in the room. Some of the members of the Girls Steering Committee asked them to leave, explaining that the session was closed to media. Several women backed up the girls' request, and the media did leave, only to go out to the hall and appeal to the conference organizer (a woman), who permitted them to go back in, thinking that the benefit of media coverage outweighed the girls' concerns. The Girls Steering Committee felt deeply disrespected and powerless. It was a woman with good intentions who gave them that feeling. Without realizing it, she reinforced the culture's devaluation of girls' needs. Even though the girls on the committee were frustrated, they told me later that they appreciated the support given to them by some of the women present. In this case, the girls clearly saw two different responses to their power: unconscious denial and conscious alliance. Although they didn't achieve the result they wanted, they did see the possibility of a different kind of relationship with women.

Too often, adults dismiss girls' search for justice as naïve and unrealistic, not even giving it the dignity of calling it a search for justice. Girls get the message, loud and clear, that they should think less about their own needs and more about how to accept an unjust world and get along in it. In fact, teaching a girl to get along in the world on its terms, rather than on her own terms, has been the cultural task of mothers, grandmothers, and aunts for centuries. It's reasonable to think that it's helpful for girls to be taught how to "go along to get along." After all, they can't expect the world to change, can they? And if they can't expect it to change, perhaps they're better off making their peace with that at an early age.

Girls learn how to "go along to get along" from mothers, grandmothers, aunts, and older sisters; this lesson is often cloaked in the guise of protecting girls. For instance, mothers frequently caution daughters to "be careful what you wear." The implication is that if a girl wears revealing clothing, she's "asking for trouble" in the form of sexual harassment or assault. At the same time, girls receive the direct message that they should mold their bodies, through dieting and/or exercise, to be sexy and attract attention from boys and men. They are also taught to be quiet and polite and to let boys and men take "center stage," by expressing interest in the things boys and men are interested in.

This kind of daily, often unconscious tutelage gives girls a clear message that they need to change themselves to fit into an unsafe and disrespectful world. They are taught that, if they don't stifle their own dreams and expectations, they will lose important relationships and connections and put themselves at risk emotionally and physically. The anxiety created by trying to learn and follow so many conflicting cultural rules can overwhelm a girl's previous awareness of her self, her goals, and her rights as a person. When we—adult women—are the surgeons who clip girls' wings (by passing along the conflicting rules rather than challenging them), we directly contribute to an undermining of girls' feminism.

And the larger culture supports women acting in this way, to the detriment of both girls and boys. The need for aspiration and passionate commitment to a life dream exists in every person. Boys are taught to express their aspirations through actions in the public world, and our culture supports them in this. (A classic example is the central importance of boys' high school sports teams to their whole community.) In contrast, girls are traditionally taught to repress their aspirations as they grow up and instead attach themselves to the dreams of a boy or man. Both girls and boys lose in this lopsided equation because if their personal dreams don't fit into the culture's rules, they're out of luck. And even if their dreams seem to fit into the rules, the culture itself loses by being inflexible. As Myra Sadker and David Sadker write in *Shortchanging Girls, Shortchanging America* (1991): "What if the cure for cancer is in the brain of a girl?"[3] If it's in the brain of a girl who submerges her own dreams and knowledge, none of us (women or men) will benefit from her brilliance.

Girls need women to change the traditional dynamic in our relationships and help them hang on to their expectation of a fair world as they get older and see clearly how unfair the world still is in many ways. How do we help them to feel that they can and should change things that are unjust in the world? How do we ally ourselves with one another and bring the greater power we have in the world to bear on the concerns girls have?

First and foremost, we can listen to girls. We must take their knowledge (and their complaints) seriously. We must set aside our cynicism about the unfairness of life and believe that we and they *can* change things. And then we need to stand with them and help them change things. We must do this even when we're not sure that our actions will really make a difference. In Eleanor Roosevelt's words, "You must do the thing you think you cannot do." Women, after all, have been doing things we think we cannot do for ages.

Recently, *New Moon* received a package containing a handwritten letter from Summer, a third grader, and a book from her school library. Her story shows how girls feel power when we listen to them and help them act to change the injustices they experience. Summer sent us a copy of her letter to Stephen Cosgrove, the author of the book *Catundra*. The story is about a cat who "had always been just a little bit plump; you could, in fact, call her downright fat."[4] Catundra is teased and shunned by the other animals because she is fat. She's miserable. When she loses weight, she suddenly feels happy. Summer wrote to Mr. Cosgrove to tell him that the book "really hurt my feelings. It made me cry because it was a very mean story, and I do not like the way Catundra only gets friends after she loses weight. There are lots of ways to have friends—you do not have to be skinny to have good friends. Your book should not be in school libraries because kids will get their feelings hurt just like me."

At the bottom of the page, below Summer's signature, are the signatures of her mom, Robin; her guidance counselor, Ms. Jaye; and her school librarian, Nicole. Without even talking to Summer, we could see that she was well supported by these three important women in her life. When Summer was upset by the story, they encouraged her to take action and let others know how she felt. The seemingly simple acts of writing to the author about her feelings and getting the book removed from the library so it wouldn't hurt other kids are the essence of what I call "everyday feminism."

Summer—along with her mom, counselor, and librarian—took her response to the book seriously and found a way to use that response to make things better for herself and others. The women who supported Summer didn't tell her simply to ignore the book, and, most important, they didn't tell her that her feelings didn't matter or were somehow "wrong." Instead, they took Summer's experience of injustice, found its cause out in the world, and figured out how to change what they could by standing beside her and using their adult authority and skills.

Contrast this response with the way many other kids must have felt reading that book since its publication in 1978: they internalized Catundra's feelings of shame and determined to change themselves (by trying to lose weight) rather than change the injustice of a culture that discriminates against fat people. Summer's relatively small actions take on huge significance when you consider the positive energy for change that's generated each time a girl who experiences injustice is supported by adults in fighting that injustice. It strengthens her sense of her own value, it reinforces the validity of her perceptions and knowledge, and it makes her a hero as she helps others.

It's a cliché to tell girls to believe in their dreams. In order to do that with any kind of credibility, we first have to believe in our own dreams. This means that we have to remember what our own dreams were and are. So, we have to do our homework first. We need to know what we want, and we need to be consciously working to reach those dreams, so girls can see our challenges and defeats alongside our triumphs. When they see us fighting for our beliefs, they feel strengthened in their beliefs. When they see us working for justice and fairness, they recognize their own desire for justice. And when they see us succeed in making change, on however small a scale, they understand that it's possible for them, too. They can see themselves, and others, as heroes.

Women have just as much to gain in these relationships as girls. By listening deeply to girls, we can reconnect with parts of our own experience that have been lost to the past. Remembering our girlhood can be exhilarating and painful at the same time, especially for young women who've just recently left the pain of adolescence behind. Often, we've forgotten things for a reason. Spending time with girls can bring back emotional memories (both good and bad) with breathtaking power. I experienced this with my daughters when they were in eighth grade. They complained that two of their friends were "acting like they're too cool for us." Mavis and Nia's feelings were deeply hurt by the rejection, and they felt betrayed that things were changing for reasons that they did not understand.

I tried to convince Mavis and Nia that they shouldn't care what those two girls did. Real friends didn't do these things, so they should just ignore them, I said. But that advice didn't cut it. When my daughters said, "You don't understand!" and didn't immediately cheer up, I got impatient and felt rejected myself, wondering why they didn't trust that I knew what I was talking about. Their troubles zapped me right back to my miserable eighth-grade year, when I suddenly became "too cool" for my longtime friends. I was the mean and fickle one, hurting others' feelings without regard.

I knew firsthand that insecurity was at the root of "acting cool" and abandoning old friends. I hadn't told my girls this story, however, because it was painful to remember and admit how mean I had been to my friends. I still felt guilty, and I didn't want to admit the unflattering truth. Women often do this with girls. We tell them part of the truth about our experiences and ourselves but leave out some key part because it's painful to remember or we're ashamed and regret how we acted. Being less than truthful erects an emotional barrier that girls feel.

They can tell we're not being fully honest and vulnerable with them. The inevitable result is distrust. Girls feel preached at, rather than understood, and the gulf between us grows. When I eventually told my daughters the whole truth, they listened intently. My story didn't solve their problem or take away their pain, but it did restore the bond of trust and intimacy between us. And, unexpectedly, it helped me, after twenty-seven years, to forgive myself for being the insecure girl who was mean to her friends. This is solidarity, a cornerstone of feminism.

Women also have much to gain from girls' seemingly "unrealistic" expectations. Younger girls often have clearer vision than women, which explains why they say "That's not fair!" so often. Girls expect the world to treat them and everyone else fairly. When it doesn't, they are outraged. Women, on the other hand, have learned to put on cultural blinders. The blinders allow us to cope with an unjust world by blocking some of it out. We do this because it can be overwhelming and depressing to see things as they really are. Once we put the blinders on, we don't want to admit that we've compromised our own sense of justice and expectation of equality. We don't want girls to remind us of what we lost.

But when we block out reality, we are also cutting ourselves off from the good parts of it and from the energy to make it better. If we can develop the courage to listen to girls' complaints and honor their truth, we're taking the first step in changing the injustices that cause the complaints. Girls have very high expectations, and when we take their concerns seriously, we can raise our own expectations and be inspired to face larger challenges. That's what liberation is all about. And it helps us just as much as it helps them. Because when we take on larger challenges and learn from them, we are strengthened for the next challenge. When we allow girls and their vision to reinvigorate our own expectation of justice, we become sisters in the deepest work of feminism.

Girls and their high hopes help us to flex our own intellectual, emotional, and organizational muscles, just as they pull us from physical lethargy with their bottomless well of energy. We, in turn, can help girls to flex their justice muscles, as we lend our worldly knowledge to their passion. It gives us all a workout. Though the work may be exhausting at times, the reward is a changed world, for us and for future generations of girls.

NOTES

1. *New Moon* is the magazine I founded in 1992 for girls aged eight to fourteen. Girls not only create the articles and artwork in the magazine but also oversee the direction of *New Moon* through their work on the editorial board. To learn more about the magazine and its goals, go to http://www.newmoon.org.

2. Lyn Mikel Brown and Carol Gilligan, *Meeting at the Crossroads* (Cambridge, Mass.: Harvard University Press, 1992).

3. Myra Sadker and David Sadker, *Shortchanging Girls, Shortchanging America* (Washington, D.C.: American Association of University Women, 1991).

4. Stephen Cosgrove, *Catundra* (New York: Price Stern Sloan, 1978).

ROXANNE HARDE & ERIN HARDE

Voices and Visions: A Mother and Daughter Discuss Coming to Feminism and Being Feminist

Try to be worthy of your foresisters, learn from your history, look for inspiration to your ancestresses. If this history has been poorly taught to you, if you do not know, then use your educational privilege to learn it. Learn how some women of privilege have compromised the greater liberation of women, how others have risked their privilege to further it; learn how brilliant and successful women have failed to create a more just and caring society, precisely because they have tried to do so on terms that the powerful men around them would accept and tolerate. Learn to be worthy of the women of every class, culture, and historical age who did otherwise, who spoke boldly when women were jeered and physically harassed for speaking in public.

—ADRIENNE RICH, *Blood, Bread, and Poetry* (1986)[1]

Roxanne: On the one hand, Erin, I find it somewhat artificial to be writing down the essences of a conversation that began almost as soon as you could speak. While I haven't consciously tried to shape your political ideologies, I have aimed to raise you to live your life with the fullest and richest experience possible. To that end, and as a feminist mom who identifies fully with second wave agendas, I have worked to make you aware of women's history, of sexist practices and patriarchal power structures, and of the value of your own perceptions and experiences.[2] I have tried to be, and tried to raise you to be, worthy of our foresisters, as Adrienne Rich says.

On the other hand, this process makes me more aware of my perception of feminism as an ongoing conversation. I came to identify myself as feminist, not through an epiphany but through a growing recognition, largely in conversation with other women, that my beliefs and practices were overtly feminist, that feminism just made sense to me. When you were a baby, I remember contemplating the second wave credo, "the personal is political," as I became aware that one of my neighbors was a victim of spousal abuse. The attitudes of several people on the block, the police, and the social services system worked to endorse her husband's behavior at the same time that my neighbor's friendships with other women began to give her a sense of self-worth. She made the personal political and forced the judicial and welfare systems to help her out of an impossible situation.

My feminism has been built as much on my relationships with this woman, my family, and friends as on my studies of women writers and storytellers like Adrienne Rich. I understand feminism in practice as a fluid and mutable conversation, kept alive by the continual joining of new voices and visions, sometimes muffled during dark periods, but never silenced. Because of the multiplicity of women's experiences, every female voice that joins the conversation enriches and complicates it. I believe that feminism must be seen as feminisms; room must be made for feminist ideology from many different perspectives. Most especially, we must make room for third wave feminism, for without the new vitality and directions those voices add, the conversation will not flourish. You and I know many women who are part of the second and third wave, who have benefited from the women's movement and who operate as feminists in their daily experience, but who do not identify themselves as feminists or join their voices to the ongoing feminist conversation.

Erin: Mom, I know that without your presence in my life, feminism would still be an alien word to me. Although I have yet to identify fully with the politics of the second or third wave, I am starting to develop my own personal feminist flavor. I believe that your concept of feminism as a conversation is an effective way to present women with various thoughts and definitions of feminism. Rather than thinking of feminism in terms of a movement or a theory in a text, which can be intimidating, women should be encouraged to express their own feminist perspectives. In a conversation, divergence and disagreement are always possibilities, and so this format provides women with a considerable amount of freedom. I find this concept to be much more inviting than categorizing women as either second or third wave feminists.

I am interested in the dichotomy you suggest, in which feminism is enriched and complicated simultaneously. Though I agree that this occurs due to the influx of new voices, especially third wave voices, I wonder if we should accept this complication or eventually aim to create new definitions and theories. Indeed, like you, many third wave critics have said that this new complication in feminism will help it to transcend current boundaries, but isn't there a possibility that women will accept this complication without further debate, thus turning feminism into a vacuum? My aim is also to talk about my introduction to feminism, and how I was more inspired by women in popular culture and fiction than by the feminist "hall of fame." I don't want to sound defensive, but as for making room for third wave feminism, I believe that it is actually second wave feminism for which we must continue to make room.

Roxanne: I think you're right, but my own second wave ideology is still so dynamic that I don't believe that I'm becoming a dinosaur. My point is that all women's voices have a right to join in the conversation; and I think a vacuum in feminism is not possible, because in this conversation, every divergent view or complication is important. For example, I'm sure we could debate endlessly your grandmother's feminist impulse. I think she adds to the feminist conversation, although she has never identified herself as a feminist. I became aware of the general cultural practices that oppress women by listening to my mother in conversation with other women. These voices set forth a lived feminism that leveled explicit criticisms at practices that denied women and girls rights and privileges equal to those of men and boys. When my mother pointed out to her neighbors the unfairness in allowing a son but not a daughter to play hockey, she made her feminism clear through experience and praxis, not through theory, which I still find inspiring.

Erin: I am intrigued that your feminism was inspired by my grandmother, who has always seemed to be the typical "Grams," baking cookies, gardening, and taking care of Grandpa. It is only now when I observe her behavior that she seems empowered; when she says "yes, dear" to my grandfather, I see a combination of being patronizing and patient. She has endured patriarchal restrictions for a long time, but she never had a medium through which she could express a definitive feminism or identify herself as a feminist.

Your feminism, however, has always been assertive and admirable. The fact that from an early age, I was encouraged to play sports that were considered nontraditional for women attests to that. Unfortunately, when you pounced on my father for making sexist comments, I was both amused and intimidated. At the time, you seemed to represent the whole "bra-burning" stereotype. For third wave feminists, the second wave is a vexing proposition, because the third wave is shaped by both the various second wave mandates and by the cultural backlash against them. Further, the third wave is seen as both encompassing diverse activist work and as being keyed down from the militancy of the second wave. I agree with Rebecca Walker's statement that second wave feminism seems to exclude young women because it "doesn't allow for individuality, complexity, or less than perfect personal histories."[3] While I agree with Walker, I also worry that second wave mandates will be forgotten. Catherine M. Orr points out that the third wave is about feminist practice as a matter of personal style or individual choice, and that "any emphasis on organized intervention is regarded as naïve and even oppressive to women."[4] Your feminism was guided by this organized intervention, and though I think calling second wave political goals naïve is unjust, I believe that the emphasis on individual expression makes the third wave inviting and effective.[5] Even though I have never declared myself a feminist, I realize that as a third waver, there is no need for radical action or strategy to support the movement. Militant action is not needed to promote the third wave; instead, the experiences of young women construct the third wave.

The third wave is challenging because it refuses to work within boundaries or dictate them. For instance, it reads cultural production and gender politics as sites of struggle, but inhabits those sites, drawing desire and pleasure, as well as directing anger. For example, although I admire the autonomy and sexual power of the female characters on *Ally McBeal,* I resent their Barbie-doll uniforms and the way the media feeds on them. I think that whereas the second wave was more of a collective political movement, the third wave helps women work on a personal level. I may never lobby my child's school for nonbiased gender practices, as you did, but I can draw self-confidence from third wave examples and role models as I enter the job market. Naturally, if women can come to terms with their feminism on a personal level first, it will ultimately contribute to the movement. The strategy for getting to this level has changed from the days of the second wave, and I think it has improved. I am still coming to feminism on a personal level, but I eventually hope to contribute on a larger level. Unlike you, my feminism was not influenced by feminist texts; rather, like my grandmother's, it was expressed through personal choices, for example, my choice to play male-dominated sports.

This pattern of "skipping a generation" is not unique to our family. Alice Rossi comments that "the public heroines of one generation are the private heroines of the next."[6] Rossi refers to the second wave's affirmation of the original feminist movement, while noting that the third wave is more interested in reflecting upon personal feminisms than it is in organized activism. According to Rossi's theory, my grandmother and I share a feminism that prefers private, rather than public practice. However, as a third waver, my reason for a lack of public activism stems from an overwhelming confusion concerning the definition of third wave feminism, and the social stress that faces contemporary women and consumes their time. My grandmother could not live a public feminism because this option was not available to her.

Roxanne: Erin, there's public activism and there's lived feminism. You might never occupy a dean's office to make the public aware of a university administration that turns a blind eye to openly misogynist practices, or participate in rallies and campaigns against anti-abortion politicians or those legislators who find ways to discriminate against women on welfare. But you should consider taking part in the annual Take Back the Night march and observing December 6.[7] You may see these actions as activism, but I think they are merely two ways of aligning yourself with your community—in this case, feminists in the academy. You argue for the necessity of continuing the conversation; I see these activities as part of that. Even if you never identify yourself as a feminist, you have put yourself into the feminist conversation and acknowledged that your actions are governed by a feminist impulse. For my part, I'm happy to be vocal about my feminism and how it shapes my decisions and my worldview.

It's clear that pop culture and your education have influenced how you see the world. I also think that you are able to place the second wave within its historical contexts and to see how the stereotypes and caricatures emerging from pop culture have led to a misunderstanding of the second wave's intentions. I was astonished to hear my sister tell me during a recent visit that she doesn't think she's a feminist. However, I decided a long time ago that I can best serve my own feminist interests with patient explanation and by setting a positive example. My sister understands that the women's movement of the 1960s and 1970s helped make possible her education and a career in which she was seen as equal to her male counterparts, and in which she rarely suffered from gender discrimination. While she is now a stay-at-home mother, she has every intention of returning to her career, and the women's movement has made that reentry possible as well. I know that when she confesses apathy about feminism, she holds stereotyped visions of bra-burners, even though she knows that the feminists of the 1960s caused every Western nation to rethink its labor policies. Furthermore, these images are media-constructed falsehoods, as are many of the stereotypes women today have of feminists. Even if the caricatures were wholly true, the idea of standing in front of government buildings and burning one's underwear doesn't seem as silly to me as the widespread practice in the 1950s and 1960s of firing any visibly pregnant woman—and the widespread acceptance of that practice. In short, media representations and distortions of feminism are so powerful and pervasive that they prevent women, even women who are as thoughtful and well-educated as my sister, from recognizing the obvious benefits of the second wave.

Erin: I find it ironic that my aunt, given her education and autonomy, doesn't take part in the feminist conversation, while my grandmother inspired your entrance into the conversation. I am somewhat irritated that my aunt would deny an ideology that has clearly benefited her; as Rich says in our epigraph, we need to be aware that many women have gone before us and have given us the freedom and power to criticize and defy patriarchal cultural practices. However, as a third waver, I think my aunt has a right not to participate publicly. What I expect of both my aunt and myself is that we assert our own beliefs; I think the third wave starts on a personal level. Once we are confident in our own skin, then maybe it will be time to participate in public feminism.

My current understanding of the third wave is both fuzzy and clear. I realize that the third wave is not clearly defined or separated from the second wave; it is messy and self-contradicting, but also encompassing, enlightening, and empowering, and because of the latter three adjectives, I feel that the third wave allows women to express any ideas they have about feminism without being boxed into a category or identity. In *Third Wave Agenda* (1997), Leslie Heywood and Jennifer Drake define the third wave "as a movement that contains elements of second wave critique of beauty culture, sexual abuse, and power structures while it also acknowledges and makes use of the pleasure, danger, and defining power of those structures."[8] Oddly enough, I think that both my grandmother and I are feminists within the chaos of the third wave, because it holds so many possibilities. Whether Grandma pursues her hobby as a woodworker and tells my grandpa to do the dishes, or I work toward a career instead of a family, we are functioning in the third wave. I have attempted to define the feminism of my grandmother and myself, because we've never come out of the feminist closet.

I must acknowledge, however, that my view on the third wave differs from those of some other third wavers. While my feminism remains private rather than public, many women have an "in your face" attitude about it. I have a friend who makes a point of debating every topic from a feminist perspective, both in class and in casual conversations. Unfortunately, she's become a "feminazi" caricature to many of my classmates. Although my friend may be more militant than some second wavers, I would still classify her as third wave, along with myself, even though my feminist battles are carefully chosen and taken up only with people who will take me seriously. I sometimes wonder if I am really contributing to the third wave simply by working out my own issues when other women are devoting their lives to improving social policies and ideologies about women. I think so, but I recognize that others may not. Though my grandmother will probably never declare herself to be a feminist, I'm lucky to have the opportunity to explore and assert my feminism. But unlike you and other second wavers, I will never be able to define my feminism clearly because of the erratic nature of the third wave, and I'm comfortable with that.

Roxanne: I won't apologize, Erin, for insisting that my voice be heard; one of the great things about growing up in the second wave was the new freedom women were finding as they claimed their right to self-expression. And that freedom did allow individual choice. I think that, as I have, you can define your own feminist ideology, and that definition will come from your lived experience. When I was studying for my master's degree, one of my classmates characterized me as a "raving feminist." I found that hilarious, first, because he had issues with any type of gender theory, and second, because I have never seen myself as a radical feminist—I assume that's what he meant by "raving"—although many radical feminists have inspired me. While I feel that I have never said or done enough to express my feminist ideology, I also worry about presenting my views or any feminist practice as dogma. I see the paradox that lies in being fully committed to my feminism even as I refuse to force my views on others; but just as you learn to live with third wave paradoxes, I can live with this one. I agree with Orr's suggestion that "second wave 'moms' can and should be represented as something more than just oppressive to their third wave 'daughters.'"[9] In my case, I can take her point literally. My own free expression may be seen by other women, including you, as the opportunity to learn about the multiplicity of women's voices that shaped my feminism, but moreover, my voice should invite you to freely express your own.

I feel lucky to have become an academic after women's studies departments or programs were established in most North American universities. The feminist voices that built this new discipline also brought many new perspectives to literary studies, the forum in which I developed my feminism and in which I now work. Influenced by and participating in women's studies, feminists have imported research from many disciplines to the study of literature, and they have brought the practical along with the theoretical; for example, the pedagogical strategy of forming small groups so that even the quietest may speak counteracts hierarchy and promotes the egalitarian spirit essential to feminism. I remember how exciting it was to read the theorists who helped me to articulate my own beliefs, to learn to read the text at hand but also to be able to read the sociocultural text around me.

At the same time, Erin, I think that the path of feminist theory within the discipline of literary criticism foreshadowed the messiness that you find both inherent and important to third wave feminism. By the 1970s, the voices of second wave feminism began to indicate that feminist literary theory could not be only one theory. Writing in 1980, Annette Kolodny argued for a feminist criticism from "multiple critical schools and methods, but captive of none."[10] She expected to see the history of literature altered, and it has been. She made it clear that literature is a social institution, and that reading is socialized behavior. Moreover, she suggested that when writers such as Kate Chopin and Charlotte Perkins Gilman dropped out of the literary eye, it was because their male readers could not properly interpret, understand, or appreciate women's texts. Most importantly, she has made it clear that there are several ways for feminists to read literature and culture. Even as second wave theorists like Kolodny foreshadowed the shape of the third wave and its blurring of boundaries, I think they have ensured that the boundary between the second and third waves is an indistinct blur rather than a clear break. I think you would be hard-pressed to find any idea among third wave thinkers that is wholly unique and distinct from the second wave.

My work as a feminist literary scholar has taught me that, because feminist theory is informed by many feminist voices, any consensus is necessarily equivocal and polyvocal, and dependent upon the current state of the conversation. Contradictions play out on a critical ground where the discourse is vital and among equals. All women bring to the conversation a multiplicity of approaches and assumptions that provide a multiplicity of meanings, as in the very best literature. Think, for example, of Virginia Woolf's *A Room of One's Own,* and the diverse lines of feminist thought—domestic, economic, historical—she uses to support her argument that in order to write fiction, a woman needs her own income and a room of her own. This variety in feminist schools of thought can lead to conflict and competition, but also to movement, vitality, and learning. Under this variety, however, lie some beliefs held by most feminists: that the oppression of women is a fact of life, that gender—and gender biases—leave traces on all "texts" of history and culture, and that feminist discourse is an explicitly political enterprise working to change existing power structures, both in and outside the academy. Woolf's call for women to come together to form communities of change is part of that enterprise. I further understand that the choices made by feminist literary critics, including my choices, play a part in the struggle to end oppression in the world outside texts.

Erin: Though feminist literary criticism has now become crucial in my studies and my reading of popular culture, it was initially difficult to embrace. I was not initially inspired by the writings of feminist theorists. Instead, I became drawn to feminism through two disparate bodies of work: women in popular music and turn-of-the-century American women's fiction. I wonder if we won't look back to women in popular culture, music, and film as the leading feminists of this *fin de siècle.* My studies of the struggles to transcend gender-based confinement and oppression in Kate Chopin's *The Awakening,* Charlotte Perkins Gilman's "The Yellow Wallpaper," and Edith Wharton's *The House of Mirth* forced me to consider patriarchal restrictions in my own culture. Wharton's book was released as a major motion picture starring Gillian Anderson from *The X-Files,* and I wonder if this indicates that third wave feminism is shaping popular culture. In both *The House of Mirth* and *The Age of Innocence,* Wharton criticizes societies that punish women for claiming autonomy (Lily Bart) or for being eccentric (Ellen Olenska). I'm excited that Hollywood is putting money into such stories. I only hope that the producers and audiences won't miss Wharton's points, that women should be allowed to be autonomous, eccentric, or whatever they want. Wharton's female heroes attempt and fail to transcend gender constrictions. Thanks to third wave feminism, women's choices are becoming fully accepted; I hope that contemporary audiences and readers will make the connection.

Roxanne: That was spoken like a true literary critic. While I seriously doubt that most moviegoers will connect Wharton's feminist impulses to contemporary feminist practice, when you connect the feminism in her writing to her social environment, your observations fit well with the cultural materialist tenet that all writing is a product of its culture, not the other way around. I suggest that when we look to the women who serve as historical markers for the conscious beginning of the struggle for women's rights, we must see their writing as the product of a long history of feminist impulses. Before there was the first wave feminism, there were women writers who read their culture and included the political within the creative. Their work, along with that of women like Wharton and Woolf, has as much relevance for today's feminisms as it did for earlier feminist movements, because their voices can guide us in understanding, in our own culture, the sexism that prevents women from full self-realization.

Erin: As I mentioned earlier, one of the things that attracted me to feminism was and is empowered women in popular music. You mention Woolf's beliefs that women working together in community would provide the kind of freedom needed for women to express themselves artistically. By examining this concept within women's music, it is possible not only to discover to what extent pop culture embraces and articulates the feminist thinking of the academy, but also to explore whether it enlightens those who may feel alienated by feminist criticism. According to Orr, "what feminism in the academy comes to mean in the larger society, then, is determined by those who can speak in the language talk show audiences can understand and *Cosmo* readers can appreciate."[11] The people who can best speak this language are those who shape their craft to appeal to a large and diverse audience. Because pop music informs the thinking of so many girls and women, I would argue that it is an essential text in this discussion of feminism.

Some women involved in the current music scene, like the performers and fans of Lilith Fair, may realize this medium of expression is just as fluid, diverse, and confusing as the many other platforms of third wave feminism. While this can be intimidating, it is also inviting. So many voices being heard through different media shows the different possibilities of third wave expression. And it seems inevitable that new ideologies and practices will be formed. Conforming to them is not a requirement, however, but an option. I think of Woolf's proposal that women work to provide the place where women's artistic expression may be experienced, and as long as we insist that this community allow all manner of expression, we may have something.

When examining women in the music scene, the images projected from music videos suggest that confining women to categories in order to provide one generic, artist-friendly medium is quite impossible. Consider, for instance, teen pop icon Britney Spears, who has worked very hard to objectify herself with lyrics like "Hit me baby one more time" and her song "Stronger," which seems emancipatory in its lyrics, but contradicts itself in a video that is essentially soft-core porn. One music critic writes that "women have become perpetrators of their own misogyny by letting their 'anger be negated and trivialized.'"[12] I'm not sure if Britney is angry, but she certainly cashes in on her own objectification—and once a woman is a thing, that thing is easy to abuse. Therefore, it worries me that Spears has become such a household name and that young women may see her as a role model. Indeed, what was the point of the suffrage movement, if those efforts are going to be reduced to the bare navel and "come hither" look of a former Mouseketeer? At the same time, when I interviewed the members of the Canadian rock band Scratching Post, lead singer Nicole Hughes told me that she respected women like Spears for who they are and what they do because they work really hard. But then, artists like Sarah MacLachlan and her Lilith Fair crew work really hard and promote women's issues without degrading themselves in any way. The question, then, is should artists like Britney Spears be written off as a bad phase in music and feminine representation, or should they be appreciated for achieving success in a difficult industry, even if it is by objectifying themselves? It's not a question that can be easily answered.

Roxanne: Maybe not, but the process of answering the hardest questions can be the most satisfying part of coming to feminism. And while I am happy to write Spears off as bad taste in music, I do not deny her the right to speak. Nor do I deny her the right to use her body in whatever way she chooses, although her gross opportunism offends me.

I think part of my ongoing interest in women musicians comes from my habit of reading them through the lenses of second wave theorists. For years now, we have seen Madonna use her body and sexuality in a calculated manner, but one that I find to be part of her artistic expression. A good deal of the critical commentary on Madonna has focused on her habit of reinventing herself. As Madonna has passed through her many personas, I have often done mental comparisons between her and Simone de Beauvoir; although this might seem a stretch, I often find that women who have gone before provide a means of interpreting those in the present.[13] These two rebels seem logically connected to me. Both have passed through many stages, and both are attached to the "new": Madonna as a trendsetter, Beauvoir as a revolutionary voice. Beauvoir notes with surprise in *The Second Sex* (1949) that when she wanted to define herself, the first thing she had to say was, "I am a woman."[14] Feminism owes a good deal to her articulation of how the "truly feminine" has been fashioned and how women have been defined as "other." Madonna, on the other hand, has made it clear that being female is just the beginning of the many things women are. With every pose she strikes—the bordello beauty, the new Monroe, the butch, the wayward girl, the geisha, the dominatrix, the cowgirl—she carries an awareness of self that undermines each stereotype for feminine desirability even as she works to build the persona. I think that Madonna is fully aware of the ways in which women are made "other"—Beauvoir coined the term *alterité* to describe it—because she seems to me to be the object of her own gaze. She presents the female body in the same way she presents the female voice: as tough, demanding, and self-actualized. Madonna claims attention as the speaking subject; Spears remains only an object.

Erin: For me, Madonna has always been a non-issue. She has adapted her style to whatever is trendy in popular music and has enjoyed two decades of success because of it. I have never owned a Madonna album or viewed her as a role model. However, your comments have made me rethink her as an artist, and possibly as a feminist voice. While I have been somewhat amazed that she has had the audacity to assume whatever culture or subculture she pleases, she usually does something productive with her art. For example, "Vogue" in the eighties caused unrest among members of the gay community because they felt the style of dancing in that video belonged to their nightclubs, and many gay men felt that Madonna was exploiting them for her own financial gain. On the other hand, I think Madonna has supported the gay community by using "camp" values to pay respect to this community. Her videos and concerts often portray same-sex couples, often with herself as a part of them. She is liberated in her sexuality, but as you have observed, she is the subject who controls her body and image, whereas Britney's image is constructed by men who aim to use her sexiness as a means to cash in. Even though I find some of Madonna's videos ("Music" for one) counterproductive, I can at least take comfort in the fact that they are hers—and by that, I mean her art, her design, her message, and her image, produced by her company, however much they vary from one year to the next.

One woman I do admire in rock is Courtney Love, who heads the band Hole. Her behavior is often appalling, and some of her actions are hardly proactive for feminism, but I still love her in all her mean, aggressive glory. In her song, "Doll Parts," Love sings "I am / doll eyes / doll mouth / doll legs." She criticizes the patriarchal ideology that women are only the sum of their parts, that it is acceptable to be made object. However, I find her lyric, "I want to be the girl with the most cake," troubling, in that it suggests innate competition among women to enjoy their empowerment. Clearly, for Love, not every "girl" gets to have her cake.[15] Moreover, Love has been known to bare her breasts during shows, and I question if this action is empowering or degrading. Surely the prepubescent boys in attendance do not see it as a claim to women's rights. I agree with Heywood and Drake, who suggest that Love, for better or worse, may be the third wave's Gloria Steinem, "in that she is a highly visible lightning rod for third wave issues."[16] And, I would add that, like Madonna's, Love's actions are her own; when she bares her breasts, it's not for anyone but herself.

Roxanne: I find Love's breast-baring as problematic as I did Janis Joplin's over thirty years ago, and for the same reasons you do: she may see herself as subject, but a good deal of her audience sees her as a sexual object. I think, though, that Love—like Joplin before her—finds such gestures liberating and as empowering as some of the messages in her lyrics. For myself, though, I wonder if you are attracted more by the very real talent of some of the women you listen to than by their feminist gestures, radical or otherwise. When I think about Love's rather traditional choice to marry and have a child, her plastic surgeries, and her clear desire to be pretty, or about Joplin's traditional "blues mama" persona and her similar overweening desire to be a "pretty girl," I have a hard time figuring either of them as feminist role models, in any wave. Contrast Love's choices with the radicalism of Germaine Greer's *The Female Eunuch* (1970).[17] Greer figures marriage as a form of slavery, and attacks the systematic denial and misrepresentation of female sexuality by a patriarchal society. Instead of wanting to be "the girl with the most cake," Greer demands an end to capitalism and to the current proscriptive structures of church and state, and while she insists that women must come together to make these changes, she concludes that the ends cannot justify the means. With role models like Greer behind me, I find that the third wave does not come close to matching the second in radicalism or feminist commitment. Contrasting Love's lyrics to Greer's arguments shows them to be a pale feminism indeed.

However, if I'm going to draw from Greer—one of the earliest radical feminist voices and one who had a great influence on me—I must point out that she calls for women in community and describes the cultural call for conformity as a way of drawing women away from power.[18] And Love has supported other women in rock—her tussle with Lilith Fair aside—and she has consistently flown in the face of cultural confines. Greer argues that the struggle which is not joyous is the wrong struggle, and its joy is centered in its sense of purpose, achievement, and dignity, and in radical action.[19] I think that real joy must lie in the commitment Love has shown in her struggle for self-expression. In their fine article on women who record for independent labels, Joanne Gottlieb and Gayle Wald suggest that the appropriation of the guitar, the quintessential male instrument, holds radical potential.[20] Although there are a host of great female rock guitarists, Love plays the guitar with abandon and in ball gowns—it's a memorable combination.

Erin: Radical feminism on a theoretical level bothers me. One of its aims is to eradicate gender, and I find this an unsettling, dystopic notion, and an unrealistic one at that. But I love radical feminism in music. What I like about Love is that she revels in being a woman, but in a way that affords her the opportunity to be both the prom queen and the snarling bitch who is fed up with the "Boys on the Radio." MacLachlan is always the same demure woman on stage, and while Lilith Fair made it clear that women need to be treated better by men, I don't think MacLachlan can get a crowd as worked up as Love can, and I think that, at least on occasion, women should get worked up and angry. I said before that the third wave is beneficial because you can live it as quietly or loudly as you want. I like a combination, and screaming along with Love is therapeutic.

I'm learning to be grateful for the third wave because I can express myself and my personal feminisms without the looming presence of such radical notions telling me what I can and cannot do. Consider the accomplishment of our family: you, Mom, paid attention to Grandma's tradition of lived feminism and have used it in your own writing, incorporating her ideas, yours, and now mine into writing a new tradition of feminism. Anytime the stories of women are set forth in print, on film, or on an album, other women can access them and find and understand their own feminisms. Listening to other women's voices can only give strength to feminism.

For me, some women in music present the most accessible, and therefore influential, feminist agenda of the third wave. Consider the lyrics of Alanis Morissette, who was probably one of the first women rockers to make me consider oppression and emancipation. In Morissette's breakthrough album, *Jagged Little Pill* (1995), she angrily claims her place as the speaking subject and makes clear her views of male-female relationships, the music industry, and human relations in general. In "You Oughta Know," Morissette begins bitterly, singing to an ex-boyfriend: "And I'm here to remind you / Of the mess you left when you went away." These lyrics are problematic because they show a woman who seems to depend on a man for happiness, but at the same time, Morissette makes a liberatory movement as she sings of her own powerful sexuality. Several songs into the album, Morissette demonstrates her disdain for the male-oriented recording industry. In "Right Through You," she asserts, "You took me for a joke / You took me for a child . . . You took me out to wine dine 69 me / But didn't hear a damn word I said."[21] Morissette's album forces men and women to hear her words and realize that her world is not centered around the phallocentric; throughout the course of the album, she comes to the realization, as does the listener, that she is her own woman.

Roxanne: I remember when that album first came out; Morissette's anger and the power in her expressions of her sexuality gave me chills. I'll admit I had a moment of discomfort when I first figured out the words that the radio and video people were bleeping out ("Are you thinking of me when you fuck her?"), but Morissette seemed to me to care as much about pleasing herself as her lover; I found, and still find, the record exciting and liberatory. I think she is both a solid example of postmodern feminism and a solid third wave role model. Morissette provides an intelligent and tough-minded reading of contemporary culture, and she does so with a postmodern feminism that rejects traditional assumptions about truth and reality and recognizes the shifting position of subjectivity. Her play of voices on her albums—angry rejected lover, up-and-coming musician, satisfied lover, child mimicking her stage-mother—acknowledges the discursive construction of identity. Yet Morissette presents herself as multi-voiced; she does not remove the meaning of sexual difference from her narratives and cultural readings. Moreover, her reading and interpretation of the cultural text she finds in front of her holds the kind of suspicion that I want to encourage for young women. Morissette privileges and finds empowerment in the female and feminine aspects of language. On stage and in videos, she dresses in jeans and T-shirts, but her sexuality is overwhelming, both through her lyrics and through her music, which involves many instruments and takes many voices.

Erin: Sure, Morissette plays in jeans and a T-shirt, but let's not forget the video for "Thank You," in which she appears completely nude. I remember when the video first came out: many of my male friends were totally disgusted and yelled in protest because they were accustomed to the beautiful women who so often occupy television and music. I was appalled by their behavior because Morissette has a fairly average female body, and frankly it was a welcome sight compared to the Ally McBeal–types ruling prime-time television. Morissette bares her body, and it is shocking not just because she is naked but because she uses her nudity in a positive way: she is not dangling herself over a man as is often demonstrated in rap videos; instead, she presents the female body as a wholesome image. I only hope that other men who saw the video were not as pigheaded as my friends. But I have a feeling that just as I originally believed that all feminists were raving bra-burners, many men, and women for that matter, are still misinformed. Take, for example, Lilith Fair; a fraction of the audience was men, and I never attended the event, partly because I didn't want to be associated with that kind of atmosphere. Even now I would rather attend a festival with male rock bands, and I think that this is a result of ingrained social values.

Roxanne: Well, Erin, I suspect that your preference for male rock bands should lead you to further challenge ingrained values engendered by a patriarchal society. There is a reason I buy you so many albums by women, you know. However, my own feminist ideology has never been about engaging or alienating men. I believe that like-minded individuals, working in community, can make changes through their action, reaction, and influence. I choose to live and work as a feminist, and I work in community with other feminists, just as I choose to study literature by women. I tend not to focus on male-oriented cultural texts; of course, I should qualify this by noting that I take everything seriously and that, for example, overt misogynist or feminist lyrics by a male rock artist probably wouldn't escape my scrutiny. But I don't go looking for them. Men's cultural production is not of interest to me, and, frankly, I think it gets more than its fair share of attention and energy. I hold as one of my basic tenets Catharine MacKinnon's point that men have literally capitalized on reproductive difference: "their needs have defined auto and health insurance coverage . . . their perspectives and concerns define quality in scholarship, their experience and obsessions define merit . . . their images define god, and their genitals define sex."[22] MacKinnon's anger was both justified and productive; she was a founder of the Furies Collective, a radical lesbian commune, and she exemplifies the combination that motivates my feminism: my anger at the disadvantages girls and women suffer because of gender bias, and my need to be in community with other women. I think both anger and the need for community were in evidence at Lilith Fair, in the merchandise row run by and catering to women, in the ways women's issues were promoted alongside women's music. Further, by donating to domestic violence shelters in every town the Fair visited, MacLachlan reminded us of the appalling fact that every town *needs* domestic violence shelters.

You mention Lilith Fair as an example of what women can achieve and how they can make their voices heard. I think that even as it set forth feminist theory in a practical forum, Lilith Fair embodied the ideal of women in community. I loved it that MacLachlan organized such a thoroughly eclectic lineup: she included all genres of popular music (and some that weren't so popular), she featured new as well as established artists, and she kept women's issues front and center. I appreciate the mix of third wave voices like the Dixie Chicks hollering their lusty claim to be "ridin' on a sin-wagon," just as much as the strong second wave practices of the Indigo Girls. From Fiona Apple's "Sullen Girl," to the Chicks' claim that young women need "Wide Open Spaces," to the Indigo Girls' instructions that women will be a lot "Closer to Fine" when we stop looking to the old definitions for answers, Lilith Fair provided concertgoers with a spectrum of feminist voices. The festival literally was a matrix of feminist discourses, and it interwove the ideological with the practical in a way that one doesn't often find in the course of daily life.

I want to close with this idea that I see as central to feminism in any wave: the idea of women in community. Every theorist I have drawn from touches on how important it is for women to come together to listen and be heard. As these women help shape my ideologies, they shape my daily choices. For example, my many different types of volunteer work support projects and organizations that enable women and girls. I follow the example of Adrienne Rich, whom I see as the essence of second wave experience and praxis. Rich contends that for our work we need a community of women, "on which we can draw; whom we envision as our hearers, our co-creators, our challengers; who will urge us to take our work further, more seriously, than we had dared; on whose work we can build."[23] I believe that I build on the work of my foresisters; I hope that other women may build on mine.

Erin: Well, Mom, I've drawn from your work, and I'm sure many other women will do the same. Just having this discussion on paper has been enlightening and thought-provoking for me. I suppose that since I have represented the third wave in this discussion, it is appropriate I have the final word. Before we started this, defining myself as a feminist had been problematic because of the stereotypes and ambiguity that accompany the term. I realize now, however, that being a third wave feminist affords me the opportunity to adopt the term or to refuse it. It is our practices that matter, not how we describe ourselves. As I have been saying, Mom, defining yourself as a second wave feminist implies radical thinking and a commitment to voicing that thinking. Being a third waver, however, allows me the opportunity to express feminism simply by being disgusted at a music video that objectifies women. If young women come to understand this, then maybe they will be encouraged to become involved and express themselves. However, I do not believe that we must be limited to these quieter expressions; second wave ideas must be kept in the third wave, and perhaps reinvented, in order to challenge society and third wave feminists, because there can never be one feminism. The wider the range of personal expressions, the further this movement will take us. Our discussion has led me to realize that feminism has endless possibilities, and that it always has and always will. Since the feminist conversation began, women have encouraged each other's reflection, discussion, and action. At any rate, I believe that any woman aware of her own feminist practice will contribute to the ongoing conversation and empower herself at the same time.

NOTES

1. Adrienne Rich, *Blood, Bread, and Poetry: Selected Prose 1979–1985* (New York: Norton, 1986), 290.

2. I (Roxanne) want to be clear that when I discuss women's experiences, I am doing so from the perspective of Erin and myself: white, middle-class North Americans. We do not intend to present women's experiences as undifferentiated and universal. Although we recognize the need to consider the differences as well as the similarities of women's experiences across the boundaries of race, class, ethnicity, and nation, this essay is written from our personal perspective.

3. Rebecca Walker, "Being Real: An Introduction," in *To Be Real: Telling the Truth and Changing the Face of Feminism* (New York: Anchor, 1995), xxix–xl, xxxi.

4. Catherine M. Orr, "Changing the Currents of the Third Wave," *Hypatia: A Journal of Feminist Philosophy* 12, no. 3 (1997): 29–45, 34.

5. Like other young women trying to give voice to their awakening feminism, I (Erin) have found the definitions of third wave feminism and postfeminism somewhat confusing. I think my confusion is understandable in light of Judith Stacey's definition of postfeminism as "the simultaneous incorporation, revision and depoliticization of many of the central goals of second-wave feminism" (Orr, "Changing the Currents," 34), which sounds very like a definition of third wave feminism. In this paper, I've tried to define the third wave and have abandoned any discussion of postfeminism. After my mother and I presented a short version of this dialogue as a paper at the Canadian Women's Studies Association's annual conference, we took part in a lively discussion that helped me to

understand the term postfeminism in both its meanings. As Orr suggests, "postfeminism assumes that the women's movement took care of oppressive institutions, and that now it is up to individual women to make personal choices that simply reinforce those fundamental societal changes" (ibid.). Thus, postfeminism may be seen as what comes *after* feminism and as part of the backlash that argues against feminist cultural critiques, especially second wave readings of rape, sexual harassment, pornography, and abortion. The second view of postfeminism sees it as part of the poststructuralist, postmodern cultural critique. With my mother, I find this problematic, in that this type of criticism tends to remove the meaning of gender from cultural analysis, and therefore reproduces the assumption that feminism is no longer needed. While I owe many a debt for the ability to come to this understanding, I especially want to thank Professor Mary Carpenter of Queen's University for her insight.

6. Alice Rossi, *The Feminist Papers: From Adams to de Beauvoir* (1973; rept., Boston: Northeastern University Press, 1988), 616.

7. On December 6, 1989, fourteen female engineering students were murdered in their classrooms at the University of Montreal's Ecole Polytechnique. Their murderer was a solitary gunman with a grudge against women—those who were successful in the sciences in particular and feminists in general, according to his suicide letter. December 6 has been declared the National Day of Remembrance: most Canadian communities observe the "Montreal Massacre" in some way, while virtually every postsecondary institution in the country cancels classes and finds several meaningful ways to commemorate the women who died and to further the campaign to end violence against women.

8. Leslie Heywood and Jennifer Drake, eds., *Third Wave Agenda: Being Feminist, Doing Feminism* (Minneapolis: University of Minnesota Press, 1997), 3.

9. Orr, "Changing the Currents," 42.

10. Annette Kolodny, "Dancing through the Minefield: Some Observations on the Theory, Practice, and Politics of a Feminist Literary Criticism," *Feminist Studies* (1980): 19.

11. Orr, "Changing the Currents," 43.

12. Donna Lypchuk, review of *Anti-Diva: An Autobiography* by Carole Pope, in *National Post*, November 25, 2000, D1.

13. Beauvoir's highly literary discussion of *alterité* (otherness) remains a crucial work for feminists and still provides a touchstone for postmodernist and postcolonial feminism. Her view of the great writers remains essential to feminist literary criticism. I find just as valuable her criticism of women's own complicity in being made "other," and we see feminists today criticize the same type of complicity. And where Beauvoir concluded by declaring she is not a feminist, she went on to be a leading feminist voice, eventually prioritizing feminism over her long-held socialism, which makes a case for the dynamism of women's voices as they are shaped by women's experience.

14. Simone de Beauvoir, *The Second Sex,* trans. H. M. Parshley (French orig., 1949; New York: Vintage, 1952), xxi.

15. Courtney Love, "Doll Parts," recorded by Hole (Caroline, 1995).

16. Heywood and Drake, *Third Wave Agenda,* 6.

17. Germaine Greer, *The Female Eunuch* (London: Paladin, 1970). Greer acknowledges her debt to first wave feminism and self-consciously places her book within the "second feminist wave" (p. 11). She looks to the first wave in her attack on marriage: "The opponents of female suffrage lamented that women's emancipation would mean the end of marriage, morality and the state. . . . When we reap the harvest which the unwitting suffragettes sowed we shall see that the antifeminists were after all right" (p. 12).

18. Ibid., 21.

19. Ibid., 20.

20. Joanne Gottlieb and Gayle Wald, "Smells Like Teen Spirit: Riot Grrls, Revolution, and Women in Independent Rock," in *Microphone Friends: Youth Music and Youth Culture,* ed. Andrew Ross and Tricia Rose (New York: Routledge, 1994), 250–74.

21. Alanis Morissette, "Right Through You," *Jagged Little Pill* (WEA/Warner Bros., 1995).

22. Catharine A. MacKinnon, *Feminism Unmodified: Discourses on Life and Law* (Cambridge: Harvard University Press, 1987), 36. MacKinnon has made Marxist feminism relevant by arguing that the personal is political, that women are socialized early to accept themselves as lesser beings, that sexuality defines gender and represents the focal point of men's domination over women. She further argues that sexuality is domination, that it always involves a power dynamic, and that when we understand that dynamic and the relationship between gender and sexuality, we can make sense of much of previous and present aspects of society: pornography, sexual harassment, rape. I disagree with MacKinnon's premise that women's existence is wholly constructed under the conditions of male supremacy, that the essence of the feminine gender is victimization. Nor can I support her suggestions that women must break the ties of sex and love with men as part of the movement away from oppression, or that lesbianism is a central element of women's liberation.

23. Adrienne Rich, *On Lies, Secrets, and Silence: Selected Prose 1966–1978* (New York: Norton, 1978), 214.

SARAH BOONIN

Please—Stop Thinking about Tomorrow: Building a Feminist Movement on College Campuses for *Today*

PROLOGUE: LESSONS FROM SENECA FALLS

It was in Seneca Falls, New York, during the 150th anniversary celebration of the historic convention of the summer of 1848, that I first realized what it meant to be a "young feminist" working within the national feminist movement—and how profoundly my work at the Feminist Majority Foundation (FMF) was challenging that notion. I had been working at FMF for less than a year; in this time, my colleagues and I conceptualized the content and structure of FMF's campus program, *Choices,* and then traveled from campus to campus refining and reconstructing the program.

The organizers of the Seneca Falls anniversary celebration asked Ellie Smeal, the president of FMF (who was my mentor there), to speak at the National Organization for Women's (NOW) rally and to participate in a weekend of meetings and press events. In particular, they wanted Ellie to join other prominent feminist leaders in drafting the "Declaration of Sentiments for the 21st Century." My three colleagues and I immediately recognized the potential for a road trip. We had studied that historic summer in our college women's studies courses and were deep in the process of reflecting on our first year at FMF. We were beginning to wonder where our work fit into the larger feminist movement, and we were trying to make adjustments to the campus program for the following year. We were eager for the opportunity to listen and learn from the greatest activists of our time. So, the four of us asked Ellie if we could take time off from work, pay our own way, and volunteer and observe at the convention. Always willing to share information and experiences with us, Ellie not only agreed but also let us stay with her.

When we got to Seneca Falls, we were starstruck, mingling with the academics and activists who made up the syllabi of our women's studies courses. Although we expected to attend only the weekend's public events, Ellie invited us virtually everywhere she went—to dinners, to meetings, and even backstage at the rallies. While we knew this was an unusual opportunity for women of our age and experience, we had gotten used to Ellie's inclusive style. It wasn't until we started interacting with the other activists that we understood how unusual our experience was, especially in terms of the way young women are treated within the larger movement. We were the only women under twenty-five to be found behind the scenes at many of the closed events and meetings. Everywhere we went, prominent feminist scholars and activists would approach Ellie, and then be surprised and somewhat entertained by us—this group of young and excited women who were keeping her company. They would greet Ellie, smile warmly (if not somewhat patronizingly) at us, and then ask Ellie, "Who are the interns?" Ellie would reply, meeting their smile, "They aren't interns; they are my colleagues." Then she'd introduce us one by one. To that, her peers would say, "Oh, how fantastic! Where did you find them?" It was as if we were feminist aliens imported from a faraway planet. They were amazed that Ellie had found us and wanted to know how many more of us there were and where they could get some of their own. They gave us their cards and took ours. They usually made sure to mention how lucky we were to have a mentor and role model like Ellie to inspire our future careers. These interactions occurred repeatedly throughout the weekend—often with the same women, who still didn't remember our names, even after the third or fourth meeting.

Initially, when Ellie would refer to us as her colleagues or invite us to sit in on a closed meeting, I felt embarrassed and unworthy. I was looking at these new women of Seneca Falls and secretly hoping I'd be like them *someday* but feeling unsure if I fit in right then. It had never occurred to me that I could be a valued participant alongside such great academic and activist leaders. But as the weekend progressed, so did my thinking about my place among these leaders. I visited museums and historic sites, listened to speeches, attended meetings, and read the history of Seneca Falls. I learned about how Elizabeth Cady Stanton, Lucretia Mott, and other early feminists had spent their time during the first convention 150 years before. Through all of this history and observation, I was struck by the degree to which the work of Seneca Falls (both conventions) actually reminded me of my own work. The meetings and discussions were very much like those in which I participated with Ellie and with my young colleagues at FMF. They were even similar to the debates I had had with my feminist classmates in college. Rather than the seamless problem solving I expected to witness upon the coming together of my feminist idols, I heard passionate and insightful, but also flawed, discussion. Meetings were imaginative and productive, but also disorganized and even heated.

It was with a mixture of disappointment but also relief and excitement that I thought to myself, "If given the chance, *I could contribute* to this conversation." I began to see these feminist leaders gathered around me as I saw myself and my friends—as women with vision and courage but with no clear answers.

At the same time, in the shadow of the rich history of Seneca Falls, I wondered, "What has changed?" Women in the United States and abroad still don't have adequate access to safe and legal abortion and family planning. We still face rampant discrimination in the workplace and inadequate political representation. We still suffer from epidemic levels of sexual assault and domestic abuse. Child care and elder care remain undervalued and are still disproportionately the responsibility of women caregivers. And that is just a sampling of the inequity. As I listened to the speeches and attended the meetings at Seneca Falls, I would close my eyes and imagine myself there in 1848. I would hear the protesters gathered at every event, with their gruesome and violent posters chanting nothing more original than "Baby Killers!" or "Go back to the kitchen!" Then I'd open my eyes and see hope in the faces of the women around me. So little had changed, yet so much more seemed possible.

Toward the end of the weekend, it was clear that most of the feminist icons of my college years—the women who had inspired me to take my frustration to the streets, the women who declared my experience relevant and trusted me to change the world through their books and their speeches—did not really consider me a colleague. They were more interested in what I might do after they were gone from the front lines than in what I might contribute that weekend. More important, my colleagues and I had something worth saying—something that was being wasted at a time when the movement had no such luxury.

Late the night before the final day of the conference, Ellie asked the four of us if we would stay up with her, Charlotte Bunch, and some other women to help complete the drafting of the "Declaration of Sentiments for the 21st Century." The document needed to be ready early the next morning for a press event and still required substantial work. We were excited to be a part of the action in any way and were ready to start typing their dictation when we arrived at their meeting place. But rather than simply having us take notes and type, these leaders asked us for our opinions. They relied on our answers to their questions as much as they relied on each other's. Together, we reviewed and refined the Declaration—an agenda for equality in virtually every sphere. By the end of that night, though I'd contributed only a small amount to the final product, I felt as if I had been a part of history and not merely an observer. The amount of work still to be done in order to achieve equality, though tremendous, somehow seemed possible in that room in the company of such strong and accomplished women—my young colleagues included. I felt engaged in a way that I hadn't at any other point during the conference.

Although Seneca Falls did not necessarily change my approach to campus organizing, it illustrated the unique nature of my opportunity and obligation within the movement. As a campus organizer at FMF, not only was I one of a very small group of young women at the time with a paid job in the national feminist movement, but I was also one of an even smaller group of young women considered a leader and entrusted with genuine responsibility. I had the chance to help build a new model for campus activism that would engage young feminists not only because we rely on their support but also because we need their talent.

I was twenty-one years old when I took a job working as a campus organizer for FMF. Through my work at FMF, I helped to develop, coordinate, and later direct *Choices,* the nation's largest pro-choice, feminist campus program. From the beginning, Ellie Smeal and the entire staff at FMF viewed the new campus program not as a preconceived project to be implemented by young activists, but rather as an experiment to be created and inspired by young activists from its grass roots up through its leadership. The program was built step by step, not by a series of decisions or assignments handed down by Ellie or then-director Dee Martin (herself in her early twenties), but through long days spent in FMF's conference room sharing, challenging, and refining our collective vision for a student-based pro-choice movement on college campuses. We built on our own experiences as organizers and consulted with countless students and faculty members regarding theirs. Throughout this process, Ellie had the courage to let a team of recent college graduates be leaders *alongside her* at a time when few others were ready to give young women the same opportunity. She viewed us not strictly as students or young women, but as feminists—women who, like her, had the desire to work toward women's equality. In the end, the vision we arrived at seemed simple enough: to build a permanent, feminist, pro-choice presence on college campuses that would train young activists to make substantial contributions to the ongoing feminist movement. The campus groups would be fueled by the brightest and most motivated students. The groups would be proactive and would be ready to mobilize in times of crisis. Figuring out how to make this vision a reality was the far more difficult task.

While we never completely answered all of our own questions about campus organizing in my time at FMF, we made substantial progress. We implemented a two-pronged approach. We launched permanent campus groups, called Feminist Majority Leadership Alliances, and unveiled a national organizing campaign called *Choices,* which provided cohesion and a collective mission. Our approach in building the campus program, even more than the model we finally arrived at, can offer substantial insight into the complexities and challenges of campus organizing. In sharing some of my own breakthroughs in understanding campus activism, I do not intend to dictate how to imagine or implement other people's activism. Rather, I hope to describe how imagination and reconceptualization are uniquely possible within the feminist movement. Through my journey at FMF, as I had the privilege of helping young women come to their feminism, I strengthened my own.

RETHINKING LEADERSHIP

Every one of us who formed the original team of campus organizers at FMF shared a basic belief in the power of young leadership. We discussed feminism as a dynamic movement of ideas—constantly changing, expanding, and being refined. We questioned the relevance of chronological age as a predictor of a person's potential contribution to the movement. We shared a commitment to breaking down the false (but very deeply ingrained) undercurrent that serves as the basis for the vast majority of feminist campus organizing ventures—that student activists are primarily a long-term investment. That is not to say that student organizing isn't a long-term investment at all. Of course it is. However, the fundamental assumption that students could and would make major contributions as young leaders *today* ultimately led to the success of the program more than any other programmatic breakthrough.

What do I mean when I say that young feminists aren't the future of the movement? Well, what does it mean when someone says that young people *are* our future? Does it mean that we are not a part of the present, that there is no urgency in the work that must be done today? That the work can wait? Does it mean that we young people can take our time and make a difference at some point in the future? Does it mean we have nothing worthwhile to contribute right now? The implied answer to these questions is yes. By welcoming our participation at some future date, the establishment (even the feminist establishment) shuns any meaningful role we might have alongside them on the front lines of the current movement.

Like many of my colleagues, I grew up inundated with the concept that I if I worked hard enough, I could be a future leader. I tended to clump those public service–like messages about changing the world "someday" with those messages about saving for my retirement and drinking milk to prevent osteoporosis. Those messages went in the "long-term-but-not-all-that-interesting-right-now" category of information, or sometimes into the "insulting-advice-from-older-people" part of my brain. In other words, when people talked to me about doing great things with my life "someday," I really heard them telling me that I did not exist today. So I simply tuned them out.

I used to wonder why it is that young people are so frequently pushed out of the inner circles of decision making and leadership—not just within the feminist movement, but also throughout many progressive movements. After all, every time I look at the faces around me at a march or rally, it is young people who seem to be the "marching millions." So why are we so often left out and cast aside as naïve and unrealistic? Perhaps it is because we threaten the establishment of institutions—even if those institutions are feminist. Perhaps it is because we are risk-takers and have less at stake in taking those risks, or we have not yet built our careers, and so mistakes seem less devastating. We think big and frequently aren't as jaded as some of our mentors who have lived through intense disappointments.

However, for the same reasons that we are written off, we have a greater ability to transform the status quo than any other generation. We have grown up with the progress of our mothers and our mothers' mothers behind us. Although this privilege can lead to the illusion that all the battles have been fought and everything is okay, it also makes it possible for us to imagine and believe in an entirely new level of change. We are less reined in by our past experiences and more willing to take risks. As there is no blueprint for equality, success in the movement is a process of trial and error. We never know when, where, or from whom we might hear the very concept that will transform our work. In such a setting, imagination is just as important as experience.

Grounding our approach to student organizing in the belief that young feminists *can* be leaders was only part of the transformation our work required. As we began interacting with students, we ran up against a major obstacle. On campus after campus, we encountered young feminists who did not consider themselves leaders. While we were ready to embrace these young activists as equals, they believed that leadership was for older people and, worse yet, that it was inherent. Since they didn't think they "had it," they felt they shouldn't even bother trying to be leaders. I cannot count the number of times I approached a young woman about taking on a leadership role within a group and heard back, "I'd love to, but I'm not really a good leader." Fair enough. I'll admit that some people are good leaders and others aren't. But when I would ask her why she didn't consider herself a good leader, she would simply say, "I don't know, I'm just not a *natural* leader." It was as if scientists had isolated a leadership gene. The assumption seemed to be that some of us are born with it and can be leaders if we choose, and the rest of us are not and can only aspire to follow along.

Rather than combating these false notions of leadership, many organizers in the movement reinforce them. (I have fallen into this trap myself when I'm not paying close enough attention.) Rather than developing effective leadership training tools, we wait for the few young self-defined leaders to step forward, or we spend our time trying to identify the one or two "natural leaders" on campus (who are already overcommitted). We discount potential leaders because of their lack of experience, and we assume that experienced leaders don't need any additional training.

Through our efforts to recruit leaders for our campus groups, we realized that we must teach leadership skills. As part of the campus program, we now make that training available to all members of the group, rather than to just a select few. With the help of students, we have developed an extensive curriculum that enables activists on campus to learn effective leadership skills and then to teach those skills to their peers. We teach everything from public speaking to talking with campus administrators and the press to running effective meetings. This curriculum has proven invaluable in encouraging and training new leadership for FMF's campus groups year after year. Consequently, I have seen some of the most unlikely students develop into outstanding campus leaders with only a year or two of experience.

YOUNG FEMINISTS—WHO ARE WE?

At the time we launched FMF's campus program, many national organizations, having bought into the fear of a fading feminism, were shying away from using the term "feminist" in hopes of enlisting the support of more students. Similarly, they were carving out the "hottest" subset of their issues to advertise to students without disclosing their larger agendas. In stark contrast, at FMF, we made the decision to use the opposite strategy to re-energize student activism. We emphasized our identity as explicitly "feminist" and were extremely up-front about our multi-issue agenda.

After four years of travel to dozens of campuses all over the country, extensive conversations with hundreds of students, academicians, and activists, and scores of conference panels and dialogues involving young feminists, I have come to an unsurprising conclusion: despite tireless efforts to convince us otherwise, feminism isn't dead! Campuses aren't post-anything yet, and feminism, when innovatively presented, is as relevant to students today as it has ever been. Although I initially struggled with the approach, having been inundated by the national media's assault on our movement throughout my childhood, I found that our choice to use the term "feminist" in our name has been one of our biggest assets. If anything, the label "feminist" does more to draw students out of the woodwork than to drive them away.

This is not to say that education about feminism is not necessary. It is. In fact, I've given many a lesson on the definition of feminism. I've been on campuses where the first thing I do is define feminism as the pursuit of the social, political, and economic equality of women. On other campuses, I've started by asking students to define the term for me, then have gone on to dispel their myths about man hating or the idea that we have already achieved all the equality we need. Finally, I've spoken at length with other students about how racial discrimination and sweatshop labor are feminist issues because they are perpetuated by the same fundamental patriarchal structures.

Whatever the starting point, by clearly and honestly embracing the label "feminist," we have invited our student allies to share a common identity, terminology, and agenda with us and with one another. Rather than spending energy convincing members to embrace the "feminist" label or its underlying goals, we help the self-identified feminists on campus to come together and educate their peers about the movement. Through public education campaigns, guest speakers, and events, the Feminist Majority Leadership Alliances reach out to their communities. As the groups establish reputations for making positive contributions, so does the larger movement. Equally as important, when group members hear about feminism on other campuses, or in the news or in class, they feel a part of it. By sharing a portion of their identity with other feminists, students are a part of something far larger than their group, their campus, and even their country.

We made a similar decision with respect to the mission and principles of our campus groups. Many of our colleagues warned us against including too many issues in our campus mission statement, citing the potential alienation of members who agreed with some but not all of our positions. Despite this warning, we were unwilling to bury some of our issues on the campus level while maintaining a fuller agenda on the national level. In launching our campus groups, we proudly highlighted all of FMF's principles—pro–gender equality, pro-choice, pro–LGBT rights, pro–civil rights and affirmative action, pro-environment, pro-nonviolence, antidiscrimination, and pro-labor. This was both an honest decision on our part and ultimately a wise one in terms of recruitment. Through women's studies courses and women's centers, students on campus have a much fuller and more complex concept of feminism than ever before. Far more women on campuses than ever before have been educated in the history, language, and philosophies of the struggle for equality. As a result, young feminists think and speak both critically and globally. To be relevant, the feminist movement cannot speak about "choice" in this country without also speaking about poverty and lack of access to basic health care both in the United States and abroad. We cannot talk about abortion without dealing with HIV/AIDS, LGBT rights, or even sweatshop labor.

Our multi-issue approach has not only resonated with feminists but also enabled many of our groups to bring together activists working on a variety of different issues under the umbrella of feminism. By agreeing on a broad set of issues from the start, our campus groups are able to maximize productivity, recruitment, and coalition building on campus. The response has been both empowering and validating.

While we at FMF had a clear sense of the role we hoped campus feminists would play within the national movement and were confident that they existed in significant numbers, we had to answer the questions "How do 'they' see themselves in relation to 'us'?" "How do they see themselves?" "How do they see us?" Answering these questions has been perhaps the most dynamic, intriguing, and elusive aspect of the work for me. Just as there is no one prevailing "young person" identity, there is no monolithic "young feminist" identity. Having straddled the worlds of campus feminism and the national movement, however, I have noticed a tension between young feminists and their predecessors, which I think is among the most destructive forces in the movement today.

Frequently I hear other young feminists talk about "our movement" or our "wave" of feminism. Many of the students I work with speak about "our kind of feminism" as though it is in response to, or even in spite of, the work of older feminists, rather than building upon or in coordination with that work. It is as if our goal as young feminists is to break free of the work done before us rather than to use that work as a lever. The "we" of young feminists too often excludes older feminists, just as the "we" of older feminists too often excludes younger feminists. This rhetorical and theoretical rift has very real implications for campus activism. As I met with countless young feminists and professors on college campuses, I noticed an attitude of distrust among some campus feminists toward national leadership and older mentors. Students are often hesitant to involve professors and community members in their work because of a very legitimate fear of being dominated. As a result, students fall into a trap: either they accept their roles as "helpers" to those making the decisions and end up feeling disempowered, or they falsely "set themselves free" to work on their own. Although this "freedom" seems liberating at first, it simply marginalizes young activists further and virtually ensures that they needlessly repeat mistakes. Students ultimately feel defeated and further alienated from the "we" of the movement, and older feminists are discouraged by what they perceive as a lack of young faces in feminism.

I think that is why I've grown to dislike the wave metaphor so intensely. Why must the feminist movement be characterized in terms of "waves"? I think many of us use the wave metaphor to represent the growth and progress of the movement through time. But inevitably, the "waves" simply become labels that separate one age group of feminists from another. Doesn't the word *movement* already imply change? Doesn't a movement, by its very nature, show progress and build as it evolves? In naming first one "wave" and then another, are we implying that there is stagnation within each wave? And don't waves come one after another? What happens in between them? Can two or more waves arrive at the same place simultaneously? What about moving both forward and backward, fast and slow, and even in circles at times?

I've heard many of the newer interpretations of the wave metaphor—about how waves can blend into one another, how waves are powerful and progressive. Still, I think—whether intentionally or not—this metaphor feeds into the feminist movement's need to emphasize the distinction between one generation and the next rather than fostering collaboration. In my experience on campuses, this has been the single biggest challenge to true partnership between the national movement and campus feminists.

I don't deny that feminism today differs from that of the past and that this difference is good. The language, strategies, and scope of feminism have evolved tremendously. However, I view the uniqueness of my generation of feminists largely as a matter of progress and growth, rather than as a rejection of the past. The movement today is more mature in ways that are a credit to its history, its openness, and its encouragement of new ideas and philosophies. Too often, we create new labels for ourselves to justify our progress and forgive our mistakes. In the process, we forget the very basic connection we all share as feminists. While feminism does not need to—and should not—mean sameness, it does imply a certain philosophical and ideological connection. We share a commitment to the pursuit of equality. That common pursuit forms the basis of our community and must be nourished by national organizations as we work with students on college campuses.

Unless we think of ourselves as a "we"—a community of students, activists, scholars, and national leaders—we can never be true partners in change. Older mentors must be willing to share experience and knowledge while welcoming the input and co-leadership of younger feminists. At the same time, young feminists, despite our fear of losing autonomy, must not turn our backs on the guidance and support of those who did the work before us. The feminist movement won't survive without an empowered and active young constituency. At the same time, a young constituency won't do much good without the help and input of more seasoned mentors. This is not to say that we shouldn't do some things differently. We should. However, it is destructive to our ultimate goal of equality to try to do the work alone.

The more my colleagues and I traveled from campus to campus, the more we became convinced that FMF needed to play a major role in changing the interaction between campus activists and the rest of the movement. Rather than building a "student arm" (translate: auxiliary or periphery) of the movement with its own identity, we hoped to promote a larger collective—a diverse and nonmonolithic "we." We fostered strong, reciprocal mentoring relationships as a major component of FMF's campus program. As partners with young activists, we encouraged mentors to make room for young leaders at the decision-making table. We've tried several methods of bringing together younger and older activists on campus—joint actions, internships, faculty and community councils, activist-based course work, dinner meetings, and even parties. When most successful, the partnerships have been honest, reciprocal, and fostered from both ends.

Perhaps our first and best illustration of a successful partnership came in the aftermath of the tragic murder of the abortion provider Dr. Barnett Slepian in November 1998. As soon as we learned about Dr. Slepian's murder, we all agreed that the most important first step was to notify members of our campus groups immediately. We quickly suggested what students could do to respond to the brutal murder and prepared some materials they could use to conduct their activities. While some of us assembled the materials, the rest of us called everyone on our lists. As we provided students with our ideas, we listened to theirs. As the night wore on, we refined our own strategies and increasingly referred students to one another for support and advice.

The response from our student colleagues was unbelievable. In fact, it was the single best response we'd gotten from the campus groups since starting the program. Within days of the murder, nearly every one of our campus groups at the time (on over thirty campuses) conducted marches, candlelight vigils, and other activities. They wrote letters to the editor, placed articles in their local papers, and circulated literature and petitions. With one round of phone calls and some emergency planning, our students dramatically affected the national response to this horrific event. Moreover, our students felt empowered.

Because we immediately contacted them, they felt like "insiders" in the national response. Because they played a key role in shaping our response and advising one another through this national crisis, they felt like—and were—our *partners*.

WHAT CHANGED FIRST—THE CAMPUS OR THE FEMINIST?

Whatever issues describe our feminism, whatever our theoretical background, and whether or not we consider ourselves leaders, we don't "do" feminism the way we used to. Campus feminism is different today than it was in the late 1960s and 1970s, not simply because of theoretical transformations within the movement, but because college campuses are different places today than they were back then. Much of the perceived "lack of interest" in feminism at the time we started our work on campuses had more to do with outdated methodology than with outdated issues. For nearly thirty years, the feminist movement had been relying on virtually the same approaches to campus organizing. It is no wonder that students weren't packing the meeting halls.

On campuses today, women make up more than half of all students. We are graduating at the top of our classes, and we are increasingly going on to pursue higher degrees. The concept of a woman going to college to get an "M.R.S." degree is mostly ancient history. Moreover, Title IX and the feminist movement have led to a surge in extracurricular opportunities for women. Academic, professional, and sports clubs vie for women's attention. Today, a female student can be the editor of the newspaper, president of student government, or captain of a varsity sports team and still be a feminist. Although these changes have been tremendously beneficial to women, they have also contributed to the marginalization of campus activism.

So many feminists I spoke with while recruiting for the program early on—students, faculty, and community members—thought of our work as "only campus activism." At first, I didn't have an answer for them. I remembered having that feeling myself as a student leader. I had come to internalize my place on the margins as an activist. While student government, the campus newspaper, and varsity sports teams enjoyed legitimacy, attention, and credit, the activist groups I was a part of were cast aside as nonessential. It didn't seem to matter that I was working thirty hours a week with these activist groups or that we were making as much of a contribution on campus as they were. Eventually, rather than fighting our identity as insignificant and struggling for the credit we deserved, we rejected the pursuit of legitimacy. Believing we could never gain recognition for our positive contributions on campus, we falsely dismissed the recognition as antifeminist anyway. Somehow, my fellow feminist activists and I had bought into the notion that to think of ourselves as important was to be the enemy. Now, working with student feminists nationwide, I have witnessed this self-deprecation in epidemic proportions.

As we worked to get FMF's program off the ground, we knew we needed to address this problem. How did we expect to recruit and retain students to a movement that they viewed as only marginally important? Moreover, how would campus groups be effective in their work if they weren't taken as seriously as other groups on campus? In order to do the kind of work we hoped to do and to involve a significant number of students, we needed to address the issue of poor self-image among many feminists on campus.

We found that the more we emphasized students' importance on campus and their contribution to the national movement, the more they viewed themselves as important. We began building this mindset into our recruitment and training strategies. We taught our students to analyze closely the resources allocated to other groups on campus and then demand as much for themselves. We challenged them to look at the enrollments of sororities, student governments, and social clubs and then to decide that their feminist organizations were worthy of at least as much participation. We built in awards programs and national recognition for the groups as a way of acknowledging students' hard work and talent. We worked with faculty members to take a more active role in the groups, which underscored their legitimacy.

At the same time we realized that women on campuses have more opportunities today than in the 1970s, we also recognized that they have more obligations. College is more expensive now than ever before. Consequently, more students are working part- or full-time in addition to taking a full course load. For these students, volunteerism is a luxury that time won't allow. In order to adapt to all of these changes on campus, the old model of campus organizing had to change.

When I first tried to recruit students for the program, I was struck immediately with an almost universal question from students. "What's in it for me?" At first, I was somewhat disappointed by this. I would think to myself, "What do they mean, 'in it for them'?" In theory, isn't feminism more about "we" than "me"? But the more students I spoke with, the more I realized that my reaction to their question was rooted in my own privilege. It isn't that students today aren't generous with themselves and their time; it's that they simply have other realities to deal with. Given that their time is limited, how can they combine feminist activism with their other goals and responsibilities? For example, can they fulfill their internship requirement through the activism? Can they do feminist work instead of working in student government or on the school paper and still have something to put on their résumés? Will they have access to national conferences and events?

Therefore, in working with students, FMF considers things such as résumé building and internships, training and support, and even the prestige of the program. This was a big adjustment for some of us—especially those of us who disliked acts of self-promotion. However, by building into our program elements such as career development, we not only enable more students to participate but also help them get jobs at feminist organizations further down the line. In broadening the appeal and benefits of participation, we can recruit students from all walks of life. We work with students who have families, full-time jobs, and health concerns as well as with nontraditional students and students who have dramatically different interests and skill sets. We also made a commitment to working with community colleges, which frequently have enrollments that are upwards of 60 percent women. For these students, free time is often especially scarce.

Our adaptation to the changing landscape of college campuses has had a tremendously positive effect on student response to our campus program. By thinking in terms of the benefits of participating in campus feminism, we have fostered a respect for student work and time, and the students themselves have developed a sense of worthiness. Recruitment has shifted from begging students to participate to offering them an *opportunity* to participate. As the groups have taken themselves more seriously, they have demanded and received better treatment—more space, more funds, and better coverage in campus press.

Many of our groups and student colleagues even began receiving awards on campus for their work—as "best campus group" or as outstanding student leaders.

Now when I speak with students on many of the campuses I work with, especially at community colleges and on rural campuses where investment by national organizations is rare, students take pride in their campus reputation. They feel honored to be working with their feminist colleagues on campus and across the country. Similarly, students increasingly report that their involvement with the program has inspired them and helped them to receive internships, scholarships, and job offers in the nonprofit sector.

EPILOGUE: LESSONS FROM FEMINIST EXPO 2000

Just as that road trip to Seneca Falls set the stage for so many of the lessons I learned at FMF, Feminist Expo 2000 brought them all together for me. At first, I couldn't understand why Ellie was so driven to host the Feminist Expo for Women's Empowerment in March 2000. Her idea was to bring together feminists from every sector of society to exchange strategies and information and to demonstrate the breadth, depth, and diversity of the movement. As a part of Expo, she wanted to recruit thousands of college students to attend. The concept was noble, but was it worth all of the effort?

From September 1999 through March 2000, I, along with the ten-member campus team I directed at the time, took on the greatest organizing challenge of our lives. We conducted months of field travel, sometimes organizing three major speaking events on different campuses per day. We worked fourteen-hour days and nearly every weekend. We set up dozens of large and small campus events to get the word out and participated in countless conferences and panels. We distributed tens of thousands of flyers and took down thousands of names and e-mail addresses. Additionally, we invited some of the most talented young feminists in their fields to speak during more than 150 panels, workshop sessions, and plenaries on virtually every aspect of feminism imaginable. We planned a series of ten sessions that were specifically geared toward youth organizing involving young leaders from nearly every major national feminist organization. We constructed an enormous campus hub in our Exhibit Hall, where students could speak with us, attend training sessions, and access campus organizing materials.

By the time the first day of Expo rolled around, I felt numb. I was tired, hungry, and able to see almost nothing but typos in the program book and mix-ups in the room setups. But when I walked up onstage during the plenary session to welcome the thousands of feminists sitting in the audience, I finally understood Ellie's dream about the event. It was as if everything I'd been telling myself and students about the movement was actually right there in front of me—the size of the movement, its power, its harmony, its diversity. I saw older women with their daughters and granddaughters as well as younger women with their siblings, friends, and families. I saw professionals, students, artists, and activists. But mostly, I saw one thing—young feminists. We were everywhere! Over one-third of the attendees were college-aged women. It was as if all the outstanding women I'd had the honor of meeting on campuses over the past three years descended upon the same space at the same time. As I approached the podium, I was shaking. I was so proud. It wasn't just that I was proud we had succeeded in getting so many students there; I was proud to be considered a part of this movement. I was proud because, as I looked at all of the young faces staring back at me from the audience, it was clear that the event would have been incomplete without them.

Feminist Expo demonstrated what I had set out to help create when I took my job with FMF's Campus Leadership Program: a movement where young and old, campus and community blended together seamlessly and powerfully. In the end, it wasn't the speakers, the celebrities, or the national organizations with their booths that made the students flock to Expo. The thousands of students who came to Expo— by the busload and vanload, via trains and planes, all the way to Baltimore from every corner of the United States—didn't come to witness someone else's movement. They came to Feminist Expo because they felt a part of the discourse and felt they had something to contribute. They came to Expo because the movement felt like home to them. They came because this was *their* movement.

Ultimately, the magic of the feminist movement isn't in the pages of its charters, bylaws, or books; it isn't within the walls of its nonprofit organizations. It is in its vision. Vision, as I've learned through my work with students, has no age limits. This has been the single most important discovery for FMF's campus program. And it has changed my life.

PART THREE

Recognizing Feminism

JENNIFER BAUMGARDNER
& AMY RICHARDS

Who's the Next Gloria? The Quest for the Third Wave Superleader

In the mid-1990s, the *New Yorker* did a special issue on that fa-vorite niche subject: "Women." Tina Brown, who was editor-in-chief of the magazine at that time, hired Roseanne, the star of a popular televi-sion show, to consult for the issue and reached out to all manner of leaders from various walks of life. Amid it all, the editors of the *New Yorker* put in a call to the writer and activist Gloria Steinem—generally considered to be the "it" girl of women's lib. The *New Yorker* wanted to get the "skinny" on who would be "the next Gloria"—the superleader who would take up the feminist charge. Because Steinem believes that no one person represents feminism, she listed a handful of younger women, including a journalist, an activist, and an artist. Her sugges-tions must have appeared too lackluster for Tina Brown, however, since the *New Yorker* ran no story about feminism's new leaders.

It's not so surprising that the ritzy and venerated magazine of the mainstream media didn't share Steinem's interest in the various and plentiful leaders of the third wave. (Actually, the media's search for one star—such as Steinem herself—who could be plucked from the many organizers of the women's movement and anointed as a leader is an old story, one that has dogged feminism throughout its existence.) It is likely that the editors of the special issue on women were disappointed that Steinem named a range of feminists rather than one "star." After all, she could have cited Naomi Wolf, Katie Roiphe, or anyone else who was already a media favorite. But Steinem was right on: it is exactly that multiplicity—of individuals and of expertise, among other qualities—that we believe defines third wave leadership. For too long, this narrow definition of "leader" has made it impossible for women, people of color, and gay people to have their vision and impact acknowledged. So, we'll say it once and for all: women and people of color do not lack leaders. What we lack are structures that identify and support different forms of leadership.

Activists who fall outside the white/male/heterosexual/Ivy League model are below the radar of most establishments, not just the mainstream media's. There isn't an infrastructure within foundations or electoral politics that identifies, nurtures, and supports multiple, nonhierarchical, authentic leadership. When this kind of leader actually finds a way to get to a journalist or grant officer, it is all too rare that his or her leadership is recognized. If you are a female working for human rights legislation, for instance, you are likely to be defined as an activist or community organizer, but not a leader. Complicating matters further, unless you are white, male, and heterosexual, it is presumed that your sphere of influence includes only those who are like you. Ergo, Jesse Jackson represents African Americans, while Ralph Nader can speak for consumers. The leader of a minority, in this view, can never represent the majority.

In 2003, we are faced not with access—with getting one person inside the power structure to represent all of us who are on the outside—but with building a new structure for equality. The fact that access isn't equality plagues our understanding of modern feminism. The women's movement is perceived as a white, middle-class movement (run by and for the same) mainly because the gains of feminism have been measured by our entry to the privileged white male sphere. It doesn't take Cornel West to tell you that white women have more plentiful and direct routes to the white male sphere of influence than women of color do. Yet, if we measure feminism by what might be thought of as a quality of life standard rather than by access to elite institutions, feminism's story changes. How much do women of all ages, races, ethnicities, and income brackets think that they are capable of? Is it significantly more than what women of those same subgroups thought they could do forty years ago? *Yes.*

But let's go back to our bumper-sticker slogan: Women and people of color do not lack leaders. Given an expanded perspective on leadership, it's clear that the problem isn't leadership per se, but how we define the ability to lead. Here's an example of what we're talking about: At a lunch with the director of the Next Generation Leadership Network Initiative at the Rockefeller Foundation, a thirty-something staffer complained about the dearth of interesting and qualified female applicants for the Initiative. The remedy her team came up with was to extend the age range for "future leaders" from twenty-five-to-forty to twenty-five-to-fifty. Her guiding assumption was that women come to leadership later in life. Through our jobs as feminist activists and writers (and the fact that we've been traveling around the country since the fall of 2000, promoting a book called *Manifesta: Young Women, Feminism, and the Future*), we meet a diverse crowd of creative leaders, most of whom are female and under the age of forty. Therefore, we had to ask how the Next Generation Leadership Network Initiative was measuring leadership.

Is a leader the person who helps other people to reach their potential or the person scrambling for face-time on CNN? In the next generation of leadership, will a leader be valued for transforming his or her community as much as ruling a country? Not surprisingly, the Rockefeller Foundation based its definition of leadership on the most traditional rules of hierarchy, not to mention patriarchy. Criteria for selection as a future leader included publication in a narrow array of acceptable journals and magazines, Ivy League academic credentials, career achievement determined by job title and salary, and networking potential (which seemed to be based primarily on how one might do at a reunion of *Mayflower* descendants); in short, success as defined by the *Wall Street Journal*. The problem, it became clear, was not with young women but with this huge granting body's stodgy definition of leadership. The Rockefeller Foundation, like the *New Yorker,* clearly fell prey to what might be called the Clone Syndrome of leadership.

The Clone Syndrome makes it impossible to value trailblazers who don't replicate the traditional model for leadership, even if these individuals are creating change and affecting hundreds of people. The Clone Syndrome rewards what are, in effect, the least innovative pathfinders and paths. It ignores the most basic element of leadership—a person's ability to move other people and new ideas forward. When the editors of the *New Yorker* called Gloria Steinem, they presumed that the third wave's leader would mimic Steinem's example. "Who is the new miniskirt-wearing journalist who makes feminism appealing to women and men alike?" they asked. By not expecting the new leader to possess her own unique qualities and style, they missed the point: Steinem's own originality and ability to speak to the particular demands of her time are precisely what made her effective—a detail lost on those who were looking for a Steinem clone.

It's not just the mainstream institutions, such as the Rockefeller Foundation and the *New Yorker,* that are affected by these cookie-cutter expectations. Even feminist institutions worry that we don't have a next generation of leaders. This means that we are believing our own bad press, to be sure, but we are also looking to the Clone Syndrome for our values. To deal with this perceived lack of young female leaders, leadership programs are cropping up in every minor and major foundation. "The Feminist Majority Foundation (FMF) is committed to training the next generation of pro-choice leaders," states the Feminist Majority Foundation's Web site in typical phraseology. That organization's Feminist Leadership Alliance is active on dozens of campuses and hosts "Rock for Choice" concerts. Choice USA conducts an annual Gloria Steinem Leadership Initiative, which trains the next generation of pro-choice leaders. The Women's Campaign School at Yale and the National Women's Political Caucus both take young women through campaign curricula, hoping to groom the next freshman class for the U.S. Senate. Meanwhile, the Woodhull Institute for Ethical Leadership, founded by Naomi Wolf and Margot Magowan, has quarterly retreats and an active alumni network for younger women.

Amy is a co-founder and Jennifer is a very active member of the Third Wave Foundation, the only national organization for young feminist activists between the ages fifteen and thirty. In 1996, Third Wave started calling its routine work "leadership training" because that had become a foundation catchphrase, that is, a phrase you had to use to secure grant money. The name change worked; money started coming in to help the organization tap and nurture the "next generation of feminist leaders," even though Third Wave had been doing this work for years under a different label. For instance, every summer Third Wave hires an intern to plan our annual info-party, an event featuring activists, spoken-word artists, and musicians to raise participants' consciousness while they are having fun. The interns begin the summer with little direction and a vague sense of how to organize. Before long, they discover artists and extend invitations to them; they find locations for the info-party; and they secure food and beverage donations. By the time the event comes along, the interns have been transformed by the experience and are ready to take on their own projects. This position is now filed under "Leadership Training."

There are several problems with traditional leadership training programs, especially those for women. First, the programs use a conformist structure to produce people who are by definition required to be iconoclasts. These leadership training programs mislead the participants by promising them that they can be a leader in five easy steps, just like the other fifty people who signed up for the symposium. What all of this ignores is that true leaders, after all, aren't waiting for the media or anyone else to anoint them. They are identifying problems and mobilizing people to participate in the vision for change—even if the media and funders don't recognize them as leaders. Second, trying to find a new Gloria (or the next Angela Davis or this decade's Martin Luther King Jr.) is also part of the Clone Syndrome, and it excludes women and people of color disproportionately. The only women and people of color who are rewarded are those who act like white men. After all, the leadership of "out groups" tends to be rooted within our communities, churches, families, and jobs—in other words, within our everyday lives, not in elite structures. Third, and finally, this "next generation" view is stuck hopelessly in the utopian future, refusing to deal with leaders right now.

In contrast with the tired old Clone Syndrome or even with the better, but still limited, Women's Leadership Paradigm, we want to lay out a Third Wave Paradigm. What we are calling the Third Wave Paradigm of leadership is, in fact, plain old feminism. It inspires individuals to take the initiative to create change in their own lives and in their own communities.

We argue in *Manifesta* that this generation was born with feminism "in the water" of our culture.[1] Whether we have embraced it or rejected it, experienced it as a torrent or a trickle, the goal (if not the reality) of equal pay for equal work or a network of services for battered women already existed for us. In a way, this means that we can benefit from feminism's achievements without having to join "the movement"—that is, until we are slapped in the face with a sexist injustice. Whether we are battered women or machinists fired after getting pregnant, whether our employers don't grant paid parental leave or we learn that 80 percent of the homeless population is female—whatever the cause, the day comes for each of us when we need feminism. And the opportunity arises in that moment to become a leader in our own lives and our communities.

In this way, feminist leadership models itself after community and issue-based leadership, and it isn't terribly different from one generation of feminists to the next. However, by dint of sheer numbers and having grown up in a feminist-influenced culture, third wave leaders are better positioned to actually succeed in maintaining different—and multiple—models of leadership. Third wave feminists are scattered throughout many professions rather than concentrated in traditionally feminist occupations. Furthermore, the issues on which we focus are broader than those historically identified as feminist issues, such as environmental issues, prison reform, and fair housing. And with the current convergence of so many movements that are simultaneously working to reframe leadership, such as political groups and the media, this generation of feminists is ripe for this transition.

In spite of our clear relationship with and similarity to second wave leadership and values, we have assigned a few unique qualities to the third wave's model:

- *The leadership emerges from the leaders' real lives and acknowledges expertise grounded in experience.* Thus, Catherine Megill, a twenty-seven-year-old clinician at Western Women's Medical Center, an abortion clinic on Manhattan's Upper West Side, is a crucial leader in the field of reproductive freedom, partly because it is her generation that is utilizing reproductive health services. After working at the National Abortion Federation for several years, Megill noticed that a disproportionate number of women came to New York City for their abortion, because of the more woman-friendly policies in New York, such as the ability to get a later-term abortion.

Megill rightly assumed that these women were often coming to New York City alone and on a limited budget and that they probably could benefit from having someone accompany them to and from the clinic, and house them if they needed to spend the night. This is exactly what her organization Haven facilitates—and it's a transforming experience for the patient and for the escort.

- *Third wave leaders are leaders wherever they are, not necessarily "within the movement."* Generally speaking, being a feminist in the 1970s took people outside of their "regular" lives and the mainstream. For a second wave feminist, being part of the movement might have meant joining a consciousness-raising group or a big organization such as NOW (National Organization for Women) or subscribing to *Ms.* magazine or participating in a state ERA ratification campaign. As part of the third wave, feminists can work at NOW but they can also be feminists at Wal-Mart or at an advertising agency. The power of being a feminist is no longer relegated to women's studies departments, national women's organizations, and *Ms.* magazine. This means that we have to look at how feminist leadership has become almost mundane. We must be willing to be confident and entitled in nonfeminist spaces, as well as to be subversive in them when necessary. For instance, the woman who works at an ad agency may have more power to change ads than do the feminists sending protest e-mails from the outside. The feminist man who sits on the board of a research facility has more power to insist that new medical breakthroughs be tested on women (not just white men, as is usually the case) than does the woman hoisting a placard outside the National Institutes of Health. If you have an insider's perspective and relationships with those on the inside, you have a greater investment in this change, and you have a greater understanding of how a system can be changed. In other words, third wave leadership maximizes feminism's strength and diversity via our existing feminist institutions but, more important, it increases its scope and effectiveness through insiders in workplaces and government.

- *We have no superleader.* The fact that there is no one third wave leader tapped by the media is progress, even if it makes things . more difficult for the editors of the *New Yorker*'s issue on "Women." The advantage is that we have a chance to define ourselves, one of the tenets of feminist theory. We have to have faith in our pure mass, rather than hunting for an individual who can stand in for all of us. Besides, if one of our messages is about bringing down corporate power, then why should we measure our success by whom the *New York Times* or the *New Yorker* covers? It's up to third wave feminists to recognize this contradiction and to begin to value the alternative forces that we nurture.

• *Third wave leadership embraces individual responsibility and self-worth.* In many ways, a traditional definition of leadership has included the condition that most people give up responsibility. Abdicating responsibility (or not realizing that one can be responsible) might be especially contradictory for women who are looking for feminist leaders. For instance, take the 2000 presidential election. You might have been devastated that Gloria Steinem endorsed the two-party system by stumping for Al Gore. Or, you could have been furious that Barbara Ehrenreich would support Ralph Nader, given the threat of a Bush presidency. Either way, you are undermining your own power to vocalize your opinions about a candidate and not realizing your own sphere of influence. Your five friends are more influenced by your choice of candidate than a remote celebrity figure's choice, anyway. Conversely, if we think of leaders as people to blame when things don't work out as we planned, then it's no surprise that more people haven't assumed these leadership positions. For some, it's easier to look for feminist inspiration or disappointment in someone else than to realize our own need to be a leader. This issue comes up all the time when we travel. People will say, "I am a feminist, but . . . ," and go on to list how feminists haven't prioritized child care or a living wage or transgenderism or whatever the person's own priority might be. Our response encourages people to own feminism for themselves. We say to them, "feminism is as much your movement as anyone else's, and it's up to you to prioritize what you value."

A theme of our Third Wave Paradigm is multiplicity. Ironically, the women's movement we were born into didn't really have the luxury or space to define itself in multiple ways or to envision its approaches to leadership being popularized. When the modern women's liberation movement, the second wave, was getting started in the 1960s and 1970s, there was a need to blast feminism into the culture. The movement needed prominent and "acceptable" individuals who could announce its ideas to the masses and expose the urgency of the need for change. Betty Friedan fit the bill because she was coming from a place of middle-class privilege. She was a married woman with children and thus didn't pose a threat to the patriarchal stronghold. Feminism at mid-century was a new identity for women; the focus was on getting the word out about experiences and injustices that affected millions of women but were previously kept behind closed doors. Having a single woman leader as the primary representative of the women's movement was less problematic back then than it would be now, when recruitment or spreading the word about feminism is not the primary task. (It should be noted, however, that radical feminists critiqued Friedan's middle-class approach almost immediately; women of color critiqued radical feminists' approach soon thereafter; poor women critiqued the other approaches; and bisexual women and lesbians had another angle of criticism.) Even in the 1960s and 1970s, feminism was never truly represented by one person, but the media found a few good women for their purposes.

By comparison to Friedan's experience as the mass media's Everywoman, Johnnie Tilmon, an early welfare rights advocate, was recognized as a leader only after the women's movement created separate (and marginalized) media- and politically directed women's organizations. Tilmon represents the feminist idea of acknowledging that poor women on welfare are the real experts on poverty, broadening the focus from previously anointed experts such as Senator Daniel Patrick Moynihan. Eventually, this personal-is-political perspective was sought out in the mainstream, too. Tilmon is not a "superleader." A superleader is often tokenized, is often isolated from the community she is supposed to represent, and is often resented for her privilege. In this context, the idea of a leader might be better described as an effort to reduce thousands of perspectives to the perspective of one individual. It's far more effective and feminist to have five thousand people who each influence five others than to have five people each address five thousand individuals.

This brings us to the most important part of this essay: examples. How are young women being third wave–style feminist leaders? When Emily Alexander was a nineteen-year-old freshman at Oberlin College in Oberlin, Ohio, she positioned herself to be the paid liaison between the school's health center and the students. The health center provides Pap smears, STD (sexually transmitted disease) testing, abortion referrals and counseling, and emergency contraception to students in this relatively rural town. The clinicians are permanent residents of a town that is historically less progressive than the institution that resides there. Alexander made the case for creating this job after several students had complained about one female practitioner who was insensitive to students seeking STD testing and treatment.

Then there was a junior by the name of Brooke Baker, who was resolving a huge issue for her college, the University of North Carolina at Chapel Hill. An older female administrator brought up her concern that young feminists don't talk about child-care issues, although many of them will soon be faced with a need for child care themselves. The administrator's daughter was struggling to find decent and affordable care for her two-year-old and was facing the painful decision of either leaving a job she loved or compromising her work. The university, which has 26,000 students and several thousand employees, provides about eighty day-care spots at a price that only faculty—not staff or graduate students—can afford. There is a temp service on campus, however, and Brooke noted that many undergrads were in dire need of employment. Brooke is now exploring the possibility of adding babysitting to the list of services provided by the temp agency. There is a babysitting service at Barnard that may serve as a good model for one at Chapel Hill. When we meet women at one school who are working on a problem that has already been tackled successfully by students at another, we always try to hook them up, another way of enabling feminist leadership.

Lateefah Simon was twenty-one when she became the director of the

Center for Young Women's Leadership in San Francisco. In 2000, she received a grant from Third Wave Foundation and has since mentored countless other women who are looking to create change in their communities. Simon doesn't have a college degree, nor does anyone on her staff; and the Center relies on its collective real-life expertise to run the organization.

Purvi Shah is a graduate student at Rutgers who sits on the board of SAKHI for South Asian women. In the wake of the September 11 tragedy, Purvi and others created a network for South Asians who are experiencing racial prejudice. Her network doubles as a safe haven for women whose already-violent domestic situations have escalated owing to increased tension stemming from September 11 and our crumbling economy.

Sarah Jones is an actor and spoken-word artist whose one-woman show, *Surface Transit,* launched her career as a powerful artist four years ago. All of her work pushes at racial and gender stereotypes. Jones captured national attention when KBOO, a radio station in Portland, Oregon, was fined $7,000 by the Federal Communications Commission for playing one of her "indecent" songs. The irony was that Jones's spoken-word piece called "Your Revolution" is actually a comment on the sexism and racism of hip-hop. "Your revolution will not happen between these thighs," Jones says in the song. "The real revolution ain't about booty size."[2] Jones was using words and images used routinely by Eminem and LL Cool J, but because a black woman was doing the talking—and delivering a feminist message—she was censored. But Sarah fought back. Lucky to get pro bono representation from the People for the American Way, Sarah is holding a mirror up to white people and men of all colors, making the sexism stand out.

These women and the thousands of others who are like them aren't superheroes, celebrities, or ridiculously privileged. They are just feminists who are rooted in their communities, who were nourished by a feminist culture (one that taught them they were as good as the boys), and who know that they are entitled to both rights and responsibilities. Each woman identified an injustice and took steps within her own power to solve it. No need to kiss any frogs or wait for the next superleader to arrive. As Alice Rossi put it in her book *The Feminist*

Papers: "The public heroines of one generation are the private citizens of the next."[3] In other words, don't wait for the new Angela Davis to tell you what to do. You are the superleader of your life.

NOTES

1. Baumgardner and Richards, *Manifesta* (New York: Farrar, Straus and Giroux, 2000), 17.

2. Sarah Jones, "Your Revolution" (Ninja Tune USA, 2000).

3. Alice Rossi, *The Feminist Papers: From Adams to de Beauvoir* (1973; rept., Boston: Northeastern University Press, 1988), 616.

MICHELE BYERS

Buffy the Vampire Slayer: The Next Generation of Television

Yes. Date and shop and hang out and go to school and save the world from un-speakable demons. . . . You know, girl stuff.
        —BUFFY SUMMERS, "Faith, Hope, and Trick" (Season Three, 1998)

Since its first season, *Buffy the Vampire Slayer* has continually raised the specter of the strong, independent woman/girl who can never sit passively by but must actively engage the world around her. It is this active quality that interests so many young women (and men) in the show. What has been missing in both feminist and popular commentary about Buffy, however, is the recognition that the artifacts of popular culture that are directed at young adults should be taken seriously and tied—when possible—to feminism, the study of gender, and activism. Media texts like *Buffy the Vampire Slayer* are moving to the forefront of critical inquiry and are being taken seriously by third wave feminists. One of our jobs is to recognize feminist moments in these texts.

Buffy the Vampire Slayer is a prime-time television series about a group of somewhat misfit young adults in the town of Sunnydale, California. Their leader is the lovely Buffy Summers (Sarah Michelle Gellar), a former cheerleader and prom queen. In her television incarnation, Buffy is more action hero than *Seventeen* magazine cover girl. She is a power-house of strength and skill, and her purpose is to save humanity from the powers of darkness; she is also an anxious young person moving cautiously into adulthood. Buffy, unlike earlier "Slayers," is a contemporary young woman who constantly questions her work and her role as savior. Although the traditional hero of mythology is inarguably male, with *Buffy* the heroic becomes not just reconciled with the feminine but ruled by it.[1] And though Buffy, like the more traditional hero,

171

must often stand alone, she is aided at every turn by her friends, known affectionately as "the Scooby gang." Together with their creator, Joss Weedon, these characters have opened a televisual landscape that offers a potentially radical revisioning of gender.

There are several important areas *Buffy* occupies in contemporary popular culture, especially as the show relates to the interests of third wave feminism. The critical acclaim the show has achieved in the popular press and in the more general population seems to prove its success. But what is it about *Buffy* that marks it as different? What makes it distinguishable from other contemporary texts aimed at the youth market? I would suggest that we attack this question by looking at two major factors—the reconstruction of notions of contemporary girlhood and young womanhood and the question of diversity in the television landscape.

Buffy's redefinition of girlhood and womanhood intersects with the question of feminism. The most explicit link I see between *Buffy* and feminism as a political ideology and practice is that both espouse a belief in the rights of women and, significantly, the right to equality in all things. The series dramatizes the struggle that many young women face to be strong, independent, articulate, ambitious, and powerful. And this is done without erasing women's desire for connection. The feminist inclination of this show also appears in its refusal to make its female characters masculine. Instead, the supernatural opens up possibilities for female power as well as empowerment. The show's feminist impulse says that women should be able to protect themselves and their loved ones, to be respected for their intellectual and physical capabilities, to insist on their right to emotional and bodily integrity, and to desire to be nurtured as well as to nurture. This vision of girlhood and womanhood as articulated by *Buffy* is what makes the series a feminist text.

The emergence of the small-screen action heroine raises new question for viewers and critics; for instance, must the contemporary media heroine forgo heroism or enact it only as some kind of masculine masquerade? Margery Hourihan asserts that the hero is embodied, essentially, in the body of male youth. Heroines, she writes, tend to be relegated to the status of "honorary men."[2] But in *Buffy*, there is no need for the heroes to adopt male gender status, since girls do just fine as heroes in their own femininely gendered skins. For instance, in the episode "Gingerbread," Xander and Oz rush to try and save Willow, Buffy, and Amy from the vicious mob that would burn them at the stake as witches. The girls, however, never think to wait to be rescued, but set about rescuing themselves. In "Graduation Day," Buffy must go even further when she offers herself as a sacrifice to save her lover, Angel. Once he is restored, however, he can do nothing except rush her to the emergency room in hopes that someone else can save her life. Both of these examples show that in *Buffy*, the feminine enacts the heroic.

Feminine adolescence is a paradoxical space, and although adolescence is a difficult field to navigate for both sexes, it represents particular problems for young women.[3] Adolescent girls, wavering at the brink of adulthood, are told that they can do and be anything they want, and yet they feel compelled to fit into archaic images of womanhood and femininity. This is in part an aesthetic question—what does a "woman" look like?—but also an active one—what does a "woman" do? I believe this is where much of the secret of *Buffy*'s success lies, as well as why it is a place where young (and not so young) feminists recognize themselves. It provides, although not always and not easily, a radical reimagining of what a girl (and a woman) can do and be: powerful, independent, strong, smart, a slayer, a witch, an activist. And in this reimagining, the potential for heroism belongs not to an honorary man but to girls and women.

Buffy the Vampire Slayer represents a departure—though it is not alone in this endeavor—from the male-centered superhero narrative. Many of its characters, including Buffy Summers, are strong, vibrant young women. They represent a spectrum of possibilities for contemporary womanhood that includes superior intelligence, physical strength, the desire for relationship, the quest for independence, and the refusal to be dominated, circumscribed, or limited in action and mobility. The characters on the show are not supposed to represent your average California girls—they are slayers, demons, and witches after all—and yet, they are "normal," too. And it is this dialectic that makes *Buffy* resonate with so many people: the show reveals that within a mundane exterior (not just of the body but also of lifestyle) lurks the possibility of excitement, of greatness. At the end of the fifth season (2001), when Buffy is thought to be dead, the final shot closes in on a headstone, which reads:

Buffy Summers
1981–2001
Beloved Sister
Devoted Friend
She Saved the World a Lot

I think this sums up Buffy's appeal: she represents sisterhood, friendship, and the possibility of changing (and even saving) the world.

THE "FEMINIST" WORLD OF *BUFFY THE VAMPIRE SLAYER*

When I started writing my dissertation on *Buffy* in 1997, I could not find anything written about the show except by the popular press. I knew that many of my friends were intrigued by *Buffy*. Although the *Buffy* story was often thrilling, it was to the show's characters and relationships that our conversations inevitably returned. Could Buffy ever really get over Angel? Would Willow and Tara ever consummate their relationship? And what is up with Spike and Buffy? One day, I picked up the feminist magazine *Bust* and saw in its first pages a brand-new column called "Buffy Watch," complete with critical updates and links to an e-mail list devoted solely to *Buffy*. The mainstream press had already taken up *Buffy* as its latest unsung hero and often framed its discourse around the growing appreciation of "girl power"; as the column in *Bust* revealed, more explicitly feminist outlets were quick to follow suit. But I have found that some of these articles have been framed within a discourse that fluctuates between accolades for *Buffy*'s vision of strong, active women and intense criticism about the material bodies involved in this action.

I think that much of this anxiety can be traced to "the body problem" that has continually plagued women and feminist scholars. The body is "a powerful symbolic form" as well as a "site of struggle."[4] So when we study the media, we are constantly asking ourselves questions about the bodies we are seeing and the activities they are engaged in.

Often, the images of women we see in the media overwhelm the possibility of empowerment suggested by their actions. In the case of *Buffy*, critics have argued that a show that is so entrenched in idealized (and unrealizable) images of the female body cannot be read as feminist. Maybe that is true. Certainly, the cast is conventionally attractive; they are costumed and made-up in ways that emphasize their conformity to the Hollywood norm. Some articles suggest that *Buffy* cannot be feminist because of its star's body or looks. Rachel Fudge, for example, lauds the show while refuting its feminist potential by drawing our attention to the spectacle of Gellar's breasts.[5] Although I take her point that the body problem in the mass media is a crucial one for feminists, I wonder if recuperating this voyeuristic look is the answer. Are breasts really what keeps a show from being feminist?

The mass media covet and cultivate a particular type of female body—one that is young, white, beautiful, and very thin. Though it is necessary to critique the popularity of this image and to call for other bodies to be admitted into the mediascape, we cannot let our critiques end there. If we do, we run the risk of being reductive, of saying the same things over and over again without ever looking for possibilities of bodily emancipation. The televisual body is virtual; it belongs to a "dream culture of the body . . . young, beautiful, healthy and complete." The television text is polysemous; it allows the audience to decode it in various ways even as it tries to orient the viewer into desired subject positions, positions of desire.[6] Because *Buffy the Vampire Slayer* was created by the mainstream American media, the bodies it uses to articulate its messages reflect that position. But the performance of these bodies must also be considered. These characters are more than pretty bodies on the television screen; they also raise interesting questions about gender and the potentialities of third wave feminism. In "I Was Made to Love You" and "Intervention," for example, the question of the social construction of femininity is raised explicitly. A young man builds himself a girlfriend who will cater to his every whim; yet he finds that he cannot keep her from having a mind of her own. Though the experiment is disastrous, Spike insists that the young Dr. Frankenstein build a robot-Buffy (Buffybot) that will love *him*. These episodes demonstrate the social construction of femininity and how often it revolves around questions of the male ego. These episodes also problematize such constructions, however, by insisting that the "real" girl (the one who does not meet all the criteria the "builder" might want) is actually the much better model.

In May 2000, on the posting board of the official *Buffy* Web site (http://www.buffy.com), several negative and homophobic posts were made concerning the emerging lesbian relationship between Willow and Tara. Many of the people who posted not only attacked the characters but also criticized the body of actress Amber Benson (Tara). The Internet thus provided a public forum where these views could be aired. But in an unprecedented way, Benson was allowed to respond to these remarks and to reclaim the space and legitimacy of her body on television. She wrote:

> I am just a human being and I feel like I deserve to be treated with a little more kindness and compassion. I also feel that Tara deserves to be treated with a little more kindness and compassion. Yes, I am not a *stick*. I am a *normal, healthy* (I was gonna say Girl, but . . .) *woman*. I have breasts and hips and I am very happy that they are a part of me. . . . You can all judge Tara and me for being "fat," "gay," and "shy." . . . I think that being a beautiful, heavy, lesbian witch rocks.[7]

Joss Weedon also took up Amber/Tara's position when he criticized the anti-gay/anti-Amber postings. The fact that these postings are felt to be acceptable within the context of a public posting board is problematic. Nonetheless, I find it interesting that this posting board has become a space where the screened body (the actor, as opposed to the character) becomes a "real" and responsive presence. Benson does not simply enter this space as Tara in order to protect Tara from homophobia. Hers is the dual task of preserving the integrity of both her character and herself.

Buffy has a problematic legacy of body consciousness, but it also reflects the ambiguous boundaries and looming possibilities of the body. This text, with its changeable creatures (vampires, werewolves, demons, and monsters), demonstrates a fascination with the bodily mutations of adolescence, especially in the guise of the feminine. Willow, for instance, reassures Oz (a werewolf) that his moon cycles are not that different from her own (in "Phases"). *Buffy* is foundationally interested in two other "feminist" body issues: the "paradox" of feminine adolescence and the problem of "becoming a woman."[8] Although these cannot be separated from the body (of the girl moving into womanhood), they cannot be reduced to it, either. Intrinsic here is the question of what it means to be active, strong, and independent, characteristics which are often ambivalently associated with the feminine but which are central themes in this show.

The female characters on *Buffy* are interested in appearances; they long to be found attractive and to find appreciation for their bodies in the eyes of their peers. In fact, the very first episode of the series ("Welcome to the Hellmouth," 1997) focuses on popularity and Buffy's difficulty in choosing whether to befriend Cordelia and the beautiful people or the nerdy, but infinitely nicer, Willow and Xander. Especially during the high school years, these issues were recurrent on *Buffy*. The danger of being an object of desire ("Reptile Boy" and "Go Fish"), the recognition of beauty ("Homecoming"), and competition for men ("Go Fish" and "Graduation Day") are but a few examples. But each of the young women is also fiercely dedicated to her own unique powers and struggles, and all of the female characters on the show tend to reject dependency. The show even seems to reflect on these issues: in the final episode of season five ("The Gift," 2001), Xander muses that he loves smart women, and Willow (remembering how she had pined for him in the past, while he had often seemed to prefer more conventionally beautiful Buffy and Cordelia) retorts, "You couldn't have figured that out in the tenth grade?"

In order to assess a text's feminist potential, we must ask what "female identities are being made available" through a particular text.[9] The much-disputed body of Buffy Summers reveals the importance—and the complexity—of this question. The prom queen, reluctantly relinquishing her former self, moves into a new territory where she must be self-reliant, self-critical, and self-aware. As I watch *Buffy,* I wonder what possible identities are being offered as a model that viewers might identify with. I do not think that we accept (or identify with) televised characters and their identities in any direct way; rather, I think that we "try on" different identities during the viewing process, taking on (or in) different bits and pieces as we go. In the *Buffy* world, competence, strength, and independence are precisely what is being offered to women, not just breasts, abs, and lip gloss. I want to "be" Buffy when she's kicking vampire butt more than when she's sitting there looking pretty and whining about the latest rift in her love life.

The show criticizes its own portrayal of gender roles, recognizing the ambivalence of these positions. This is most interestingly shown in the character of Anya, who was originally introduced as an ancient demon sent to settle the scores of wronged women. After centuries of male-bashing, Anya finds herself stuck in the body of a teenaged girl. Having left behind thoughts of gender-neutral freedom and immortality, Anya must negotiate the slippery slope of heterosexual femininity. Anya proves that, feminist or not, our desires do not always align with what we know we should desire.[10] Her struggle is very provocative as she tries to reconcile what she has known about "men" for centuries with her growing desire to be attractive to them. It is a struggle many of us know only too well.

Yet does any of this allow us to recognize *Buffy the Vampire Slayer* as a feminist text? In *Rolling Stone,* Joss Weedon, the writer, director, producer, and general enfant terrible of the *Buffy* universe, says, unequivocally: "I definitely think a woman kicking ass is extraordinarily sexy, always. . . . If I wasn't compelled by the archetype, I wouldn't have created the character. I mean, yes, I have a feminist agenda, but it's not like I made a chart."[11]

Apparently Weedon did not set out to make *Buffy* a feminist text or to make Buffy a feminist icon. But the fact that he publicly makes this claim to feminism says, I think, that he sees *Buffy*'s recognition as "feminist" as a positive thing. "Feminist" is not a word that has been widely reclaimed by the popular press or by much of the general population.[12] It is an active word that suggests an equally active consideration of women's oppression, diversity, and position in society; as such, it is an interesting word for Weedon to use.[13] Since it seems unlikely that *Buffy the Vampire Slayer* was created as an explicitly feminist text, then some criticisms of it—especially those that stem from its refusal to meet feminist expectations—are problematic. Does the show have to be all or nothing? Can't we take up those aspects of *Buffy* that we recognize as feminist and be critical of those that we do not? We can be critical of the show while we look for possibilities of emancipation within it, for moments that appeal to us as we read them through our feminist lenses. I think that we have to remember that there is very little—if any—explicitly feminist material being produced for mainstream television today. When a show offers us feminist potentialities (even if they are not fully realized), we should not dismiss it, even if it does not fully meet our desires and expectations for feminist television.

WHOSE FEMINISM IS IT, ANYHOW?

In discussions of feminism, there is, increasingly, a desire to recognize diversity in relation to race, class, sexual orientation, and ability, for example. It is therefore important to look at how *Buffy* does (or does not) address this issue. Certainly, as with many "Hollywood" series, there is a lack of visible diversity in the cast; it has been an almost unvaried landscape of white faces. There is the possibility, however, of reading *Buffy* as reflecting diversity both through its use of vampires and demons and through the supernatural facets of its main characters. The characters have also diversified with the introduction of Tara (Amber Benson), Willow's lesbian lover. For the most part, however, *Buffy*'s terrain remains firmly white, middle-class, heterosexual, and able. And although I do not think that the absence of more obvious diversity makes *Buffy* either unworthy or unfeminist, I think it is important to remark upon it. Further, it may also indicate that *Buffy* (and mainstream television shows like it) expresses a contradiction, a tension that exists between second and third wave feminism on a much larger scale. *Buffy* is in some ways an excellent example of the third wave, displaying and attracting young, empowered women. At the same time, the retention of a focus on the struggles of privileged girls and women (white, middle-class, and so on) ties *Buffy*, as a cultural text, to the second wave.

Many women have felt that second wave feminism addressed the concerns only of white, heterosexual, middle-class women and thus excluded most women from its activism and discourse. Feminism, some critics have insisted, cannot adequately address questions of gender if it considers them separately from other categories of difference that affect women's lives. This has become of increasing importance for media scholars who look for and try to understand what sorts of images of diversity are being produced. Many see the most problematic issues in the mainstream American mass media as being the absence of images of diversity and the fact that many of the images that do exist rely very heavily on representational and narrative stereotypes.[14] It is necessary to ask what version of feminism and what vision of women *Buffy* may be articulating and what may be omitted from this vision.

One of the most problematic aspects of the *Buffy* text is that it never incorporates or interrogates difference within its fictional world. The specter of difference is not entirely absent from this text. However, in reading the materiality of the characters, it is impossible not to recognize the evidence of privilege that ties the characters together. I am speaking of their whiteness, their lack of ethnic affiliation, and their conformity to the standards of Western beauty. Given that the characters represent the way in which real actors are included or excluded from television, this text makes obvious who the players are and who they are not.

It is impossible not to remark on the absence of visible diversity from this text as from so many other televisual landscapes. The omission of diverse images of women is problematic because it is so pervasive in the most frequently viewed texts of contemporary television. Theorist Ann DuCille states that the "absence of black images in the 'social mirror' leaves the black child with little other than white subjects of self-reflection and self-projection."[15] DuCille goes on to suggest that this absence does not of necessity initiate in the black child a desire to be other than she is, but that it does, however, set up the viewer to recognize the limitations of her own body. On the most basic level, one of these limitations is the lack of access nonwhite bodies have to the spaces of television and other media. Yet will this lack of comparable images or role models on the screen also make it difficult for many viewers to identify with the more radical visions of femininity the *Buffy* text offers? It becomes even more critical for us to ask not only where are the images of girls and women who do not conform to the Hollywood ideal, but also where are the girls and women who are not white, middle-class, able, and Judeo-Christian.[16]

There are two primary ways that difference is reinserted into the *Buffy* text, neither of which completely addresses the questions of bodily diversity I have just raised. In the first case, difference is presented as an ongoing evolutionary process that exists within the individual. That is, the characters are shown as literally unstable, and this changeability becomes linked to difference. Buffy the empty-headed, shopaholic cheerleader becomes Buffy the Vampire Slayer. Willow the "brain" morphs to a vampiric doppelgänger; demon Anya must live as an "ordinary" teenager; spoiled Cordelia is revealed to have bravado and wit; Faith finds that playing at being the perfect girl is less rewarding than embracing her bad self. These "differences" are revealed within the male characters as well. Angel fluctuates between his good and bad personas; Oz must give over his identity to the cycles of the moon; boy-next-door Xander finds himself infused with machismo and, in turn, becomes a hyena-boy, army commando, and vampire; Giles is shown to have a dark and secret past; even Spike (the soulless one) is shown to have a tender side. Thus, while the characters appear to conform to the norm on the surface, they are continually called upon to address interior difference. Their superficial lack of difference is shown to be a disguise that masks the complexity of the true or secret self beneath.

The second way in which visible diversity is reinserted into the *Buffy* text is through the figures of Buffy's nemeses and sometimes allies, the vampires and demons. These figures lurk in the dark corners, sewers, and back alleys of Sunnydale, preying on the unsuspecting citizens of California suburbia. In a media text that tends to exclude bodies that are visually different, difference returns with a vengeance in the bodies of these characters. But this is what makes this reading problematic. Aside from the characters of Angel and Spike—who "pass" unnoticed among the living—and a small number of "good" demons, the undead tend to be dispatched forthwith. The vampire, in all its visual difference, becomes the frightening "other" that the heroes in this text must eliminate.[17] If Buffy and her friends represent "goodness," then the vampires and demons must be not only "other" but also "bad."

The possibility of reading these un-dead figures against the background of what is almost unilaterally a white, middle-class norm is important: it sets up these characters as members of a visual or ethnic minority group or as an underclass, even a homeless class. In either interpretation, the implication is that these bad characters prey on the good suburban citizens of Sunnydale. When viewed in this light, the actions of the slayer become unquestioningly heroic. Throughout her tenure as television's premier vampire slayer, Buffy has done away with hundreds of demons, vampires, and monsters and yet remains repelled by the idea of taking a human life. That is left to those whose "goodness" is more ambiguous than hers.

If we accept the possibility that the un-dead and immortal characters represent difference in the *Buffy* text, then we must also critique the show's representations of whiteness and white privilege. Despite the text's attempt to reinsert diversity within the bodies of its main characters, we are still left with "real" bodies that are mostly devoid of visible difference. If this text raises the specter of visible difference as terrifying and in need of removal from the screen, we must also ask what the images of sameness evoke. DuCille writes that "one fantasy of whiteness is that the threatening Other is always a terrorist. This projection enables many white people to imagine there is no representation of whiteness as terror, as terrorizing."[18] In this context, it becomes possible to see Buffy as an avenging figure of terror, wielding her stake not only in the service of feminine independence but also in the eradication of visible difference (and, in truth, she does evoke fear in the hearts of many). Like many supernatural texts, *Buffy the Vampire Slayer* works hard to legitimize the hunter's position, to naturalize it and make it empowering rather than terrifying. Those who attempt to analyze this show from a feminist perspective must beware of both the ways in which it naturalizes whiteness and the fact that the assertion of white privilege is a feminist issue.

The mass media enjoy taking up oppositional discourses like feminism and "repackag[ing] them within dominant terms."[19] Sometimes this can have positive effects, but at other times these discourses may lose their oppositionality as they become incorporated into television or other media forms. *Buffy the Vampire Slayer* represents both of these possibilities. On the one hand, the show establishes a terrain where women are empowered, where they take action and evidence physical strength, intellectual temerity, and independence. On the other hand, *Buffy* articulates a world devoid of visible difference or where difference must be eliminated, raising the specter of racism. This is not unlike the criticisms leveled at some more traditional versions of feminism in which all visible difference is similarly absent. It may be that today's televisual texts are able to articulate only this type of feminism, which has not yet caught up with the more complex feminisms and femininities that take difference as an integral component of their expression. This makes *Buffy* once again a space of contradiction and feminist tension, which is not necessarily a bad place to be. But the manifestation (or lack of it) of difference as an internal component of the show's main characters is an issue too important to be sidelined or ignored. Television is a complex medium, one that cannot be supposed to interpolate differences between viewers as if all viewers were the same. That is, viewers are not homogeneous and do not engage with one (unified) text, a text that has only one possible reading. We need to develop strategies for reinserting genuine diversity into the text, which will help viewers locate more and different things, people, and places with which to identify.

FEMINIST POSSIBILITIES OF CONTEMPORARY TELEVISION

Douglas Kellner writes that "television today assumes some of the functions traditionally ascribed to myth and ritual."[20] Television viewing, certainly, has become very ritualized, and television has created a vast number of contemporary myths. Some of these myths have to do with the emergence of a new vision of girlhood and young womanhood that may not be explicitly claimed or coded as feminist but can be linked to feminist agendas that support and encourage girls and young women to be strong and independent. As far as I am concerned, *Buffy the Vampire Slayer* is still one of the leaders of the pack. Although the show, like other contemporary media texts aimed at young women, continues to marginalize difference and diversity, *Buffy* is important in the possibilities it reimagines for youth. Whether this makes the show explicitly feminist is still not clear.

It is important to think about what it means to claim the label *feminist* and what a text that claims this label might look like. Feminism can be about many things, but central to it is the idea of advancing and rendering visible the lives of women, in all their diversity. Feminist work may be done without claiming the label feminist. However, if people engaged in emancipatory work reject being called "feminist," then we must ask why. Sometimes the label feminist may be claimed to gain legitimacy for works that are in opposition to what are traditionally seen as feminist agendas. Sometimes being a feminist implies being narrowly cast in archaic stereotypes that mean little (or are downright alienating) to young women (and many older women, too). What I mean to suggest here is that "feminist"—like any other label—is paradoxical, ambivalent, and fluid. It means different things to different people at different times and it is and has been used to advance different political agendas. Contemporary American television is rarely seen as a place that fosters feminist expression, although many people, including myself, keep looking for moments where some version of "feminism" is being articulated. This does not mean that feminism can mean anything at all or that it can simply mean whatever we want it to mean. It does, however, endorse the attempt to make feminism more expansive and diverse, and thus less limited and elitist.

I find it problematic when *Buffy* is criticized for failing to meet feminist standards. Television shows are rarely activist, in the sense that as entertainment, they rarely set out to address political issues that affect women (or any other social group). Some people would charge that those of us who spend our time studying television do not engage in activism, either, whether our work has an explicitly feminist agenda or not. Nonetheless, television is a pervasive medium in our culture, and, increasingly, it is a space where people learn about what it means to be women and men. In this context, actively reading and deconstructing television texts, taking them seriously, and offering them up for critique (as opposed to simple criticism) become important tasks.

Buffy the Vampire Slayer and other texts that depict strong, independent young women do not necessarily do us a disservice when they do not articulate the version of feminism that we would most desire to recognize on the small screen. We have to look at these shows as offering instead a space for some nascent televisual feminisms. Shows like *Buffy* allow a "tiny space [to be] created by the mismatch of dominant visions with muted ones."[21] In this case, at least some of those visions are feminist. I do not think that this is accidental, either. I have no doubt that feminism has a place in the lives of *Buffy*'s viewers (and in Buffy's life, too).

It is hard not to recognize *Buffy the Vampire Slayer* as articulating a vision of feminism, albeit one that is primarily white and middle-class. The radical images of femininity it offers its viewers are linked to this idealized version of womanhood and girlhood. *Buffy*'s popularity in critical and feminist circles must thus also be understood within this particular context, within the particular version of feminism that is being produced for the show's viewers. There are exciting and interesting things happening in the contemporary mediascape, and I think that *Buffy the Vampire Slayer* is one of them. As a series, *Buffy* offers an interesting perspective on the possibilities of young womanhood (and manhood) as strong, independent, and complicated. But I can say it no better than by letting the youth market speak for itself, at least in one voice:

> For some, Buffy's appeal is the brutal portrayal of high school. For others, it's the pop-culture references. . . . And for some, the lure is the Wonderbra'd blond chick fighting vampires, and that's fine by me. Because the basic truth about Buffy herself is known to all who appreciate her: She is the intelligent, youthful hope that anyone, when confronted with life's little ghouls (metaphorical or otherwise), will be able to—as Willow put it—kick some serious demon ass.
>
> —Hannah Tucker, age seventeen[22]

NOTES

1. Margery Hourihan, *Deconstructing the Hero: Literary Theory and Children's Literature* (New York and London: Routledge, 1997), 67.

2. Ibid., 68.

3. Mary Celeste Kearney, "'Don't Need You': Rethinking Identity Politics and Separatism from a Grrrl Perspective," in *Youth Culture: Identity in a Postmodern World,* ed. Jonathon Epstein, 148–88 (Malden, Mass., and Oxford: Blackwell, 1998).

4. Susan Bordo, "The Body and the Reproduction of Femininity: A Feminist Appropriation of Foucault," in *Gender/Body/Knowledge: Feminist Reconstructions of Being and Knowing,* ed. Alison M. Jaggar and Susan R. Bordo, 13–33 (New Brunswick, N.J.: Rutgers University Press, 1989), 13, 28.

5. Rachel Fudge, "The Buffy Effect, or a Tale of Cleavage and Marketing," *Bitch* 10 (1999): 18–21, 58.

6. William Bogard, *The Simulation of Surveillance* (Cambridge: Cambridge Uni-

versity Press, 1996), 163; Julie D'Acci, "Defining Women: The Case of *Cagney & Lacey,*" in *Private Screenings: Television and the Female Consumer,* ed. Lynn Spigel and Denise Mann, 169–200 (Minneapolis: University of Minnesota Press, 1992); Teresa de Lauretis, *Alice Doesn't: Feminism, Semiotics, Cinema* (Bloomington: Indiana University Press, 1984).

7. http://www.buffy.com (May 2–4, 2000).

8. Kearney, "Don't Need You," 143, 155.

9. E. Graham McKinley, *Beverly Hills, 90210: Television, Gender and Identity* (Philadelphia: University of Pennsylvania Press, 1997).

10. Bronwyn Davies, "The Problem of Desire," *Social Problems* 37, no. 4 (1990): 301–16.

11. Mimi Udovitch, "What Makes Buffy Slay?" *Rolling Stone* 840 (2000): 60–64, 66.

12. Then again, maybe we could argue that it is easier for a male television executive to "own" feminism than a female one. If *Buffy* had been created by a woman, we might have even higher and more unrealistic expectations of the show.

13. It might have been read differently if this quote had been made to a magazine like *Bust* or *Bitch* or even *Ms.,* all of which aim to address a feminist audience. It is not clear that linking *Buffy* to feminism was going to score Weedon any brownie points with the readership of *Rolling Stone.*

14. Think about the shows that make up the contemporary landscape of youth-oriented television. They are almost exclusively populated by characters who are not only beautiful and thin, but also white, straight, able, upper middle-class young women and men.

15. Ann DuCille, *Skin Trade* (Cambridge, Mass.: Harvard University Press, 1996), 13.

16. I insert "Judeo" here because Willow's character is Jewish. Although her religious affiliation has been remarked upon only a few times during the years that this show has been on the air, the fact that Willow is Jewish is important even though it does not become a central part of her character. Because the vampire story is intrinsically linked to Christian culture, Willow periodically raises the problematic quality of this connection. For example, in one episode Willow expresses her anxiety about having a crucifix affixed to her bedroom window because it will upset her father. The naturalization of Christian iconography in the vampire story is disrupted here by the insertion of a narrative in which Christian icons are not seen as normal, natural, or possibly even acceptable. However, this question of religion is only an incidental point in the *Buffy* story; Willow often uses crosses and holy water herself without questioning it. It is also interesting that in this text—as I have argued in relation to *My So-Called Life*—one type of difference becomes linked to multiple differences, as if they could exist only in one character (Byers, 1998). Willow encompasses this religious difference but

also becomes different in other ways in the fourth and fifth seasons (1999–2001), when she decides to become involved with another young woman.

17. This itself is something of a paradox, however, because the show is predicated on the destruction of the vampire yet, at the same time, the serial nature of the television series means that the show is also founded on the impossibility of this eradication.

18. DuCille, *Skin Trade,* 174.

19. Caren Deming, "For a Television-Centered Television Criticism," in *Television and Women's Culture: The Politics of the Popular,* ed. Mary Ellen Brown (London: Sage Publications, 1990), 37–60, 203.

20. Douglas Kellner, *Media Culture: Cultural Studies, Identity and Politics Between the Modern and the Postmodern* (London and New York: Routledge, 1995), 237.

21. Deming, "For a Television-Centered Criticism," 58.

22. Hannah Tucker, "High School Confidential," *Entertainment Weekly* 505 (October 1, 1999).

SUSAN MUADDI DARRAJ

Third World, Third Wave Feminism(s): The Evolution of Arab American Feminism

> *My grandmother's voice says nothing can surprise her.*
> *Take her the shotgun wound and the crippled baby.*
> *She knows the spaces we travel through,*
> *the messages we cannot send—our voices are short*
> *and would get lost on the journey.*
> —NAOMI SHIHAB NYE, "The Words under the Words"

Let me tell you a story . . .

Many centuries ago, there lived a powerful sultan named Shahrayar, who had become so disillusioned by love that he established a tradition by which he married a new woman every night and ordered her to be beheaded the next morning. This continued for years, until the walls of the palace ran with blood and there was a scarcity of unmarried girls in the kingdom. Terrified parents fled with their daughters, while others buried theirs.

Into this chaos stepped Scheherazade—young, intelligent, witty, and brave. She was the daughter of the vizier, the sultan's prime minister, and much to her father's horror, she insisted on marrying Shahrayar. On her wedding night, as they lay in bed together, she asked the sultan if he would like to hear a story. She wove action, love, and beauty into this tale, but stopped at its climax once the dawn appeared. The sultan, eager to hear the story's end, suspended her execution until the next morning. However, once she had completed it, Scheherazade was ready that evening with a new story, which she also left unfinished. And so this continued for 1,001 nights, at the end of which Scheherazade had started a family and Shahrayar had regained his morality and repented for his earlier crimes. Thus did Scheherazade, with the power of her words, save a kingdom and a man's soul.

This is the story of one of Arabia's most famous heroines—at least, this is how this tale is told in the Middle East, where people grow up hearing stories about women like Scheherazade; Aisha, the prophet Muhammad's favorite wife, who led his army into battle after his death;[1] and Cleopatra, the Egyptian queen who brought Julius Caesar and Marc Antony to their knees.

However, this is not how such women are portrayed in the West.[2] Scheherazade and Cleopatra share a similar fate, having been reduced to nothing more than harem kittens and the sex toys of sultans. The reputation of Aisha has gone in a much different direction; it has metamorphosed into the stereotype of the meek Muslim woman, veiled and silenced by a domineering husband. Indeed, these two stereotypes are still widely accepted and applied to modern Arab/Muslim women by Western nations. In particular, Cleopatra, the queen who was considered the most dangerous and powerful woman in the world by the ancient Romans, has been portrayed in ways that diminish her historical significance and reduce her to nothing more than a Mediterranean Playboy Bunny. Furthermore, with an almost schizophrenically stereotyped vision, the American media, when it covers stories in the Middle East, tends to show only images of mysterious women, clad in black from head to toe, who move like eerie shadows across American television screens.

The recent "war on terrorism" that followed the September 11 terrorist attacks on New York and Washington featured much media coverage of Afghan women: clad in their *burqas,* these women represent a medieval silencing of women. More problematically, their plight is depicted as the norm for Muslim women, all of whom are viewed as members of one monolithic category. Much to its credit, the American feminist movement has been trying to educate others about the oppressive restrictions on women imposed by the Taliban, but the focus has been somewhat misdirected, with the result that many people have been led to think that all Muslim women live under such conditions. Something similar happened during the Gulf War in 1990, when American news stations and newspapers bombarded their viewers with "peeks inside" the land of Saddam Hussein.[3] Most of the views captured these same black-clad women, rather than the multifaceted female Iraqi population. Although many Muslim women choose to veil themselves, many do not. Before the Gulf War began, many Iraqi women thrived right along with their country's economy, holding high positions in government, education, and business; many of these women, whether Muslim or Christian, did not wear any form of the veil. Thus, unveiled women abound on the streets of these nations, but they never seem to catch the attention of the news cameras.

In October 2000, I attended a rally in Philadelphia; the rally was a peaceful one, held by over one thousand Arab Americans and their supporters to show solidarity with Palestinians in the West Bank and Gaza Strip.[4] The rally was described by the Philadelphia police as orderly, and I was proud to have attended. The next morning, when I opened the newspaper, I was startled to come across these lines: "Men chanted in the streets while veiled women walked behind them, pushing baby strollers." Since I had been there, I knew that the majority of women in attendance had been unveiled, because many women there, including me, were not Muslim; many participants in the rally were not even Arabs. Furthermore, many of the Muslim women there did not veil. One such woman, my friend Amal, was amazed and disappointed to read the article. "That's how they always want to portray us," she said, "as if all we do is walk behind our husbands and keep our mouths shut."

These double (and contradictory) images of Arab women—the meek, veiled wife, on the one hand, and the harem kitten on the other—disrupt any clear understanding of the lives of Arab women, both in Arab countries and in the United States. Indeed, it comes as a surprise to many Western women and Western feminists to learn that there is, and has been, a strong Arab feminist movement in the Middle East at least since the beginning of the twentieth century. Whenever I use the term "Arab feminism," it generally elicits such comments from American feminists as "That sounds like an oxymoron!" and questions such as "Can you be a feminist if you're still veiled?" and "How can a Muslim woman be a feminist if she shares her husband with three other wives?"

Along with many other women, I have grappled with the eyebrow-raising self-identification as an Arab American feminist. The American feminist movement, which has recently opened its doors to so many other versions of feminism, seems not to understand Arab women's brand of women's rights. Indeed, American society seems inclined to lump all women from Muslim countries into the category of "Arab" (as in the case with Afghan women) and to view their various situations from the same perspective. Americans also tend to view all "Arabs" as "Muslims"; furthermore, all Muslims are seen as practicing a particular, conservative brand of Islam. This puts Arab American women in a unique position because we are faced with the conflation of ethnic and religious identity. We are also caught between two historical feminist movements: the one in the United States and the one in the Arab world. I, for one, am proud to be associated with both movements, but I have quickly realized that American feminism frequently misunderstands its Arab counterpart, or perhaps is unaware of its existence.

Much of this confusion and misunderstanding stems from the fact that Arab women generally live in third world countries, which are stereotyped as being "backward."[5] It is incomprehensible to many American feminists, for example, that Arab women could have independently developed a feminist consciousness. As Kumari Jayawardena explains: "In the West, . . . there is the Eurocentric view that the movement for women's liberation is not indigenous to Asia or Africa, but has been a purely Western European and North American phenomenon, and that where movements for women's emancipation or feminist struggles have arisen in the Third World, they have been merely imitative of Western models."[6]

Simply put, women in third world countries confront gender-specific issues that are different from those faced by their first world counterparts. Nawal El Saadawi, an Egyptian doctor and leading feminist thinker, writes about the widespread practice of female genital mutilation (FGM) in rural parts of her country. The practice can range from a slight nick on the clitoris for symbolic effect to a full removal of the clitoris and a sewing up of the labia, which makes future menstruation, sexual intercourse, and childbirth difficult, painful, and dangerous; the practice results in the deaths of many young women. In Jordan, women's rights activists are trying to cope with the horror of honor killings, by which a man will kill a female relative who has apparently brought shame upon the family through some kind of sexual indiscretion. South Asian women also face weighty obstacles, especially a lack of control over their own bodies. At the conclusion of her novel *Fire on the Mountain* (1977), the Indian writer Anita Desai describes the murder of a local women's rights activist who tried to educate young women in a small Indian village about their sexuality and the protection of their bodies.[7] Neighboring Afghanistan also copes with many gender issues; feminists there, including the Revolutionary Association of the Women of Afghanistan (RAWA), are still trying to address the human rights infractions of the former Taliban government. Although the future is still uncertain, many men still favor veiling; indeed, some women don't even consider the *burqa* to be their biggest problem, opting instead to focus on their struggle against poverty in an economically crippled nation. And, of course, women in many third world countries face the universal dilemma of poverty, poor health and medical care, and war. Yet, despite what many Westerners think and despite the problems besieging third world women—indeed, *because* of these problems—feminism is not a language unspoken in the Third World, especially in the Middle East.

PART ONE: THE HISTORY OF ARAB FEMINISM

When I was an undergraduate, I attempted to join a women's union on campus and was encouraged to attend an open house. I had a conversation with the union's president, a senior who had been involved since her first year. She asked about the specific feminist issues that concerned me, and when I mentioned Arab women's issues, she nodded thoughtfully and replied, "Yes, we really have to start educating them about women's rights. Their lives are very difficult." She continued by discussing the way in which many Arab women in the United States still wore the veil and how American values, she hoped, would "trickle down" to them. She seemed to imply that feminism and Islam—the assumption is that all Arab women are Muslims—are in conflict. When I told her that I was an Arab American, she seemed confused and uneasy, murmured a few neutral, polite words, and moved on.

What I wanted to tell her was that there was no need to educate Arab women about feminism, because it already exists in the Middle East and among Arab American women—and it has already been defined and has a long, controversial history. During the Age of Imperialism, when European countries—especially Great Britain and France—colonized much of the third world, the Middle East was divided among various European powers that exploited the people as well as the natural resources of the land. Most Arab countries attempted, at some point, to shed Western colonialism and nationalize their land by bringing it under the control of Arabs and investing it with an Arabic national character.[8] Women largely joined the struggle; in turn, their participation led to the self-recognition of their power as a political and social force. As Margot Badran and Miriam Cooke state in the introduction to *Opening the Gates: A Century of Arab Feminist Writing* (1990),[9] Arab feminism was beginning to be articulated while the Arab world was still under Western colonial rule, and, therefore, the feminist perspective has always run the risk of being dismissed as antinationalist or antireligious, as succumbing to Western influences. As a result, the battle against sexism fought by Arab women is more layered and intricate than the one fought by Western feminists because Arab women are simultaneously fighting patriarchy in their own societies, colonialism by Western nations, and nationalist forces in their own societies who interpret feminism as another branch of imperialistic domination.

One of the most oft-used symbols in this debate is the veil: Arabs who oppose Arab feminism claim that feminists who don't wear the veil have assimilated Western culture and thus betrayed their Arab heritage. In addition to the internal debate over the veil in Arab society, Western women tend to pity Arab women who wear a form of the veil, whether it's a full *chador* or a *hijab,* which usually covers one's head. However, the veil—whatever its form—cannot be interpreted simply as a marker of oppression or loyalty to one's culture. In the United States, Arab, Muslim, and Middle Eastern women who veil themselves withstand much criticism, but for many of them, the veil is a choice. It was explained best by Heba, a young Libyan American woman I had the good fortune to befriend one summer in Ramallah, who said that she chose to wear the veil when she was in her late teens because it symbolized her commitment to her faith, much in the same way that I, a

Christian woman, often wear a small gold crucifix around my neck. Heba is an independent woman who does not feel that either her veil or her religion conflict with her feminism.

But how is Arab feminism *different* from American and Western feminism? Are the goals and ideals of Arab feminism separate, and if so, why? More important, how can these differences be reconciled, and how can they be used positively to influence the "third wave" of feminism?

I have already indicated that Arab feminists often face different and complicated issues. This is also true of Arab American feminists like myself. When I was a teenager and an undergraduate in college, I identified myself as a feminist because I had been attracted to the writings of various Western feminists. Part of me, however, believed that the ideas of these women did not relate to the concerns of the average Arab woman who, whether she is a lawyer, doctor, or stay-at-home mother, nevertheless faces poverty, political unrest, and perhaps even neocolonialism. For instance, how did Virginia Woolf's insistence on a "room of one's own" apply to my grandmother, who wore housedresses, barely spoke English, and raised nine children in a three-bedroom New York apartment? And how did Betty Friedan's "feminine mystique" relate to my mother, who *was* a housewife for many years, but who could also claim the roles of account manager and bookkeeper for our family business as well as school and community activist in our Philadelphia neighborhood?

When I spent the summer of 1998 in the West Bank of Israel, I met with women who lived in refugee camps and whose lives were in crisis. Most of them had fled their homes during the 1948 Arab-Israeli war, having escaped with only the clothes on their backs and some hastily collected jewelry or cash (some even took the deeds to their homes, anticipating their return). Their houses in the camps were simple, square buildings, erected as temporary abodes. Families of twelve and fifteen lived in rooms no larger than the typical college classroom. On most nights, some children told me, they slept on the roofs of their homes in order to avoid sleeping on top of each other. In small workshops, women made crafts and embroidered pillowcases and purses to sell. This was often the family's sole income, as the Israeli occupation had crippled the economy in the territories and sent unemployment rates through the roof. The women also worked in their homes, preparing their small meals as best they could, boiling every drop of water before serving it to their families in order to kill any bacteria. Was there anything that Catharine MacKinnon, Carol Gilligan, or Gloria Steinem could say that would directly relate to *these* women and their lives?

There was no direct connection, of course, because Arab feminism had a different history of development from those of America and Europe. While the latter were influenced by Cartesian philosophy, the former has always been a part of nationalism and the third world politics of war and poverty. In her book *Re-Orienting Western Feminisms: Women's Diversity in a Postcolonial World* (1998), Chilla Bulbeck explains that Western feminism inherited a tendency to emphasize "individual freedoms—of thought, to acquire property and so on" from the theories and forces of democracy, capitalism, and secularization. She adds that Western feminism developed from this philosophical tradition and utilized the notion of individualism "to construct its understanding of (white western) women's place in the world."[10] In other words, Western feminism has a highly individual focus.

Arab feminism is reluctant to prioritize the self and the individual above all. Palestinians, and Arabs in general, exist within a well-established family structure; most Palestinians, including Palestinian women, identify themselves strongly with family, both immediate and extended. Barbara Epstein writes that a focus on individualism and the pursuit of success has become prominent in American culture, and although most feminists would reject it, "most of us live according to these values anyway: we measure our value by our success at work, and we let little stand in the way of it."[11] Perhaps this is a direct result of capitalism and economic success, but Arab women and society generally do not measure their value by these factors. Owing to widespread poverty, neocolonialism, and the resistance to Israeli occupation, the goals of individual wealth and personal success have been generally replaced by nationalistic aims and attempts to ensure family survival and progress. Thus, Arab women generally have other priorities, including family, which perhaps a capitalist system does not reward, and they often feel that American feminism devalues them because of this.

While Western women asserted independence from Western men, Arab women, by and large, asserted independence from both Arab men and Western colonial forces: Palestinian women fought and still fight against British and Israeli colonizers; Algerian women waged war alongside their men against French imperialism; and Egyptian women struggled to oust British colonizers from their nation. Thus, the rise of Arab feminism is rooted in a context of nationalistic struggle at a time when men needed women to take on stronger social and political roles. Since Arab women live in so many different countries and encounter various social and political issues, it is difficult to trace the rise of a monolithic Arab feminism, just as it is difficult to identify the agenda of the third wave. I will focus therefore on one example, that of Palestinian women and Palestinian feminism.

Many Palestinian feminists are personally involved in the struggle against the Israeli occupation of the West Bank and the Gaza Strip. I had been used to separating "feminism" from my own Palestinian-Arab heritage because I had assumed that, as Kipling said, "East is east, and West is west, and never the twain shall meet." While American feminists focus on issues such as abortion, gay and lesbian rights, equal health care, and financial and emotional independence, Palestinian women are fighting for Palestinian autonomy and have struggled from the beginning for the independence of a Palestinian state. In January 2002, the second uprising of the Palestinians against the Israeli occupation was dramatically altered when a suicide bombing attack in Jerusalem was carried out by a young Palestinian woman; the attack has changed the entire atmosphere and increased already high tensions between Israel and Palestine. But the fact that even women are now desperate enough to become militants and suicidal killers should not surprise anyone familiar with the conflict. The frustration experienced by Palestinian women has led some of them down the immoral and destructive path of terror.

Most, of course, have taken a more humane and practical approach to resistance. During my various trips to the West Bank, I have observed the Palestinian women in my family as they spoke about the years during the first Intifada, in which they dealt with the successive blows of school closings, high unemployment, and a general social stagnation.[12] My cousin's wife, who teaches at Birzeit University in the West Bank city of Birzeit, taught in the basements of buildings and in people's homes to make sure that her students did not fall behind in their studies. This was part of the campaign of most college professors and schoolteachers at the time, in reaction to the closing of schools by the Israeli military authority. An aunt told me about the days that the Israeli soldiers used the roof of her house as a watch post and demanded food and drink from her at all times of the day and night. Sometimes, she told me, they urinated in her water tank to antagonize the family, knowing that the tank was their sole water supply. Palestinian women have been known to throw their bodies on youths about to be arrested or beaten by soldiers. As Maria Holt writes, "Palestinian women, against all the odds, have developed a reputation for toughness."[13] It seems to me that the assertive protests of Palestinian women against occupational forces and their intense political involvement in shaping a future autonomous state constitute one aspect of feminist awareness.

Palestinian women have had a history of organizing around not specifically women's issues but national issues, that is, around the politics of war and poverty. Women's organizing has not always been widely recognized as feminist. In *Opening the Gates,* Badran and Cooke describe what they call the "invisible feminism" of early Arab feminists: "Early feminist consciousness and voices were for the most part hidden from the 'larger world' or confined to the world of women while female seclusion and the segregation of the sexes prevailed. Much of the Arab women's feminist expression has eluded people because of its invisibility."[14] In 1921, the Palestine Women's Union, the first Palestinian women's political organization, was established to involve women in the Palestinian nationalist effort—and it continues to be active today.

However, since the early part of the twentieth century, other women's groups in Palestine have begun to adopt a more overtly feminist agenda. Maria Holt writes, "There are now a number of women's resource centers, in Ramallah, Nablus and Gaza, which produce written material, run practical courses and, in general, seek to bring women from different backgrounds together, with the objective of ascertaining women's needs, educating them about their rights and preparing them for a future Palestinian state."[15] Palestinian women's organizations have worked to ensure that there is a feminist movement that operates parallel to the nationalist movement for an independent

Palestinian state. These feminists strive to prevent women's issues from becoming secondary to national ones, perhaps because they have seen what befell Algerian women who fought a similar struggle for independence. After having borne arms with their male colleagues against French colonialism, Algerian women lost many of their hard-won rights when the postrevolutionary government, backed by a radical Islamic movement, enforced a patriarchal code in the country.

Once focused almost exclusively on relieving Palestinian suffering through charitable organizations, Palestinian women's groups have, in the last thirty years, become more engaged in political, social, and economic challenges, and have established initiatives that tackle women's issues on many fronts. One of the most significant has been the articulation of women's rights. As Adrien Wing describes, the General Union of Palestinian Women published a Declaration of Principles on Palestinian Women's Rights in 1994; the Declaration affirms women's equal civil, political, economic, social, and cultural rights.[16] Women's marches to protest Israeli occupation of the West Bank and Gaza are regularly held in refugee camps and on college campuses throughout the territories. Also, women's groups have initiated successful wage-earning projects, which both train unskilled Palestinian women to provide for their families (as many of their husbands are unemployed because of the economic stress of the occupation) and foster a sense of their independence and economic survival skills. The hope is that this sense will remain with them even after the political situation improves. These groups include the Federation of Women's Work Committees, which offers women vocational training in sewing, weaving, knitting, and the creation of ethnic and heritage crafts. Ghada Talhami notes, "More importantly, it runs nurseries, kindergartens, and medical clinics. Village women are provided with literacy training and working women are urged to become unionized and instructed about their economic rights."[17]

Yet another initiative seeks peace: for decades, Palestinian feminists have met and opened dialogues with Israeli women and feminists (these include a Palestinian professor, Hanan Ashrawi, the former spokesperson for the Palestinian delegation at the Madrid peace talks in the early 1990s). This interaction is probably one of the most positive and powerful moves designed by the Palestinian feminist community, one that sets a tone for a potential sense of security between Israel and its future neighbor, the independent Palestinian state.

Finally, Palestinian women have developed initiatives on a more scholarly and academic level: writers and literary critics have sought to share the treasures of Arab culture and have made sure that women's literature is part of that effort. For example, the poet and critic Salma Khadra Jayyusi founded the Project of Translation from Arabic (PROTA), which seeks to translate the best in Arabic literature into English. Literature is, after all, one of the best methods of connecting cultures and ideologies, and Jayyusi's project has translated both prominent and obscure feminist voices in the Middle East. The point of all these initiatives is not just to achieve a national, autonomous Palestinian state, but to ensure that women remain active and influential players in its administration, culture, and society.

PART TWO: RECONCILING MY IDENTITY AND CATCHING THE THIRD WAVE

As I grew up in the United States, reconciling Western and third world feminisms seemed impossible. Is it possible to be an Arab American feminist, especially when the two affiliations seem to oppose one another? Since second wave feminism seemed largely mired in the pit of East versus West and caught up in national and international politics, I often sought refuge in the words of Katha Pollitt, who writes, simply but powerfully, "For me, to be a feminist is to answer the question 'Are women human?' with a yes."[18] This is the spirit that should propel third wave feminism; the question now is to find the mechanism. What is the best way to bring Arab and Western women to the table to begin reconciling their feminisms? I realized that I had to answer that question for myself before extending it to others.

The work of black feminists like Barbara Smith and bell hooks has influenced my perspective on dismantling the idea of a monolithic feminism. When I read how they and other black feminists dared to assert that American feminism was a predominantly white, capitalist movement that needed to be broadened, I believed that I *could* identify myself as an Arab American feminist and be neither untrue nor inaccurate. The situation of Arab American women is, as I realized, similar to the experiences of African American women. Smith writes about the invisibility experienced by many African American women:

> This invisibility, which goes beyond anything that either Black men or white women experience and tell about in their writing, is one reason it is so difficult for me to know where to start. It seems overwhelming to break such a massive silence. Even more numbing, however, is the realization that so many of the women who will read this have not yet noticed us missing either from their reading matter, their politics, or their lives. It is galling that ostensible feminists and acknowledged lesbians have been so oblivious to the implications of any womanhood that is not white womanhood and that they have yet to struggle with the deep racism in themselves that is at the source of their ignorance.[19]

The racism and ignorance that Smith describes are evident not only between white and black women but also between Western and third world feminisms. Like Smith, I found it appalling that Western feminists do not have a good working knowledge of the issues and problems that challenge Arab feminists and Arab women. Arab feminism and Western feminism should not be remote, "foreign" movements. Feminism should embrace the struggles of all women, but it currently does not. Increasingly, I have noticed that Western feminists, especially American feminists, consider and treat their Arab counterparts as "other," that is, as third world women who do not understand the struggles of women in the first world. Much of this is due to politics; in the current political climate, the United States and most of Europe (on one side) and the Middle East (on the other) are ideologically farther apart than ever before. I also understand that Arab feminism is not totally innocent and often views American feminism as another agent of colonialism—a notion that is perpetuated by opponents of Arab feminism in the Arab world. Nonetheless, I contend that there needs to be a bridging and even a synchronization of Arab and Western feminisms if the term "feminism" is to maintain its integrity and address the experiences of all women; by "synchronization," I mean a way of bringing both movements up to date with each other.

Literature, I believe, is one way to do this. By immersing themselves in the cultural expressions of women from backgrounds other than their own, individual feminists can understand the particular problems faced by women. In the preface to their book, *Opening the Gates,* which translates into English many documents of Arab feminism, Margot Badran and Miriam Cooke write, "We became excited about what might happen if more Arab women's feminist voices spoke directly to western audiences."[20] Likewise, modern Arab women writers have been targeting Western audiences, and literature has proven to be one method to build bridges. The honesty and accuracy in the work of these writers, many of whom write in English and other Western languages, paint a picture of Arab women's lives that seeks to dismantle and clarify the prevalent stereotypes of Arab women as either meek and veiled or overly sexed.

Barbara Smith describes "how much easier both my waking and my sleeping hours would be if there were one book in existence that would tell me something specific about my life. One book based in Black feminist and Black lesbian experience, fiction or nonfiction. Just one work to reflect the reality that I and the Black women whom I love are trying to create."[21] As an Arab American woman, I understand Smith's wish, as the voices of Arab women tend to be erased from the pages of world literature, sometimes for and by feminist readers. Lately, however, some of these voices have emerged. These voices tend to be both political and nationalistic, as these two forces mark the lives of most people in the third world and certainly the lives of women.

One of these emerging voices is that of Ahdaf Soueif, whose novel *In the Eye of the Sun* (1993) I purchased when I read the rave reviews it received as an exploration of Middle Eastern gender politics. When I began this eight-hundred-page novel, I had no clue that I was about to read a book that would make such a lasting impression on me. When I finished it I knew that *here,* finally, was a woman who wrote about the way I felt. Of course, I was well versed in feminist writings and theories. I had taken several women's studies classes as an undergraduate and, after graduate school, I took it upon myself to read the works of and about the lives of Simone de Beauvoir, Charlotte Perkins Gilman, and Virginia Woolf, among others. I admired them. I was interested in their lives and struggles. But Ahdaf Soueif's novel had spoken to me not only as a woman, but as an Arab American woman. I literally could not stop reading about the struggles of Asya, the young Egyptian main character, who is desperate to assert herself as an emotionally, intellectually, and sexually independent woman.

After Soueif, I read works by other Arab women and came across *Nadia, Captive of Hope: Memoir of an Arab Woman* (1999) by Fay Afaf Kanafani. In the introduction to the book, the scholar and writer Lisa Suhair Majaj says that Kanafani "gives voice to a feminist awareness grounded not in Western discourse, but in her own experiences and identity as an Arab woman."[22] Kanafani writes in the persona of "Nadia," a Palestinian woman who, after a series of personal and political struggles, develops and lives her feminist ideology. She writes, "Only men had the power to map the destiny of women and children in those days. Up to that point very few women had been strong enough to challenge this tradition. I didn't mind being one of them."[23]

Another Arab woman—one of the few to "challenge this tradition" and to have an impact on the way that Western women think of their Arab counterparts—is Nawal El Saadawi, the Egyptian feminist and doctor. She has made it her task to educate women in rural parts of Egypt about the oppressive aspects of their culture, such as FGM. She was jailed from 1981 to 1982 by the administration of President Anwar Sadat and has, not surprisingly, been the target of Islamic extremism: her medical offices were bombed by fundamentalists who opposed her efforts, and she has received various death threats. El Saadawi also writes fiction and nonfiction. In her most recent book, *A Daughter of Isis: The Autobiography of Nawal El Saadawi* (1999), she details the first two decades of her life. This autobiography (one of several she has written) is more about finding one's feminist identity through the craft of writing: "Ever since I took hold of a pen in my fingers, I have fought against history, struggled against the falsifications in official registers. I wish I could efface my grandfather Al-Saadawi from my name and replace it with my mother's name, Zaynab."[24] El Saadawi's feminist writings, although they have won the praise and notice of Western feminists, have been criticized by Arab feminists for being too "accommodating" or for "reinforcing" the stereotypes that the West holds of Arab women and Arabs in general. Such arguments among Arab feminists, however, indicate the strength and vitality of the Arab feminist movement. The current debates are not unlike the debates among American feminists; indeed, the existence of a lively and active dialogue indicates the perpetual development of the movement.

Reading a selection of works by Arab women would make it apparent how ridiculous the stereotypical images of Scheherazade, Cleopatra, and Aisha are, as well as how these stereotypes can be re-created into the heroine, the queen, and the religious scholar and leader. The treatment of these figures reflects the attitude of the West toward Arab women, whose different feminism can never be understood in the face of such opposition. Once Arab women are restored to their true dignity, once they are viewed by other feminists as full human beings and not as dark, silent shapes on a television screen, then the real work can begin.

I believe that studying Arab women's literature is one of many ways to spark curiosity and open active dialogues among women that can bridge the chasm of misunderstanding between Arab and Western feminisms and lead to a synchronization of the two movements. Arab feminism, which is susceptible to the postcolonial reaction of interpreting American feminism as a new form of imperialism, would also benefit immensely from such dialogue, which would rejuvenate the spirit of feminism and positively affect women catching the third wave by offering them a chance to deal with *real* women and not with misleading images of one another.

Furthermore, another important step will have been taken: real links will have been created between Arab feminists and other women of color. Here exists a fertile ground, waiting to be planted, and it can yield a rich harvest if Arab feminists form coalitions with other women of color, as well as with other branches of the feminist movement in the United States. Right now, women of color generally operate in small pockets, not as a collective whole. On a number of occasions I have been told by another woman of color—Latina, Asian, or Indian—that our conversations about the status of women in our respective parts of the globe helped her to envision more clearly what the next wave of feminism should look like. The third wave is a global wave, but it must sweep through and carry back messages from women all over the world—and those messages should, in their own words, articulate their visions, their concerns, and their histories.

NOTES

1. Aisha, the Prophet Muhammad's youngest and favorite wife, became a religious scholar and interpreted many of the *hadith*. She also led the armies of Muhammad into battle against the forces of Ali in the Battle of the Camel.

2. In this essay, I will be relying on the terms "East" to mean the Middle East and Asia and "West" to mean Europe and America. These terms, I should mention, have rightly raised some suspicion about their uses. Edward Said and other scholars note that it is difficult to use the term "West" and apply its meaning to the entire West, for example, and that it is not wise to use such blanket terms.

3. The fact that Iraq was portrayed as Saddam Hussein's territory is another subject of debate. Many called this an example of the way that the American media tend to "demonize" its enemies to make the idea of war more palatable to U.S. citizens.

4. In late September 2000, Palestinians and Israelis clashed as a result of a visit by Israeli Ariel Sharon (who was responsible for the massacre of hundreds of Palestinian refugees in southern Lebanon in 1982) to the Haram al-Sharif, one of the holiest Muslim shrines in Jerusalem. Sharon entered the shrine with two thousand armed bodyguards, an image that Palestinians interpreted as an invasion and a sign of disrespect. The ensuing clashes between the Israeli military and Palestinian youths have, as of this writing, resulted in the deaths of over one hundred people, all but seven of them Palestinians.

5. The term "third world" is a highly controversial one; it "originally signified a 'third force' of non-aligned nations which would wedge themselves between the Cold War oppositions of first world 'democracy' and second world 'communism'" (Kateryna O. Longley, "Fifth World," in *Striking Chords: Multicultural Literary Interpretations,* ed. Sneja Gunew and Kateryna O. Longley [Sydney: Allen and Unwin, 1992], 20, as cited in Chilla Bulbeck, *Re-Orienting Western Feminisms: Women's Diversity in a Postcolonial World* [New York: Cambridge University Press, 1998], 34). Over the years, however, the term third world has come to develop broader connotations, that is, to include countries thought to be largely unmodernized and nonprogressive.

6. Kumari Jayawardena, *Feminism and Nationalism in the Third World* (London: Zed Books, 1986), 2.

7. Anita Desai, *Fire on the Mountain* (New York: Harper and Row, 1977).

8. Great Britain was given a mandate over much of Egypt, Palestine, and parts of Jordan. France controlled and colonized Algeria, Lebanon, and other places.

9. *Opening the Gates: A Century of Arab Feminist Writing* is a significant work because it translates for the first time many important essays, speeches, and other writings by Arab feminists and makes them available for Western readers. It traces the history of Arab feminism back one hundred years.

10. Bulbeck, *Re-Orienting Western Feminisms,* 12–13.

11. Barbara Epstein, "What Happened to the Women's Movement?" *Monthly Review* 53, no. 1 (May 2001): 13.

12. The Intifadah ("uprising," in English) was a popular revolt by the Palestinian people of the West Bank and Gaza Strip that started in December 1987. It was characterized mostly by Palestinian youths throwing stones at Israeli soldiers, who often fired back with live ammunition. Hundreds of people died during the Intifadah, which lasted until approximately 1992.

13. Maria Holt, *Half the People: Women, History and the Palestinian Intifada* (Jerusalem: Palestinian Academic Society for the Study of International Affairs, 1992), 50.

14. Margot Badran and Miriam Cooke, eds., *Opening the Gates: A Century of Arab Feminist Writing* (Bloomington: Indiana University Press, 1990), xv.

15. Holt, *Half the People,* 14.

16. Adrien Katherine Wing, "A Critical Race Feminist Conceptualization of Violence: South African and Palestinian Women," in *Global Critical Race Feminism: An International Reader,* ed. Adrien Katherine Wing, 332–46 (New York: New York University Press, 2000), 341.

17. Ghada Talhami, "Women under Occupation: The Great Transformation," in *Images and Reality: Palestinian Women under Occupation and in the Diaspora,* ed. Suha Sabbagh and Ghada Talhami, Institute for Arab Women's Studies Monograph Series, no. 1 (Washington, D.C.: IAWS, 1990), 18.

18. Katha Pollitt, *Reasonable Creatures: Essays on Women and Feminism* (New York: Vintage, 1995), xxi.

19. Barbara Smith, "Toward a Black Feminist Criticism," *All the Women Are White, All the Men Are Black, But Some of Us Are Brave,* ed. Gloria T. Hull, Patricia Bell Scott, and Barbara Smith (Old Westbury, N.Y.: Feminist Press, 1982), 157–75.

20. Badran and Cooke, *Opening the Gates,* ix.

21. Barbara Smith, "Toward a Black Feminist Criticism," 20.

22. Lisa Suhair Majaj, Introduction to Fay Afaf Kanafani, *Nadia, Captive of Hope: Memoir of an Arab Woman* (Armonk, N.Y.: East Gate Books, 1999), xiii.

23. Kanafani, *Nadia, Captive of Hope,* 267.

24. Nawal El Saadawi, *A Daughter of Isis: The Autobiography of Nawal El Saadawi,* trans. Sherif Hetata (New York: Zed Books, 1999), 30.

PART FOUR

Redefining Feminism

Feminism's Family Problem: Feminist Generations and the Mother-Daughter Trope

Feminism has become a mother figure, and what we are seeing is a daughter's revolt.

—B. RUBY RICH, "Feminism and Sexuality in the 1980s"

▬▬▬In the summer of 1994, I read Katie Roiphe's *The Morning After: Sex, Fear, and Feminism on Campus* for the first time.[1] For months, the book had been receiving a lot of attention, but neither I nor any of my feminist friends had yet read it. I remember a fellow graduate student telling me that she would *never* read Roiphe's book, that obviously Roiphe was an idiot. I can't say I disagreed with her assessment after reading *The Morning After*. "*Whose* feminism is she talking about?" I said out loud, to no one in particular, as I sat reading. "This is ridiculous!"

I was quick to dismiss Roiphe during that initial reading in great part because, to put it bluntly, I thought she was dead wrong about the state of contemporary feminism. What she described bore little resemblance to the feminism I knew. Roiphe and I, approximately the same age, seemed to have read the same books, taken the same sort of classes, and participated in the same "feminism on campus," yet we emerged from these experiences with wildly different takes on feminism. We might share a generational label—what's been dubbed "Generation X" —but beyond that we seemed to share nothing more.

What I found most unrecognizable in Roiphe's text was the image she painted of feminism as a puritanical, regulating force. For Roiphe, feminism was like a stern mother telling women how to behave. She described feeling constrained by feminism, her individuality and freedom curbed by its long list of rules and regulations. As she writes:

> From Catharine MacKinnon to the protesters against the *Sports Illustrated* swimsuit issue to more mainstream theorists of sexual harassment, feminists are on the frontlines of sexual regulation. . . . Feminism has come more and more to represent sexual thoughts and images censored, behavior checked, fantasies regulated. In my late adolescent idiom, feminism was not about rebellion, but rules; it was not about setting loose, as it once was, it was about reining in.[2]

In Roiphe's description of contemporary feminism, it is no longer misogynist men, patriarchal attitudes, or a sexist culture that "regulates" women's behavior. The task of regulating women's lives has been taken over by feminists, the very group that was concerned with freeing women from oppressive control. Feminism, it seems, has come to stand in the place that once was occupied by the external forces against feminism. Feminism, Roiphe paradoxically suggests, is what stands in the way of women's liberation.

For Roiphe feminism represented regulation, yet for me feminism had mostly been about the opposite: a way for me to be an individual and break free of society's many rules about a woman's proper place. Feminism had profoundly shaped both my personal and professional lives, and I felt a strong sense of loyalty and gratitude toward it.

My feelings about feminism, I came to realize, were those of a dutiful daughter. Feminism was a mother figure to me as well—but an encouraging one, one that had given me much support over the years. As it had been for Roiphe, feminism had been an integral part of my life since I was a little girl. In fact, one of my few clear memories of childhood is of my mother proudly telling a friend that I was "already a real feminist" at the age of nine. Yes, feminism was a kind of mother figure to me, too, I realized, but one that I needed and loved.

As a dutiful daughter of feminism, then, I can see now that part of my original intent in writing a response to Roiphe was to defend feminism, the feminism I saw being attacked by Roiphe and her "antifeminist" feminist cohorts. Unlike so many other members of my generation, I wouldn't abandon second wave feminism. I would defend it as one would a mother maligned during a schoolyard battle. "Your mama," said Roiphe. "Them's fighting words," said I.

A few years later I began work on my dissertation, a project that developed as a way of responding to Roiphe's—and other "next generation" feminists'—representation of feminism. As I began my research, it became clear that what I had first noticed in Roiphe's text was, in fact, a ubiquitous phenomenon: writers of all ages, feminists and nonfeminists alike, were describing feminist intergenerational relationships in familial terms. As my project progressed, it increasingly centered on how the mother-daughter relation seems to be *the* central trope in depicting the relationship between the second and third waves of U.S. feminism.

In retrospect, of course, I can see that my own relationship to feminism demanded analysis. Why did I feel such a strong need to defend the second wave? Why didn't I identify more with members of my own generation, the self-described third wave? In what ways did my investment in defending feminism prevent me from identifying with these younger feminists? I was finding the representation of feminism as a "bad mother" everywhere, yet clearly my own daughterly relation to feminism as a "good mother" was itself part of the very structure I was trying to critique. Dutiful daughters or insolent ones, we all appear unable to leave feminism's "family."

In describing feminist generations, feminists seem to have difficulty avoiding familial metaphors. In an essay that both relies on and criticizes the use of the mother-daughter trope—aptly titled "An Open Letter to Institutional Mothers"—Rebecca Dakin Quinn coins the term "matrophor" to describe "the persistent nature of maternal metaphors in feminism."[3] The prevalence of this "matrophor" within myriad genres of feminist discourse suggests that there is something to be gained from turning feminism (and thus often second wave feminists) into "a mother." This "matrophor," I would argue, appears to embolden feminism's "daughters," granting them authority and a generational location from which to speak.

Before examining this "matrophor" in more detail, the term "generation" warrants glossing. In recent years, there has been an increasing tendency to speak of feminism in terms of generations. In fact, within feminism, the 1990s may well be remembered as a decade *defined by* the notion of feminist generations, so commonplace has this concept been to mark differences among feminisms—and feminists.[4] In its most oft-used form, the phrase "feminist generations" points to the existence of at least two, if not more, coexisting generations of U.S. feminists: the second wave feminists of the 1970s and a new generation of feminists—women who have grown up with feminism—who are being called the third wave. This latter term, "the third wave," has frequently been employed as a kind of shorthand for a generational difference among feminists, one based on chronological age. Yet I would argue that the term must also be seen as representing the desire of those who embrace it to signal a "new" feminism, one that is distinct from the second wave.

One of the problems with this use of the term "generations," though seemingly plural, is that it is almost always dyadic, referring merely to just two such generations. We seem unable to think of generations—or even waves, for that matter—in threes or fours.[5] In particular, I am interested in how the persistent two-ness of generations recalls the mother-daughter relation. As Mary Russo has argued, the problem with the "maternal symbolic" is that it "normalizes relations between women by limiting or privileging the difference configured in the mother-daughter dyad."[6] In other words, rather than recognizing the variety of "relations between women," the "matrophor" reduces these potential *relations* to a single *relation:* that of mother and daughter.

Describing second wave feminists—and second wave feminism—as a "mother" to the third wave may have been inevitable, given that the age difference between each wave's representatives is roughly the equivalent of one familial generation. Yet even within the second wave's imagined relationship to the first wave—a generational relationship that cannot so easily be represented as familial—the language of the family was already being deployed. In *The Dialectic of Sex* (1970), for example, second wave writer Shulamith Firestone refers to second wave feminists as "the rebellious daughters of [the] wasted generation" of women who came of age immediately after the 1920s,[7] while in Jo Freeman's terms, second wavers are "the granddaughters of those suffragettes."[8] While stressing the importance of affiliating with feminists of the past, ironically it was only by disconnecting themselves from other women in their immediate present that feminists in the late 1960s were able to construct their identification with feminism. The regularity with which writers from this period describe feminist generational relationships in familial terms suggests that differentiating themselves from their mothers was an intentional effect of stepping onto the stage of history. These imagined familial relationships position second wave feminists as feminism's heroic daughters gaining wisdom through their connection to the past—to their figurative "grandmothers," the suffragists. Second wave feminists emboldened themselves as political agents by identifying with one group of women at the same time that they disidentified with another. Yet their reliance on the language of the family to make this break is revealing for what it suggests about the symbolic value of "the daughter" as an agent of rebellion. In their desire to, as one commentator put it, "extricate themselves from the role that their mothers had occupied," some second wave feminists described generational relations among women generally in familial terms—a device in which "mothers" are inevitably lacking so that "daughters" may succeed where they have failed.[9]

At first glance, the metaphor of the wave seems to offer an alternative model for describing feminist generations. What has since come to be known as the first wave encompassed such a long period of history that multiple generations of women were engaged in its struggle. Within pro-suffrage families, for example, it was not uncommon for three generations—grandmothers, mothers, and daughters—to have participated in this one "wave." Yet the emergence of feminism's "third wave" seems to profoundly alter our use of the metaphor of the wave. Given the easy mapping of "mother" and "daughter" onto "second wave" and "third wave," the wave metaphor and the mother-daughter relation increasingly have become synonymous within recent feminist discourse. While initially seeming to offer a nonfamilial understanding of generations, feminism's wave metaphor has increasingly come to resemble the familial structure with its understanding of generations based on the human life cycle.[10] In fact, the third wave's launch is easily read as the start of a new feminist generation precisely because it adheres to this thirty-year model of generational birth: the second wave came of age in the 1960s, the third wave in the 1990s.

Such a view of regeneration ensures that feminists who came of age in the late 1970s to mid-1980s—and who thus fall in the middle of this thirty-year period—must necessarily go missing from feminism's narrative of its generational structure. Subsumed under the category "second wave," the inability of these women to be read as a distinct generation is compounded by the dyadic mother-daughter relation used to represent feminist generations. Unable to be understood as either "mothers" or "daughters" within feminism's imagined family structure, such feminists are often missing from recent discourse on feminism's "generations."

So far I have been speaking of generations as though they should—or even could—be understood as coherent. However, the unity or coherence of any generation or "wave" is always as much a deliberate creation as it is a representation of reality. My intention is to interrogate precisely this imagined unity of generations, exploring how and why feminists represent generations, or waves, in monolithic terms. As Joan W. Scott argues, "the emphasis on generational differences, in fact, seems to me to displace or paper over these other [ideological] differences, creating an illusory unity for feminism, taking as representative of feminism whatever discourse seems dominant at a particular moment."[11] In other words, a cohesive generational unit is itself always a fiction. A generation is an imaginary collective that both reveals truths about people of a particular age and tries to mold those people into a unified group. Even as we use the often-productive concept of generations, we must be wary of the ways in which it provides a reductive image of relationships between women, feminisms, and historical periods.

Although one is invariably placed within a generation by accident of birth, in fact, generations also constitute what Karl Mannheim has called a kind of "identity of location."[12] Generational identification is not merely the product of one's date of birth, but rather involves a deliberate identification and, in the case of feminism, a political commitment. Each generational unit must bring itself into being through an active identification with its particular historical moment. For political generations, in particular, this active identification is crucial. Within recent feminist writing, however, such a vision of political generations is rarely articulated. Rather, it is all too frequently assumed that feminists of a certain age will, by virtue of their age, *naturally* share a generational identity. Political generations, unlike familial ones, however, require intentional identification. What gets lost in the use of the "matrophor" is precisely the will behind this identification, for once feminism becomes a "mother," the generation that follows her will consist (merely) of her "daughters." When young women's identification with feminism becomes naturalized in this way, we lose sight of what is, in fact, a deliberate political act: choosing to identify with feminism.

The act of identification—both with and against other feminists—has been crucial to the formation of feminist generations. The second wave's identification with the first wave granted feminists in the 1960s a group identity: women involved in the historic struggle for women's rights. For third wave, or "younger," feminists of our current period, their simultaneous identification with and rejection of second wave feminism is what grants them an identity to call their own. What interests me here is how such intergenerational identifications—and dis-identifications—have been politically emboldening to feminists of both waves.

In using the term *disidentification,* I mean to suggest an identification *against* something. My understanding of this concept is based, in great part, on the work of Diana Fuss in *Identification Papers* (1995). Building on the work of Judith Butler, Fuss develops the following account of disidentification. "What at first may appear to be a refused identification," she writes, "might in some cases more accurately be termed a disavowed one—an identification that has already been made and denied in the unconscious." A disidentification, in other words, may actually represent "an identification that one fears to make only because one has already made it."[13] Fuss's definition of disidentification is useful in understanding how the construction of feminist generations involves an identification both with and against particular forms of feminism and feminist identities. For third wave feminists, this "refused" identification, or disidentification, is frequently with or against second wave feminism. In fact, it appears that for many younger feminists, it is only by refusing to identify themselves with earlier versions of feminism—and frequently with older feminists—that young feminists seem to be able to create a feminism of their own.

In its suggestion of a "disavowed" or "feared" identification, the concept of disidentification resonates with the mother-daughter relation, or "matrophor," used to describe feminist generational relationships. Many second wave feminists—white, middle-class women, in particular—have described how joining the women's movement enabled them to escape their mothers' fate. Ann Snitow, for example, remarks: "Some of us early [feminists] were too afraid of the lives of our mothers to recognize ourselves in them. But I remember that this emotional throwing off of the mother's life felt like the only way to begin."[14] In her description of her "fear" of "recognizing herself" in her mother's life, Snitow offers an illustrative example of disidentification, particularly as it connects to the mother-daughter relationship. As Fuss implies in her description of disidentification as "an identification that one fears to make only because one has already made it," Snitow suggests that the desire to escape her mother's life was particularly strong because she could—all too clearly—recognize herself in this life and in the limited female role it mandated. Thus, for many white, middle-class feminists of the second wave, according to Marianne Hirsch, mothers "become the targets of this process of disidentification and the primary negative models for the daughter."[15]

The noted second wave writer Phyllis Chesler provides another example of this disidentification process in her book *Letters to a Young Feminist* (1997). The volume is a collection of twenty-two letters addressed to an imaginary reader—"a young woman, possibly a young man, somewhere between the ages of eighteen and thirty-five." In her first missive to this "young feminist," Chesler writes, "when I was your age, I did not know what I needed to know in order to understand my life—anybody's life. Perhaps in writing to you, I wish to correct that, to make amends."[16] Chesler envisions that her collection of letters will pass down some of the wisdom she has gained in her over thirty years in the feminist movement. Yet as the above passage suggests, she also sees her letters as "correcting" something that was missing from her own life; she imagines that she can give "young feminists" something she never had; she assumes that "young feminists" will want to hear what she has to say.

The presumptuousness of Chesler's volume is worthy of more discussion, to be sure, and it is illustrative, if not typical, of a particular kind of generational relationship, one in which "young feminists" are expected to learn from the wisdom of their elders. As one such "young feminist," Devoney Looser, so aptly writes, "Second wave feminists—like it or not—are destined to fail in their mission to 'pass on' feminist knowledge."[17] Chesler seems unaware of the patriarchal nature of this model of authority in which it is the duty of the sage old ones to "pass on" knowledge. Nor does she seem aware that her book's very format of a series of letters written to an unnamed, unspecified, and (most important) unresponsive "young feminist" posits the exchange of knowledge not as dialogue but rather as instruction. As Jennifer Baumgardner and Amy Richards write in their critique of Chesler's collection: "You have to stop treating us like daughters. You don't have the authority to treat us like babies or acolytes who need to be molded."[18]

Putting aside my reservations about *Letters to a Young Feminist* for a moment, one of Chesler's letters may be instructive here for what it reveals about the process of disidentification. She argues that the women who initiated the second wave of U.S. feminism experienced their movement as a motherless one, driven by the power of sisterhood.

> Like the goddess Athena, newly hatched from her father Zeus's brow, we, too, wanted to experience ourselves as motherless "daughters." We were a sibling horde of "sisters" . . . we lived in a universe of same-age peers. We knew of no other way to break with the past. . . . When we stepped out onto the stage of history we did so primarily as motherless daughters/sisters/sibling rivals. Psychologically, we had committed matricide.[19]

Here, Chesler implies that in order to bring their new movement to life—to make history, to effect change—second wave feminists had to imagine themselves as motherless. They had to disconnect themselves from the generation of women who came before them; they had to reject their mothers. Chesler suggests that there is something politically empowering about "psychological matricide," allowing the now-unfettered daughters to "step out onto the stage of history" as political agents and makers of change.

In the last decade, a new generation of feminists has emerged, both claiming and being given the title of feminism's "third wave." For many of these feminists, feminism also appears like "a universe of same-age peers," to use Chesler's phrase. Naomi Wolf, a key spokesperson for this new generation, said in 1991 of the then-burgeoning third wave: "It would need to be, as all feminist waves are, peer-driven: No matter how wise a mother's advice is, we listen to our peers."[20] Like Chesler, Wolf suggests that there is a power to be found in a "peer-driven" movement. More than that, in arguing that "all feminist waves are peer-driven," she, like Chesler, defines feminism as a daughters' movement. Yet, unlike the mothers rejected by Chesler's generation, the older generation described by Wolf is feminist. In fact, the mother whose advice Wolf cautions us against taking appears to be feminism itself; Wolf thus turns second wave feminism into the "mother" of the third wave. Paradoxically, then, the very advice Chesler wishes to impart to "young feminists" will not be heard—"no matter how wise"— precisely because of this "psychological matricide," which ensures that we "listen to our peers," and not to our mothers.

As feminism itself has become a "mother" to the third wave, the various imagined familial relations with feminism have transformed. When second wave feminists committed "psychological matricide," they became "motherless daughters" who could then join forces in an orphan tribe of sisters, "a sibling horde." As Chesler describes her generation, a new political "family" replaced her former nuclear one: sisterhood replaced daughterhood. Yet for third wave feminists, feminism's "family" appears quite different. As Rene Denfeld, author of *The New Victorians: A Young Woman's Challenge to the Old Feminist Order* (1995), claims, "notions of sisterhood seldom appeal to women of my generation."[21] Because they have rejected the "sibling horde," many young feminists seem to remain within the imagined mother-daughter relationship precisely in order to give them a position from which to speak—as "daughters" rather than "sisters." In rejecting a notion of collective sisterhood, but without adopting another model—familial or otherwise—to supplant it, they remain within the mother-daughter relationship, albeit as only children to a controlling "mother" feminism. "Sisterhood is powerful" has seemingly been replaced by a new slogan: "Daughterhood is powerful."

In describing second wave feminism as a figurative mother figure to the third wave, Wolf provides an early example of what was to become a ubiquitous trope within subsequent writing on feminist generational relationships through the 1990s. The reliance on the mother-daughter trope to describe the relationship between the second and third waves may have been inevitable, given that the age difference between each wave's representatives is the norm between familial generations. The effectiveness of this metaphoric familial relationship is compounded by the fact that for many third wave writers and activists, their real mothers are, in fact, second wave feminists. (This is the case for writers Katie Roiphe, Rebecca Walker, and Naomi Wolf, for example.) Many second wave feminists, then, are literally mother figures to the third wave, even as they play this figurative role in their writing.

As can be seen in much recent third wave discourse, feminism is now a given, handed to young women at birth. As Baumgardner and Richards write in *Manifesta: Young Women, Feminism, and the Future* (2000), "for anyone born after the early 1960s, the presence of feminism in our lives is taken for granted. For our generation, feminism is like fluoride. We scarcely notice that we have it—it's simply in the water."[22] Feminism, then, for younger women, is often not something one needs to seek out or fight for. "I didn't spend much time thinking about feminism," Roiphe writes. "It was something assumed, something deep in my foundations."[23] Roiphe's description of feminism as that which is "deep in [her] foundations"—like Rebecca Walker's statement that feminism "has always been so close to home"—suggests that feminism is indeed our birthright, a kind of genetic inheritance passed down at birth.[24] One critic went as far as describing Roiphe as a woman "who could be said to have imbibed feminism with her mother's milk."[25] Whether it is consumed at a mother's breast or absorbed from the water, feminism is an essential part of who we are.

To understand feminism as something we inherit rather than create on our own has significant consequences for the ways in which we take on the cause of feminism and identify ourselves as feminists. Because women of my generation often do not experience feminism as a process—that is, as something we actively choose or help to create—we have a much more ambivalent identification with it. Even for those of us who see ourselves as aligned with second wave feminism, our sense of "owning" feminism can still feel tenuous. We own feminism in the sense that it is our birthright, yet in other ways it is not ours. It belongs to another generation, another group of women: second wave feminists. They were the ones who went through the heady experience of *creating* feminism; we just get to reap the benefits.

It may be that the third wave's "reinvention" of feminism is an attempt to gain access to the heady and wonderful feelings we were denied by accident of birth. Even the naming of a new wave seems to suggest a desire for a new beginning, one that will give women of my generation *our own* origins. Paradoxically, many of these third wave writers attempt to re-create the exhilaration and freedom of the feminist past by breaking away from feminism.

The tendency within much third wave writing toward making a clean break with the past, rather than maintaining a sense of connection, may be inevitable, given the language used to describe the third wave's relationship to feminism. Conceiving of feminism as a birthright passed from mother to daughter undoubtedly influences the third wave's understanding of, and relationship to, feminism. For some women, it may be that something inherited from one's mother is likely to be rejected, no matter what it is. For these women, it may be that a birthright (bound up as it is with one's mother) is something that can interfere with one's efforts to develop an individual sense of identity. To identify with one's mother—with her feminism, with being like her—may ultimately incite rebellion, a desire to "move away," as Denfeld calls for.[26]

In fact, I would argue that the excessive focus on individualism in the work of Denfeld, Roiphe, and Wolf is more than just a sign of their preference for liberal feminism. In their descriptions of what this individuality is in opposition to, one gets the sense that, for them, individuality is a way of resisting the group identity implied by the terms "feminists" and "women." Beyond simply disidentifying with these two identity categories, women who resist this group identity might also wish to break away from their mothers, both real and figurative. In *Fire with Fire* (1993), for example, Wolf describes power feminism (the feminism she advocates) as that which "encourages a woman to claim her individual voice rather than merging her voice in a collective identity."[27] Wolf gives us a clue as to what individuality represents for many third wave feminists: it is the antithesis of "merging her voice in a collective identity." What is to be resisted is becoming merged in collectivity. Wolf's description suggests that in order to retain—or even to establish—one's identity and autonomy, one must "unmerge": move away, break free.

In the third wave's relationship to the second wave, I believe we see signs of the difficulty that individuation poses for women, particularly in the face of the powerful mother figure of feminism. In their retaining of the identity "feminist," and in the rare moments when they champion second wave feminism, women in the third wave reveal a desire to maintain a connection to their mothers' generation. As they cannot negate the shared gender identity between mother and daughter, they are not able to extricate themselves easily from the shared identity of "feminist." In their more frequent attempts to break free radically from the feminism of the past—what Phyllis Chesler might term "psychological matricide"—their desire for autonomy and their own individual identity is revealed. They want a shared connection through feminism, but they want their freedom and individuality, too.[28]

In her description of "psychological matricide," Chesler suggests that this act is essential to freeing oneself and gaining one's individuality, particularly when the mother "remain[s] in the position of dreaded other, or objects to the daughters' emerging subjectivity."[29] As Snitow's comments suggest, however, this "matricide" might also be understood as expressing a fear—a fear of recognition, a fear of identification. As outlined by Adrienne Rich in *Of Woman Born: Motherhood as Experience and Institution* (1976), the concept of matrophobia provides a useful frame for understanding this fear. Rich writes: "Matrophobia can be seen as a womanly splitting of the self, in the desire to become purged once and for all of our mother's bondage, to become individuated and free."[30] She continues: "Matrophobia . . . is the fear not of one's mother or of motherhood but of *becoming one's mother*. . . . But where a mother is hated to the point of matrophobia there may also be a deep underlying pull toward her, a dread that if one relaxes one's guard one will identify will her completely."[31] Matrophobia shares with Fuss's notion of disidentification the fear of an identification that one does not want to make, that "one fears to make only because one has already made it." What Chesler terms "psychological matricide," then, can perhaps be viewed as one form that matrophobia takes, but it masks a fear of identification that eventually becomes disidentification. This "matricide," then, keeps at a distance the disavowed identity, in this case, the mother.

One third wave writer who seems to provide a way out of the impasse that the mother-daughter trope brings to feminist generational discourse is Rebecca Walker, the daughter of the second wave feminist Alice Walker. Interestingly, the coining of the term "third wave" is frequently attributed to Rebecca Walker, who first used it in a 1992 essay in *Ms.* Later that same year, Walker cofounded a national organization called Third Wave Foundation, which is devoted to young women's activism.[32] In "Becoming the Third Wave," an essay written in response to the Clarence Thomas hearings, Walker uses the term to emphasize both that feminism is not dead and that a new generation of feminists was beginning to mobilize itself. As Walker states: "I am not a postfeminism feminist. I am the Third Wave."[33] Her claiming of the title "feminist" allows her to maintain a link with second wave feminists while simultaneously enabling her to distance herself from the generation that immediately precedes her—her mother's generation.

In her introduction to the anthology she edited, *To Be Real: Telling the Truth and Changing the Face of Feminism* (1995), Walker writes of the need for a new generation of feminists, one that is willing to challenge many of the old orthodoxies of the previous generation. Yet while simultaneously proclaiming the need for a new wave, Walker also expresses her fear that to challenge the second wave's definition of what she calls "good feminism" is to risk rejection:

> Linked with my desire to be a good feminist was, of course, not just a desire to change my behavior to change the world, but a deep desire to be accepted, claimed, and loved by a feminist community that included my mother, godmother, aunts, and close friends. For all intents and purposes their beliefs were my own, and we mirrored each other in the most affirming of ways. As is common in familial relationships, I feared that our love was dependent upon that mirroring.[34]

Walker's representation of feminism in this passage suggests that feminism is itself part of her "familial relationships"; feminism is central to what she means by "family." This is so not only because her mother and other relatives are feminists, but also because her description of her "deep desire to be accepted" by her family is intertwined with her desire to be accepted as "a good feminist." In other words, her relationship to feminism is always bound up with her relationship to her family.

"Because feminism has always been so close to home," Walker continues, "I worried that I might also be banished from there."[35] Because she is the daughter of Alice Walker and a goddaughter of Gloria Steinem, feminism is indeed "close to home" for Walker. Walker describes a fear of being cast out on her own, yet the "there" that concludes the sentence, coming as it does after a description of feminism as "so close to home," suggests that her feared banishment would be both from feminism and from her family. In identifying with a new wave, she risks being kicked out of her home, both her literal familial home and the metaphoric home of feminism. In Walker's case, however, these two homes may be one and the same.

Published a few months prior to *To Be Real*, an article in *Essence* titled "The Two of Us" has Rebecca and Alice Walker writing about their relationship on the occasion of Rebecca's twenty-fifth birthday, in 1995. Rebecca writes of her lifelong "fear of her mother's abandonment," tracing this anxiety back to something that happened when she was eight years old.[36] She describes a childhood memory of lying in bed with her mother, notepad in hand, while Alice dictated the instructions for her own funeral: "make sure I am buried in a simple pine box. And play lots of Stevie Wonder."[37] She goes on to write:

> I am not sure if the pine-box incident marked the beginning of my fear of my mother's abandonment of me, or if it was the first time that I silenced my own apprehensions in order to soothe hers. I do know that this memory captures how I have always felt, deep down, about my relationship with my mother: If I don't do what she wants me to do, she will be gone, she will leave me. . . . The plan I devised in response was simple: I would be too perfect to leave. . . . I instinctively made myself into what I perceived to be "a good daughter," often silencing or ignoring my own needs.[38]

When read alongside the passage from *To Be Real,* there are obvious parallels between Walker's relationship to her mother and her relationship to feminism. Both involve the fear of being abandoned. Both center around the idea that to be accepted, one must behave properly, whether as "good daughter" or "good feminist." In fact, the descriptions she gives of being a "good daughter" and a "good feminist" are remarkably similar: both require following her mother's wishes.

In both texts, the daughter's fear is of rejection, of being left out on her own. Yet as Walker goes on to say in the *Essence* article, the daughter must step out on her own if she is to become her own person and develop her own identity: "While I knew that I would have to stop always being the 'good daughter' in order to reach an adulthood I could be proud of, I fretted unconsciously for a few years, taking tentative steps out of my mother's orbit."[39] Here Rebecca Walker suggests that she must give up the "good daughter" role in order to create her own sense of self; she describes the difficult yet ultimately necessary process of developing an identity separate from that as her mother's daughter.

In her introduction to *To Be Real,* Rebecca Walker describes an equally necessary break—in this case, with feminism itself. Even as she worries that to do so is to be what she calls "a bad feminist," she implores young feminists to break free from their role as dutiful daughters to the second wave.[40] In order to realize a new, "real" feminism, she argues that the third wave must face "the dreaded confrontation with some of the people who presently define and represent feminism."[41] In Walker's admittedly noteworthy case, her own mother is just such a person, someone who "presently defines and represents feminism" for millions of people.

It is not just that her mother is a major figure in U.S. feminism, but that *In Search of Our Mothers' Gardens* (1983), Alice Walker's anthology of essays, has been central to feminist scholarship on mother-daughter relationships. Dedicated to Rebecca, her only child, *In Search of Our Mothers' Gardens* addresses Walker's relationship to her own mother, a woman who expresses her curtailed creativity in the one outlet granted her: her garden. In the title essay of this collection, Walker writes: "no song or poem will bear my mother's name. Yet so many of the stories that I write, that we all write, are my mother's stories."[42] The black daughter who comes of age during the women's liberation and civil rights movements, Walker says, has opportunities never given to her mother. The daughter, then, has an obligation to tell her mother's stories that would otherwise disappear.

Second wave daughters of pre–women's liberation mothers authorized themselves to tell their mothers' stories—whether to distance themselves from their mothers' lives, as in the case of many white feminists, or to celebrate their mothers as unsung heroines, as in the example of Walker and others. Because feminism had ensured her differentiation from her mother, the daughter who came of age during the second wave could unambiguously celebrate (or denigrate) her mother. She did not risk her mother contesting her version of her life story. Her mother would never be her rival.

In Alice Walker's case, for example, she could celebrate her mother's life without anxiety that her own life would be eclipsed in the process. The title essay from *In Search of Our Mothers' Gardens* honors her mother's gift to her: "And so our mothers and grandmothers have, more often than not anonymously, handed on the creative spark, the seed of the flower that they themselves never hoped to see: or like a sealed letter they could not plainly read."[43] Alice would get to reap the benefits of the creative seed planted by her mother; she could found her feminism, and her career, on the basis of celebrating her mother. Being the good daughter could serve as her entry into feminism. Alice was able to affirm her mother while simultaneously moving beyond her. She had nothing to lose in telling her mother's story.

For her daughter, Rebecca, however, defining feminism through a celebration of her mother will never entail the same rewards. Unlike Alice's invisible and unsung mother, Rebecca's mother is decidedly present, decidedly visible. Differentiation for Rebecca will necessarily require rejecting the "good daughter" role, since playing this role would mean merely accepting her mother's feminism and thus never moving beyond it. More important, since her mother represents feminism in the "capital F" sense of the word, Rebecca's struggle for individuation will necessarily involve feminism as well. Whereas Alice could use feminism as a way to move beyond her own mother, the only way that Rebecca can remain a feminist and yet distinguish herself from her mother is to try to chart new territory *within* feminism: "*I* am the Third Wave." It is either that or rejecting feminism altogether, and, as Rebecca says in her introduction to *To Be Real,* "neither myself nor the young women and men in this book have bowed out" from a "confrontation" with feminism.[44]

All this is not to say that Rebecca Walker's description of trying to forge a new feminism for a new generation is not without risk and anxiety. She says that completing the anthology forced her "to confront that childlike and almost irrational fear of being different and therefore unacceptable."[45] Rebecca Walker's writing provides a clarifying example of the problem of feminist generations since the second wave: the daughter who grows up taking feminism for granted sees it as her own to criticize and reshape, yet she is nevertheless always in her mother's shadow. She can never truly define feminism on her own—as her mother's generation appeared to do—because both second wave feminism and her mother continue to be dominant, shaping forces in her life. The question Rebecca Walker's example raises is how one can be a second-generation feminist daughter without, merely, being a "good daughter"? How can the daughters of the second wave continue their mothers' feminism without losing themselves in it?

In hindsight, it seems consistent that it would take the daughter of a well-known second wave feminist to proclaim the emergence of a third wave. Although in many ways Katie Roiphe shares some of these daughterly features with Rebecca Walker—both have feminist writers for mothers, and both describe feminism as "something assumed, something deep in [their] foundations"—the individualistic, almost self-obsessed bent of Roiphe's feminism has never been about generating a new movement, in the collective sense of the word.[46] In this she represents one dominant strain within much of this new feminist writing: individualism and a focus on self-definition. Rebecca Walker, in contrast, seems emblematic of other dominant strains within this third wave work: the struggle to maintain generational ties while simultaneously incorporating new identities and new complexities into feminism, the struggle to have a collective movement in the face of radical individuality.

In the *Essence* piece, Rebecca Walker describes how she and her mother eventually overcame the obstacles between them, particularly her fear that if she wasn't "a good daughter," she risked abandonment.

By articulating and talking about my childhood fears and feelings with my mother over the past few years, I have tested my childhood assumptions and found that . . . both my mother and my mother's love are here to stay. . . . I am no longer the powerless child at the mercy of my mother's moods. . . . These truths will neither kill nor divide us but will instead set us free. Being honest, being real with each other helps us to be true to ourselves and more accepting of what is real in all of our relationships.[47]

In her description that "being honest, being real with each other" is what helped to heal her sometimes painful relationship to her mother, Rebecca Walker's resolution to her personal problem resonates with what she says is needed to take feminism in a new direction. In *To Be Real*, she argues that the next generation must do "the difficult work of being real . . . and telling the truth."[48] In both her relationship to her mother and her relationship to feminism, "being real" is offered as the solution. It is "being real" that might allow third wave daughters to have a relationship to their mothers' feminism and to simultaneously reshape that feminism from within. This illustration of what it means "to be real" entails contradiction: love and fear, safety and risk, intimacy and distance, connection and separation. Rather than being suppressed in an effort to win approval as a "good daughter" or "good feminist," these contradictions can be used to transform feminism.

Writing and thinking through these contradictions—creating her own feminist identity while simultaneously maintaining a connection to second wave feminism—Rebecca Walker provides a hopeful example of the potential for dialogue between future generations. Too often, feminists writing about generational relationships within feminism have written merely as "mothers" or "daughters"—wise elders or insolent rebels. Although Rebecca Walker's work as a third wave feminist does not provide an escape from writing as a daughter within feminism's "family"—nor is Walker particularly interested in trying to do so—she suggests that there is insight to be gained in thinking through the second-generation feminist daughter's position. Unlike Phyllis Chesler's often patronizing advice to younger feminists, or Katie Roiphe's often snotty disdain for feminists of all ages, what Walker adds to the discussion of contemporary feminism is the desire to both listen and be heard. As I talk to other feminists of all ages, I sense a similar longing. When all of our voices—and all of our various ways of being feminist—can be part of the dialogue, feminism will truly move forward.

NOTES

1. Katie Roiphe, *The Morning After: Sex, Fear, and Feminism on Campus* (Boston: Little, Brown, 1993). The publisher dropped "on campus" from the title for the 1994 paperback edition (Little, Brown). Subsequent page numbers in the text refer to the paperback edition.

2. Ibid., 171.

3. Rebecca Dakin Quinn, "An Open Letter to Institutional Mothers," in *Generations: Academic Feminists in Dialogue,* ed. Devoney Looser and Ann Kaplan, 174–82 (Minneapolis: University of Minnesota Press, 1997), 179.

4. Texts from the 1990s that describe feminism in generational terms include (but are certainly not limited to): "Conference Call," *differences* 2, no. 3 (1990): 52–108; Jane Gallop, Marianne Hirsch, and Nancy K. Miller, "Criticizing Feminist Criticism," in *Conflicts in Feminism,* ed. Marianne Hirsch and Evelyn Fox Keller (New York: Routledge, 1990); Renate D. Klein, "Passion and Politics in Women's Studies in the Nineties," *Women's Studies International Forum* 14, no. 3 (1991): 125–34; Nancy K. Miller, "Decades," *South Atlantic Quarterly* 91, no. 1 (Winter 1992): 65–86; Madelon Sprengnether, "Generational Differences: Reliving Mother-Daughter Conflicts," in *Changing Subjects: The Making of Feminist Literary Theory,* ed. Gayle Greene and Coppélia Kahn (New York: Routledge, 1993), 201–8; Looser and Kaplan, eds., *Generations: Academic Feminists in Dialogue* (Minneapolis: University of Minnesota Press, 1997); Anna Bondoc and Meg Daly, eds., *Letters of Intent: Women Cross the Generations to Talk About Family, Work, Sex, Love and the Future of Feminism* (New York: Simon & Schuster, 1999).

5. For more on the dyadic nature of generations, see Kathleen Woodward, "Inventing Generational Models: Psychoanalysis, Feminism, Literature," in *Figuring Age: Women, Bodies, Generations,* ed. Kathleen Woodward (Bloomington: Indiana University Press, 1999), 149–68.

6. Mary Russo, "Aging and the Scandal of Anachronism," in *Figuring Age,* ed. Kathleen Woodward, 20–33, 24.

7. Shulamith Firestone, *The Dialectic of Sex: The Case for Feminist Revolution* (New York: Bantam Books, 1970), 30.

8. Jo Freeman, "The New Feminists," *Nation* 24 (February 1969): 241–44.

9. Barbara Epstein, "Ambivalence about Feminism," in *The Feminist Memoir*

Project: Voices from Women's Liberation, ed. Rachel Blau DuPlessis and Ann Snitow, 124–48 (New York: Three Rivers Press, 1998), 128.

10. Karl Mannheim, "The Problem of Generations," in *Essays on the Sociology of Knowledge,* ed. Paul Kecskemeti, 276–320 (New York: Oxford University Press, 1952). In his influential work on generations, sociologist Karl Mannheim argues that a new generation appears roughly every thirty years. While his understanding of generations is founded on their emergence within society, culture, and politics, he argues that "the sociological phenomenon of generations is ultimately based on the biological rhythm of birth and death" (278, 290). Political or cultural generations, then, in some ways imitate the familial generational model with its regeneration around the thirty-year point.

11. Joan Scott et al., "Conference Call," *differences* 2, no. 3 (1990): 52–108, 83.

12. Mannheim, "The Problem of Generations," 292. A book that makes feminism a "mother" in just such a way is Rose L. Glickman, *Daughters of Feminists* (New York: St. Martin's Press, 1993). See also Christina Looper Baker and Christina Baker Kline, eds., *The Conversation Begins: Mothers and Daughters Talk about Living Feminism* (New York: Bantam Books, 1996); Louise D'Arcens, "Mothers, Daughters, Sisters," in *Talking Up: Young Women's Take on Feminism,* ed. Rosamund Else-Mitchell and Naomi Flutter, 103–16 (North Melbourne, Australia: Spinifex Press, 1998); Andrea O'Reilly and Sharon Abbey, eds., *Mothers and Daughters: Connection, Empowerment, and Transformation* (Lanham, Md.: Rowman & Littlefield, 2000).

13. Diana Fuss, *Identification Papers* (New York: Routledge, 1995), 7.

14. Ann Snitow, "A Gender Diary," in *Conflicts in Feminism,* ed. Marianne Hirsch and Evelyn Fox Keller, 9–43 (New York: Routledge, 1990), 32. The next line of this passage is "Black women whose ties to their mothers were more often a mutual struggle for survival rarely shared this particular emotion." For more on how feminism allowed second wave feminists to escape their mothers' fate, see many of the essays in *The Feminist Memoir Project,* ed. Rachel Blau DuPlessis and Ann Snitow.

15. Snitow, "A Gender Diary," 11.

16. Phyllis Chesler, *Letters to a Young Feminist* (New York: Four Walls Eight Windows, 1997), 1.

17. Devoney Looser, "Introduction 2: Gen X Feminists? Youthism, Careerism, and the Third Wave," in *Generations,* ed. Devoney Looser and Ann Kaplan, 31–54, 34.

18. Jennifer Baumgardner and Amy Richards, *Manifesta: Young Women, Feminism, and the Future* (New York: Farrar, Straus and Giroux, 2000), 233.

19. Chesler, *Letters to a Young Feminist,* 255.

20. Naomi Wolf, *The Beauty Myth: How Images of Beauty Are Used against Women* (New York: William Morrow, 1991), 282.

21. Rene Denfeld, *The New Victorians: A Young Woman's Challenge to the Old Feminist Order* (New York: Warner Books, 1995), 263.

22. Baumgardner and Richards, *Manifesta,* 17.

23. Roiphe, *The Morning After,* 4.

24. Rebecca Walker, "Being Real: An Introduction," in *To Be Real: Telling the Truth and Changing the Face of Feminism,* ed. Rebecca Walker, xxix–xl (New York: Anchor Books, 1995), xxx–xxxi.

25. Carol Iannone, "Sex and the Feminists," review of *The Morning After,* by Katie Roiphe, *Commentary* 96, no. 3 (September 1993): 51–54, 51.

26. Rene Denfeld, "Feminism 2000: What Does It Really Mean (to You)?" *Sassy* 9 (May 1996): 60.

27. Naomi Wolf, *Fire with Fire: The New Female Power and How It Will Change the 21st Century* (New York: Random House, 1993), 137.

28. While the writers who are my focus here clearly see feminism as limiting their individuality—feminism as Big Sister or, more accurately, Big Mother—there are other third wave writers who offer a different understanding of what feminism has to offer them. For these writers (such as several featured in Barbara Findlen, ed., *Listen Up: Voices from the Next Feminist Generation* [Seattle: Seal Press, 1997], and *To Be Real: Telling the Truth and Changing the Face of Feminism*), feminism is described as something that enables them to *acquire* individuality. In other words, feminism is depicted as an empowering force in their lives, allowing them to question society's rules about how they should be in the world. I would argue that this identification with feminism is much more like the descriptions offered by early second wave writers who describe the process of becoming feminists in positive terms. Interestingly, however, even this more positive third wave understanding of what feminism has to offer seems inextricably linked to the mother-daughter relation. See, for example, Sharon Lennon's "What Is Mine," in which she writes: "My mother, who had allowed and encouraged me to be who I was through most of my youth, viewed [my interest in feminism] as a major point of contention between us. . . . In my quest for individuality through feminism, there were a lot of screaming matches between my mother and me." Lennon, "What Is Mine," in *Listen Up,* 127.

29. Marianne Hirsch, *The Mother/Daughter Plot: Narrative, Psychoanalysis, Feminism* (Bloomington: Indiana University Press, 1989), 136.

30. Adrienne Rich, *Of Woman Born: Motherhood as Experience and Institution* (New York: W. W. Norton, 1976), 236.

31. Ibid., 225.

32. Rebecca Walker, "Becoming the Third Wave," *Ms.* (January/February 1992): 39–41, and "Doing the Third Wave," *Ms.* (September/October 1992): 87. According to information found on their Web site (http://www.feminist.com/3dwave. htm) (April 30, 2002), the organization cofounded by Walker, the Third Wave Foundation, is "the only organization created by and for young women." The Third Wave Foundation's first major event was to register voters in poor

communities of color before the 1992 elections; the group named this event "Freedom Ride 1992," a name that in itself pays homage to the civil rights movement of the 1960s. See also Meri Nana-Ama Danquah, "Keeping the Third Wave Afloat," *Los Angeles Times,* December 6, 1995, E1.

33. Walker, "Becoming the Third Wave," 41.

34. Walker, *To Be Real,* xxxi.

35. Ibid.

36. Alice Walker and Rebecca Walker, "The Two of Us," *Essence* (May 1995): 172, 173. See also Rebecca Walker's essay "Lusting for Freedom," in *Listen Up,* and her memoir *Black, White, and Jewish: Autobiography of a Shifting Self* (New York: Riverhead Books, 2001), both of which describe Walker's loneliness and isolation as a child.

37. Walker and Walker, "The Two of Us," 173.

38. Ibid., 254.

39. Ibid.

40. Walker, "To Be Real," xxxix.

41. Ibid., xxxiv.

42. Alice Walker, *In Search of Our Mothers' Gardens* (New York: Harcourt Brace Jovanovich, 1983), 240.

43. Ibid.

44. Rebecca Walker, "To Be Real," xxxiv.

45. Ibid., xxxviii.

46. Roiphe, *The Morning After,* 4.

47. Walker and Walker, "The Two of Us," 256.

48. Walker, "To Be Real," xxxiv.

GWENDOLYN D. POUGH

Do the Ladies Run This . . . ?: Some Thoughts on Hip-Hop Feminism

——I was nine years old when the first rap record hit the airwaves. "Rapper's Delight" came out in 1979, and I memorized every line. I wanted to be an MC even then. I started making up my own rhymes: "I'm the K-I-Double-TT-Y. I'm the fresh female that ya can't deny!" I used to write rhymes and listen to rap music every day. I dragged around a miniature boom box long before LL could not live without his radio. I guess you could say rap music and hip-hop culture were my first loves. I still love the music and the culture, but I have to admit that my relationship to them has become somewhat troubled. The music that I grew up on has changed, and so have I. The music and the culture used to validate me in real and significant ways. I had no problem being a certified B-girl, with my Kangol hat, pink Lee jeans, and pastel pink Nikes (or pink construction boots, depending on the weather). I had LL Cool J crooning that he needed an "Around the Way Girl" and the Boogie Boys calling me a "Fly Girl." Hip-hop culture had me feeling like we were going to be tight forever. And then Apache started rapping about needing a "Gangsta Bitch," and rap lyrics began to be laced with more bitches, hos, stunts, skeezers, and hoochies than I could count. I did not want to go from B-girl to scantily clad video ho, so I chilled. But I still loved hip-hop; I just needed to find a way to make the culture mesh with the feminist politics I had started to develop when I took my first women's studies class as an undergraduate. Luckily, I'm not alone. There are several young black women writing about their need to combine hip-hop with feminism. They have begun to create a tremendous body of work and begun to think about what it means to be a hip-hop feminist.

There is indeed a large contingent of young black feminists who are grappling with the tenuous relationship between black women, hip-hop culture, rap music, and feminism. At the May 1999 Power Moves Hip Hop Conference at U.C.L.A., during the pre-conference in which graduate students presented their works-in-progress on hip-hop, several young black women—including myself—spoke passionately about issues of gender and hip-hop culture. We bespoke the need for a feminist critique and tried to continue the lineage of black feminist/womanist dialogue in the black community. Hip-hop feminists are trying to find ways both to be true to themselves and to listen to the music and participate in the culture that stimulates the very depth of their souls. And they are trying to be true to themselves while building on the legacies and the promises left by the black women who went before them. These black women grew up knowing freedom in ways that just a generation before were not possible. In spite of the disbelief, discrediting, dismissals, and straight-up disses these women encounter, they have begun to write about their lives in relation to hip-hop culture and the feminist movement in real and honest ways.

I will attempt to theorize and document hip-hop feminism by examining the work of black women involved in hip-hop culture for common themes and a continued legacy of black feminism. I take the stance that hip-hop is a cultural phenomenon that extends beyond rap music. Hip-hop has been defined by many as a way of life that encompasses everything from dress to speech. Hip-hop as a culture originally included graffiti writing, dee-jaying, break dancing, and rap music. It has recently expanded to include genres such as film, spoken word, autobiography, literature, journalism, and activism. I examine several of these genres in order to document a potentially activist agenda for hip-hop that is tied to feminism. I explore the hip-hop feminism that has come from the music of both women rappers and hip-hop soul artists, the essays and poetry of third wave hip-hop feminists, and music video images and representations. The images and representations are sending harmful messages about materialism and can be linked to the growing black female incarceration rate. Feminism can give young women and men of today the critical interpretive tools they need to understand the world they live in—the tools of black feminism with a hip-hop slant. Some of these tools can be found in the work of third wave black feminist writers, such as Eisa Davis, Eisa Nefertari Ulen, dream hampton, Joan Morgan, Tara Roberts, and Angela Ards, who are expanding black feminist theory and black women's intellectual traditions in fascinating ways. What started out as a few young black feminist women who loved hip-hop and who tried to mesh that love with their feminist/womanist consciousness is now a rich body of articles, essays, poetry, and creative nonfiction.

Hip-hop as a youth movement grew out of the rubble of a dying Black Power movement. Just as the Black Power movement was taking its last breath in the mid-1970s in America's inner cities, hip-hop was being created by black and Latino youth in the South Bronx. It's important to note hip-hop's proximity to the Black Power movement, because out of nationalist movements by people of color against oppression came not only hip-hop but also what we currently call woman-of-color feminisms. For example, many of the women who pioneered black feminist thought, activism, and art as we now know them started out in the Black Power movement and Black Arts movement of the 1970s. Many of them, while working to end oppression for all black people by forming alliances in groups such as the Black Panther Party, Student Nonviolent Coordinating Committee (SNCC), and the Black Liberation Army, found that the movement they thought would free them all was centered on freeing black masculinity and establishing a black patriarchy. These women began to address issues of gender and found that the women's movement going on at that time was too focused on the issues of white, middle-class women. Thus, the title of Gloria T. Hull, Patricia Bell Scott, and Barbara Smith's anthology, *All the Women Are White, All the Blacks Are Men, But Some of Us Are Brave* (1981), becomes a fitting description of the ways in which black women were marginalized in both race-based movements and gender-based movements. So they began to shape and build a feminism to fight for their needs. And the feminism they created is the feminism that hip-hop feminism grows out of. The hip-hop generation sees a link between itself and the Black Power movement. Young black feminists of today also see themselves in relation to their black feminist foremothers.

The one thing that most third wave feminists grappling with their love for hip-hop have in common is that they were all born in the early to mid-1970s and they all came of age in a post–Black Power era. This is not to say that they came of age without the outlet for black consciousness that the Black Power movement encouraged. Although they did not have the Black Panther Party and Huey P. Newton to listen to, they did have the political rap stylings of groups such as Public Enemy, X-Clan, KRS-One, Paris, and Conscious Daughters. These rappers produced rap songs with political themes of unity, racial uplift, self-definition, self-determination, and black diasporic connections. There were also mass movements to end "black on black" crime and violence with projects such as "Stop the Violence: Self Destruction" and "We're All in the Same Gang." These kinds of projects used rap as a vehicle to stop black youth from killing one another and worked to bring various rappers together for a similar cause. Thus, the connections to the ideals of Black Power remained in some form. These connections are also evident in the third wave black feminists' openly stated appreciation for the Black Power movement and the second wave black feminists who went before them.

The most striking visual representation of this connection can be seen in Queen Latifah's video for "Ladies First." At the start of the video, we see image after image of black women leaders, from Sojourner Truth to Angela Davis. Later in the video, we view a scene in which Queen Latifah is dressed as a high-ranking military commander poised over a map of the world with little white men all over it. She knocks the little white men off the map and replaces them with little Black Power fists. Queen Latifah's video visually represents the connection between this generation's black women and the black female leaders of the past. Also, by replacing the white men with Black Power fists, she is showing the connection between this generation and the Black Power movement. The two scenes from the video highlight the indebtedness that hip-hop feminists feel both to the Black Power movement and to the black feminist leaders of the past.

Although Queen Latifah probably would not label herself a hip-hop feminist—or a womanist, for that matter—she has been claimed by several hip-hop feminists as the strong black female presence in hip-hop culture that inspired their own black feminist consciousness.

Through her presence and her lyrics, Queen Latifah becomes not only a model for showing the legacy of Black Power in the hip-hop generation but also a model for contemporary black womanhood that hip-hop feminists aspire to be. And songs such as "Ladies First" and "U.N.I.T.Y."—because of their pro-woman messages—give voice to the issues that contemporary black women find most pressing. For example, in "U.N.I.T.Y." she addresses the word "bitch," domestic violence, and gang violence. In "Ladies First," she addresses the need for women to be respected in society. By documenting or demonstrating this connection, Queen Latifah enacts hip-hop feminism.

Another example of hip-hop feminism—and a visual representation of the connection between third wave hip-hop feminism and black feminism—is Erykah Badu's remix of Ntozake Shange's *For Colored Girls Who Have Considered Suicide/When the Rainbow is Enuf* (1975). In her video for her hit single "Bag Lady," Badu and six other women dress as the ladies in brown, yellow, purple, red, green, blue, and orange. Shange's 1970s response to the sexism of the Black Arts movement encouraged black women to find God in themselves and love "her fiercely" in an attempt to circumvent the negative responses that most black women internalize when faced with the multiple oppressions they encounter. Similarly, Badu's "Bag Lady" encourages twenty-first-century black women to let go of the baggage that weighs them down.[1] Badu's lyrics serve as a twenty-first-century remix of Shange's choreopoem. She tells women to hold on to themselves and hold on to love. Implicit in Badu's lyrics is the message that self-love will make life better. In addition, the messages of self-redemption, self-love, and fighting against the oppressive systems and circumstances that inhibit self-love are present in Badu's work, as they are in Shange's.

The hip-hop feminist writer Eisa Davis offers another example of third wave hip-hop feminism's indebtedness to the black women who grappled with these issues before them. Her poem "if we've gotta live underground and everybody's got cancer/ will poetry be enuf?: A Letter to Ntozake Shange" essentially questions how useful the tools that the women of Shange's generation fought with are for this generation. The poem lists the ways in which the problems that this generation faces are quite different. She notes that there is now "high definition tragedy." And she asks the questions, "if we've gone and burnt up everything in the sky/if there's nothing else to eat but landfill stroganoff/if we've gotta live underground and everybody's got cancer/ will poetry be enuf?"[2] The poem ends on the hopeful note that "poetry just might be enuf." Clearly, it is a different kind of poetry: it is poetry made to question and fight today's problems. Some of the issues are the same. But most have been amplified, and still others are totally new.

Hip-hop feminists need to create a feminism that fits their lives. Shange's generation did not have to contend with the reality of AIDS. Although the heroin epidemic was horrific, it in no way matched the trauma inflicted by crack in African American communities. Add to those differences the impact of an urban environmental poisoning that amounts to genocide and a global capitalist structure that leads to fewer and fewer jobs just as welfare is being reformed, and we can see how the issues in the poetry would need to change. And although black feminism offers useful analytical tools, I contend that these, too, have had to change. Black feminism has had to take on a hip-hop slant in order to reach the generation that needs to utilize it.

The need for a different kind of poetry leads to rap music and hip-hop culture. Countless academics have traced rap's connection to African American oral and musical traditions. Rap is the most recent addition to a culture that is steeped in history and talent. Rap has been categorized in a variety of genres, from music to storytelling to poetry. Rap is the contemporary art form that gives voice to a part of the population that would not have a voice otherwise. It is my belief that rap is the poetry that just might be "enuf." I think that rap has political potential—potential that should be honed by the feminist movement in general and by third wave hip-hop feminists in particular.

This might sound crazy, given rap music's track record of sexism and misogyny. Bitches, hos, and scantily clad women hardly make for a strong feminist agenda. Or do they? The fact is that rap music and hip-hop culture have brought issues concerning women into the public space. Rap videos that subjugate women have become fodder for much feminist activism and academic discussion and debate. We use them now to talk about what is wrong in the entertainment industry and the world. What would happen if we pushed these kinds of discussions and debates further? What would happen if we took the advice of cultural critics such as bell hooks and Cheo Coker and expanded our critique of rap music? Both hooks and Coker note that rap music does not occur in a vacuum and that sexism and misogyny are as American as apple pie. The only difference between rappers and the "suits" in the boardroom is race and socioeconomic status. While rap does give us some startling and, indeed, ugly representations of female objectification, rap is not responsible for other travesties, such as the feminization of poverty, welfare reform, and the glass ceiling, to name only a few.

I believe we can use rap music as teaching moments. Rap can help us to enact a public pedagogy that can be used not only to bring women's issues into the public sphere but also to mobilize action. One of the main things an MC does is to move the crowd. What would happen if we combined hip-hop and feminism to work toward that political end? What would happen if we had feminist MCs moving millions toward a critique of gender that motivated them toward change? We have not had any female MCs with this kind of feminist agenda. Although rappers like Queen Latifah, Salt-N-Pepa, and Yo-Yo have come close, they will not openly claim a feminist agenda or even call themselves feminists. What would happen if we could harness the power that rap music has to make people dance and make them work toward change in women's lives? The current power of hip-hop works on a variety of levels. Not only does it intersect borders of race, class, and gender in terms of its listening audience, but the messages that the music brings to its multiple listeners can influence them. Also, the power of hip-hop is worldwide; it is causing young men and women all over the world to learn English—more specifically the black English vernacular—just so that they can follow rap lyrics. When one adds to this equation the fact that an enormous number of white youths in America are buying the music and identifying with the culture, the power of rap music and hip-hop culture becomes clear.

Finding a way to combine feminism and hip-hop in politically meaningful ways is one of the premier goals of hip-hop feminism. This is not easy work. The negative lyrics of most contemporary hip-hop are enough to make even the most die-hard hip-hop feminist contemplate giving up the music and the culture. Eisa Nefertari Ulen and Tara Roberts's creative journalistic article titled "Sisters Spin the Talk on Rap: Can the Music Be Saved?" and dream hampton's essay "Free the Girls, or Why I Really Don't Believe There's Much of a Future for Hip Hop,

Let Alone Women in Hip Hop" both speak volumes about the frustration of being a hip-hop head who is also a feminist. For example, Ulen and Roberts write, "If you are a woman in hip hop, you are either a hard bitch who will kill for her man, or you're a fly bitch who can sex up her man, or you're a fucked-up lesbian. There is no fullness of womanhood."[3] Personally, I have to admit that lately I listen to some of the music on the radio and wonder how much longer I will be a hip-hop head. I contemplate how we went from the somewhat sexy compliment à la Sir Mix A Lot "Baby Got Back" to the harsh, sexually harassing rants of Mystikal: "Shake ya ass . . . bend over, show me what ya working with."

It would be easier if I didn't listen to the lyrics. But that's what I love most about rap: its clever wordplay, its witty rhymes, the way it puts words and phrases together; all of this makes me smile. In fact, I could listen to rap without all the fancy tracks and samples. Just give me that old "boom bap" and I'm fine. Lately, however, it's just not as much fun. I'm becoming more and more torn by what I hear in the music and what I believe as a feminist; I want to give up.

I want to give up until I watch the negative images and I realize all the work that needs to be done in order to give my younger sisters and brothers the tools to see these images, too. For example, when I saw Ja Rule's new video, "Down A** B**ch," I was ready to throw in the towel. Here was another video all about how women should stand by their men and be down for whatever. His rough voice crooned, "Every thug needs a lady. Would you ride for me? Would you die for me?" In the video, Ja Rule and female rapper Charlie Baltimore remix the Bonnie and Clyde theme with hip-hop flavor. They rob an unidentified rich person's mansion, taking a safe full of diamonds. However, before they can make off with the jewels, the alarm sounds and they try to escape. Charlie Baltimore is caught. The cops really want Ja Rule, but she, being a "good bitch" and a "down ass chick," does not snitch. Instead, she does the time. We next see her in her prison-issue orange jumpsuit. She goes from being scared to running the other women prisoners: she becomes a survivor in jail. We see her pushing around the very women who pushed her around when she first entered the prison. When she is released, presumably years later, Ja Rule picks her up, and all is well. The troubling message that this video sends to young women, specifically to young black women, that it is okay to commit crimes for their men, is the reason I continue to grapple with my love for hip-hop and my black feminist identity. Even if they spend time in jail, this video says, it is okay, because it will pay off in the end, when their man will take them away in a luxury car and fly them off to a remote island to lavish them with tropical drinks and beautiful clothes. The video tells young women that the only way to obtain material possessions is to let some man use them to commit crimes and then depend on him for their reward.

The fastest growing prison population statistically in this country is black women. They are going to jail largely because of their relationships with men who are involved with criminal activities. They are going to prison for things such as smuggling drugs. They are women like the recently pardoned Kemba Smith, who simply fell in love with the wrong man and was too afraid to leave. Kemba Smith recounts, "At age 24, without so much as a parking ticket on my record, I was sentenced to more than 24 years in prison—without parole. Technically, I was convicted of conspiracy to distribute crack cocaine, but I contend that I went to jail for dating a drug dealer."[4] She was finally pardoned as a last-minute act of President Clinton, but she still feels that justice was not served. She notes, "You'd think I'd have been doing cartwheels when I was released. Truthfully, my feelings were in conflict. It was tough to leave behind the incredible women I met in prison—especially since many of them were victims of the same laws that put me away."[5]

dream hampton writes of another woman, who, like Kemba Smith and the others still in jail, did time for drug-related crimes. This woman "used to be so fly, the first girl in Detroit with her own Benz. Candy-apple red and convertible, with customized plates that spelled CASH. She bought red boots to match. . . . She liked to make the trip back then. She could drive all the way without stopping (he never did like to drive long distances), but he'd keep her awake with promises about the next forty years."[6] This woman, like Charlie Baltimore in Ja Rule's video, did not snitch on her man. hampton explains: "She's proud of the fact that she never snitched. Doesn't seem suspicious that he served 18 months, went home, and has forgotten to put money on her books for the past ten years."[7] The jailed woman brags that "little girls like [Lil'] Kim are rhyming about her life."[8] However, the sad fact is that Lil' Kim, Foxy Brown, and others are rapping about their own lives. The growth in the number of black females in prison has been exponential because of stories like these.

Ja Rule's message to women about being a "down ass chick" would not be so bad if it was the only one. But the message is everywhere, and it's not coming just from men. Women rappers such as Lil' Kim and Foxy Brown also rap about the illegal things they would do for their men. And even though Alicia Keys's video for the hit single "Fallin'" somewhat flips the script on this message by having the free woman visit the male inmate in prison, the message of the song is eerily similar to those of the above-mentioned songs. Keys sings, "I keep on fallin' in and out of love with you. I'll never love no one the way I love you."[9] Her message echoes that of Ja Rule because it asks young women to live through their men: we see a field full of women—mostly black and Latina—singing the lyrics in the video.

Yet, instead of falling in and out of love with these men, young black women need to love themselves. They need to love themselves enough to recognize that no love is worth going to jail for. This is a job for hip-hop feminism. Hip-hop feminism, as evidenced by Badu's remix of Shange's choreopoem, can give young women the tools they need to realize this kind of self-love. That particular message of self-love, so central to black feminism, needs to be remixed for this generation. Feminism in general, black feminism in particular, and third wave hip-hop feminism most definitely need to be held accountable. They should give young women the tools necessary to critique the messages they are getting—messages that end in jail or worse.

In the novel *The Coldest Winter Ever* (2000), the hip-hop activist and former rapper Sister Souljah chronicles the life of Winter, a young black girl growing up in Brooklyn. Winter is the daughter of a big-time drug dealer, and as such, she has become accustomed to a high standard of living that requires designer labels, fancy jewels, and anything else with an expensive price tag. Her world comes to an end when her father is arrested and she finds that she is alone in the world with a need for material things that she cannot fulfill. She goes through a downward spiral and ends up dating drug dealers like her father in order to continue living in the manner to which she has become accustomed. She ends up in jail when she is caught in her boyfriend's car with his drugs. The novel gives fictional form to the very real growing incarceration rate of black women in America. It is an incarceration rate that can equally be attributed to extremely harsh drug laws and relationships with men who sell drugs. The novel also shows a young black woman who is highly influenced by the contemporary materialistic trend in rap music and hip-hop culture. This is the only picture of a "good life" the main character has. Winter does not have anyone giving her a critique of materialism, sexism, or gender identity construction. Winter represents many young women who are getting the same messages from hip-hop culture without a critique and without being given critical interpretive tools.

Joan Morgan, the author of *When Chickenheads Come Home to Roost: My Life as a Hip-Hop Feminist* (1999), explores the hypersexualized bad girl images of rappers Lil' Kim and Foxy Brown in an article written for *Essence* magazine. Morgan notes, "The punanny-for-sale materialism that dominates Lil' Kim's album, for example, is rampant among some young females. Sex has become the bartering chip many women use to gain protection, wealth and power. In the Black community, where women are given little access to all of the above, 'trickin' can become a way of leveling the playing field."[10] She notes that these rhyming bad girls are the result of a community "busy rescuing The Endangered Black Man"—a community where few are "willing to believe that black girls growing up in the same violent, materialistic, and economically and spiritually impoverished environments were likely to suffer their own pathologies."[11] She notes that "black women are dying in disproportionate numbers of AIDS, cancer and drug abuse, and the exploding female prison population and teenage pregnancy rate have become near cultural norm."[12] Morgan does not find it surprising that young black women, like their young black male counterparts, are trying to get paid by glamorizing the harsh realities that they face. I maintain that we need to create a space in which young women can critique these harsh realities and rap music's glamorization of them. We need to encourage dialogue between the older generation and the new, and also between men and women. I believe that we can use hip-hop culture to begin making that space.

Hip-hop feminist thought offers varying views and critiques of rap music, specifically rap music performed by black men rappers, and discusses the need for a steady, unflinching critique of the music and the culture. Joan Morgan notes, "I needed a feminism that would allow us to continue loving ourselves and the brothers who hurt us without letting race loyalty buy us early tombstones."[13] I would add that we also need a feminism that would encourage a self-love that would prohibit the internalization of negative self-images—the kinds of self-images that are fed by rampant materialism and usually end in prison jumpsuits. We are losing a whole generation of young women of color; feminism has to at least attempt to address that problem. I see the salvation of young women of color as one of the crucial goals for hip-hop feminism. Giving them the tools they need to critique, and indeed to survive, the negative images is the only way that the ladies can truly run this—*this* being our very lives. Otherwise, the messages will run and ruin us.

NOTES

1. Erykah Badu, "Bag Lady." From *Mama's Gun* (UNI/Motown, 2000).
2. Eisa Davis, "if we've gotta live underground and everybody's got cancer/will poetry be enuf?: A Letter to Ntozake Shange," in *Step into a World: A Global Anthology of the New Black Literature*, ed. Kevin Powell, 380–84 (New York: John Wiley & Sons, 2000), 383.
3. Tara Roberts and Eisa Nefertari Ulen, "Sisters Spin Talk on Hip Hop: Can the Music Be Saved?" *Ms.* (February/March 2000): 70–74, 70.
4. Kemba Smith, as told to Stephanie Booth, "Pardon Me," *Honey* (September 2001): 86.
5. Ibid.
6. dream hampton, "Free the Girls; or, Why I Really Don't Believe There's Much of a Future for Hip Hop, Let Alone Women in Hip Hop," in *Vibe Hip Hop Divas*, ed. Rob Kenner, 1–3 (New York: Three Rivers Press, 2001), 2.
7. Ibid.
8. Ibid.
9. Alicia Keys, "Fallin'." From *Songs in A Minor* (BMG/J Records, 2001).
10. Joan Morgan, *When Chickenheads Come Home to Roost: My Life as a Hip-Hop Feminist* (New York: Simon & Schuster, 1999), 77.
11. Ibid.
12. Ibid.
13. Ibid., 36.

The Transfeminist Manifesto

The latter half of the twentieth century witnessed an unprecedented broadening of the American feminist movement as a result of the participation of diverse groups of women. When a group of women who had previously been marginalized within the mainstream of the feminist movement broke their silence, demanding their rightful place within it, they were first accused of fragmenting feminism with trivial matters, and then were eventually accepted and welcomed as a valuable part of feminist thought. We have become increasingly aware that diversity is our strength, not our weakness. No temporary fragmentation or polarization is too severe to nullify the ultimate virtues of inclusive coalition politics.

Every time a group of women previously silenced begins to speak out, other feminists are challenged to rethink their idea of who they represent and what they stand for. Although this process sometimes leads to a painful realization of our own biases and internalized oppressions as feminists, it eventually benefits the movement by widening our perspectives and constituencies. It is with this understanding that we declare that the time has come for trans women to openly take part in feminist revolution, further expanding the scope of the movement.

"Trans" is often used as an inclusive term encompassing a wide range of gender norm violations that involve some discontinuity between the sex a person is assigned at birth and her or his gender identity and expression. For the purpose of this manifesto, however, the phrase "trans women" is used to refer to those individuals who identify, present, or live more or less as women despite their sex assignment at birth. "Trans men," likewise, is used to describe those who identify, present, or live as men despite the fact that they were perceived otherwise at birth. While this operational definition leaves out many trans people who do not conform to the male/female dichotomy or those who are transgendered in other ways, it is our hope that they will recognize enough similarities between issues that we all face and find our analysis somewhat useful in their own struggles as well.

Transfeminism is primarily a movement by and for trans women who view their liberation to be intrinsically linked to the liberation of all women and beyond. It is also open to other queers, intersex people, trans men, non–trans women, non–trans men, and others who are sympathetic to the needs of trans women and consider their alliance with trans women to be essential for their own liberation. Historically, trans men have made a greater contribution to feminism than have trans women. We believe that it is imperative that more trans women start participating in the feminist movement alongside others for our liberation.

Transfeminism is not about taking over existing feminist institutions. Instead, it extends and advances feminism as a whole through our own liberation and coalition work with all others. It stands up for trans and non-trans women alike and asks non-trans women to stand up for trans women in return. Transfeminism embodies feminist coalition politics in which women from different backgrounds stand up for each other, because if we do not stand for each other, nobody will.

PRIMARY PRINCIPLES

The primary principles of transfeminism are simple. First, it is our belief that each individual has the right to define her or his own identity and to expect society to respect it. This also includes the right to express our gender without fear of discrimination or violence. Second, we hold that we have the sole right to make decisions regarding our own bodies, and that no political, medical, or religious authority shall violate the integrity of our bodies against our will or impede our decisions regarding what we do with them.

However, no one is completely free from the existing social and cultural dynamics of the institutionalized gender system. When we make any decisions regarding our gender identity or expression, we cannot escape the fact that we do so in the context of the patriarchal binary gender system. Trans women in particular are encouraged and sometimes required to adopt the traditional definition of femininity in order to be accepted and legitimized by the medical community, which has appointed itself as the arbiter of who is genuinely "woman" and who is not. Trans women often find themselves having to "prove" their womanhood by exhibiting gender stereotypes in order to receive hormonal and surgical interventions and to be acknowledged as women. This practice is oppressive to trans and non–trans women alike, as it denies the uniqueness of each woman.

Transfeminism holds that nobody shall be coerced into or out of personal decisions regarding her or his gender identity or expression in order to be a "real" woman or a "real" man. We also believe that nobody should be coerced into or out of these personal decisions in order to qualify as a "real" feminist.

As trans women, we have learned that our safety is often dependent on how well we can "pass" as "normal" women; as transfeminists, we find ourselves constantly having to negotiate our need for safety and comfort against our feminist principles. Transfeminism challenges women, including trans women, to examine how we all internalize heterosexist and patriarchal gender mandates and what global implications our actions entail; at the same time, we make it clear that it is not the responsibility of a feminist to rid herself of every resemblance to the patriarchal definition of femininity. Women should not be accused of reinforcing gender stereotypes for making personal decisions, even if these decisions appear to comply with certain gender roles. Such a purity test is disempowering to women because it denies our agency, and it will only alienate a majority of women, trans or not, from taking part in the feminist movement.

Transfeminism believes in the notion that there are as many ways of being a woman as there are women and that we should be free to make our own decisions without guilt. To this end, transfeminism confronts social and political institutions that inhibit or narrow our individual choices, while refusing to blame individual women for making personal decisions. It is unnecessary—and, in fact, *oppressive*—to require women to abandon their freedom to make personal choices in order to be considered true feminists, for this view will only replace the rigid patriarchal construct of ideal femininity with a slightly modified feminist version that is just as rigid. Transfeminism believes in fostering an environment in which women's individual choices are honored, and in scrutinizing and challenging institutions that limit the range of choices available to them.

THE QUESTION OF MALE PRIVILEGE

Some feminists, particularly radical lesbian feminists, have accused trans women and men of benefiting from male privilege. Male-to-female transsexuals, they argue, are socialized as boys and are thus given male privilege; female-to-male transsexuals, on the other hand, are characterized as traitors who have abandoned their sisters in a pathetic attempt to acquire male privilege. Transfeminism must respond to this criticism because it has been used to justify discrimination against trans women and men within some feminist circles.

When confronted with such an argument, a natural initial response of trans women is to deny ever having had any male privilege whatsoever in their lives. It is easy to see how they would come to believe that being born male was more of a burden than a privilege: many of them despised having male bodies and being treated as boys as they grew up. They recall how uncomfortable it felt to be pressured to act tough and manly. Many trans women have experienced bullying and ridicule by other boys because they did not act appropriately as boys. They were made to feel ashamed and frequently suffered from depression. Even as adults, they live with a constant fear of exposure, which would jeopardize their employment, family relationships, friendships, and safety.

However, as transfeminists, we must resist such a simplistic reaction. While it is true that male privilege affects some men far more than others, it is hard to imagine that trans women born as males never benefited from it. Most trans women have "passed" as men (albeit as "sissy" ones) at some point in their lives, and were thus given preferential treatment in education and employment, for example, whether or not they enjoyed being perceived as men. They have been trained to be assertive and confident, and some trans women manage to maintain these "masculine" traits, often to their advantage, after transitioning.

What happens is that we often confuse the oppression we have experienced for being gender-deviant with the absence of male privilege. Instead of claiming that we have never benefited from male supremacy, we need to assert that our experiences represent a dynamic interaction between male privilege and the disadvantage of being trans.

Any person who has a gender identity or an inclination toward a gender expression that matches the sex attributed to her or him has a privilege of being non-trans. This privilege, like other privileges, is invisible to those who possess it. And as is true of all other privileges, those who lack the privilege intuitively know how severely they suffer because of its absence. A trans woman may have limited access to male privilege depending on how early she transitioned and how fully she lives as a woman, but at the same time she experiences vast emotional, social, and financial disadvantages for being trans. The suggestion that trans women are inherently more privileged than other women is as ignorant as the claim that gay male couples are more privileged than heterosexual couples because both partners have male privilege.

Tensions often arise when trans women attempt to access "women's spaces" that are supposedly designed to be safe havens from the patriarchy. The origin of these "women's spaces" can be traced back to the early lesbian feminism of the 1970s, which consisted mostly of white, middle-class women who prioritized sexism as the most fundamental social inequality while largely disregarding their own role in perpetuating other oppressions such as racism and classism. Under the assumption that sexism marked women's lives far more significantly than any other social elements, they assumed that their experience of sexism was universal to all women—meaning all non–trans women—regardless of ethnicity, class, and so on. Recent critiques of radical feminism from the 1970s point out how their convenient negligence of racism and classism in effect privileged themselves as white, middle-class women.

Having come to this understanding, transfeminists should not respond to the accusation of male privilege with denial. We should have the courage to acknowledge ways in which trans women may have benefited from male privilege—some more than others, obviously— just as those of us who are white should address the benefits of white privilege. Transfeminism believes in the importance of honoring our differences as well as our similarities, because women come from a variety of backgrounds. Transfeminists confront our own privileges and expect non–trans women to acknowledge the privilege of being non- trans as well.

By acknowledging and addressing our privileges, trans women can hope to build alliances with other groups of women who have traditionally been neglected and deemed "unladylike" by a white, middle- class standard of womanhood. When we are called deviant and at- tacked just for being ourselves, there is nothing to gain from avoiding the question of privilege.

DECONSTRUCTING THE REVERSE ESSENTIALISM

Though the second wave of feminism popularized the idea that a per- son's gender is distinct from her or his physiological sex and is socially and culturally constructed, it largely left unquestioned the belief that there was such a thing as true physical (biological) sex. The separation of gender from sex was a powerful rhetorical move used to break down compulsory gender roles, but it allowed feminists to question only half of the problem, avoiding the question of the naturalness of essential female and male sexes.

Transfeminism holds that sex and gender are both socially con- structed; furthermore, the distinction between sex and gender is arti- ficially drawn as a matter of convenience. While the concept of gender as a social construct has proven to be a powerful tool in dismantling traditional attitudes toward women's capabilities, it left room for one to justify certain discriminatory policies or structures as having a bio- logical basis. It also failed to address the realities of experiences for trans people, for whom biological sex is felt to be more artificial and changeable than their inner sense of who they are.

The social construction of biological sex is more than an abstract ob- servation: it is a physical reality that many intersex people go through. Because society makes no provision for the existence of people whose anatomical characteristics do not neatly fit into male or female, they are routinely mutilated by medical professionals and manipulated into living as the sex they have been assigned, usually at birth. Intersex people are usually not given an opportunity to decide for themselves how they wish to live and whether they want surgical or hormonal "correction." Many intersex people find it appalling that they had no say in such a major life decision, whether or not their gender identity happened to match their assigned sex. We believe that genital mutilation of intersex children is inherently abusive because it unnecessarily violates the integrity of their bodies without proper consent. The issue is not even whether the sex a person was assigned matches her or his gender identity; it is whether intersex people are given real choice over what happens to their bodies.

Trans people feel dissatisfied with the sex assigned to them without their consent according to simplistic medical standards. Trans people are diverse: some identify with, and live as members of, the sex different from what was assigned to them by medical authorities, either with or without medical intervention, while others identify with neither sex or with both sexes. Trans liberation is about taking back the right to define ourselves from medical, religious, and political authorities. Transfeminism views any method of assigning sex as socially and politically constructed, and advocates a social arrangement in which one is free to assign her or his own sex (or non-sex, for that matter).

As trans people begin to organize politically, it is tempting to adopt the essentialist notion of gender identity. The cliché popularized by the mass media is that trans people are "women trapped in men's bodies" or vice versa. The attractiveness of such a strategy is clear, as the general population is more likely to become supportive of us if we can convince them that we are somehow born with a biological error over which we have no control. It is also often in tune with our own sense of who we are, which feels very deep and fundamental to us. However, as transfeminists, we resist such temptations because of their implications.

Trans people have often been described as those whose physical sex does not match the gender of their mind or soul. This explanation might make sense intuitively, but it is nonetheless problematic for transfeminism. To say that one has a female mind or soul would mean there are male and female minds that are different from each other in some identifiable way, which in turn may be used to justify discrimination against women. Claiming an essential gender identity can be just as dangerous as resorting to biological essentialism.

Transfeminism believes that we construct our own gender identities based on what feels genuine, comfortable, and sincere to us as we live and relate to others within given social and cultural constraints. This holds true for those whose gender identity is in congruence with their birth sex, as well as for trans people. Our demand for recognition and respect shall in no way be weakened by this acknowledgment. Instead of justifying our existence through reverse essentialism, transfeminism dismantles the assumption that sex and gender "naturally" cohere.

BODY IMAGE/CONSCIOUSNESS AS A FEMINIST ISSUE

We as feminists would like to claim that we feel comfortable, confident, and powerful with our own bodies. Unfortunately, this is not the case for many women, including trans women. For many transfeminists, the issue of body image is where our needs for comfort and safety collide directly with our feminist politics. Many of us feel so uncomfortable and ashamed of our appearances that we opt to remain in the closet, or we endure electrolysis, hormone therapy, and surgical interventions to modify our bodies in congruence with our identity as women. These procedures are costly, painful, and time-consuming and can lead to the permanent loss of fertility and other serious complications, such as an increased risk of cancer.

Why would anyone opt for such a seemingly inhumane practice? Although we might like to believe that the need to match our bodies to our gender identity is innate or essential, we cannot, in honesty, neglect social and political factors contributing to our personal decisions.

One such factor is society's enforcement of dichotomous gender roles. Because our identities are constructed within the social environment into which we are born, one could argue that the discontinuity between one's gender identity and physical sex is problematic only because society is actively maintaining a dichotomous gender system. If one's gender were an insignificant factor in society, the need for trans people to modify their bodies to fit into the dichotomy of genders might very well decrease, although probably not completely.

However, such reasoning should not be used to hold back trans persons from making decisions regarding their bodies. Trans women are extremely vulnerable to violence, abuse, and discrimination, and should not be made to feel guilty for doing whatever it takes for them to feel safe and comfortable. Transfeminism challenges us to consider ways in which social and political factors influence our decisions, but ultimately demands that society respect whatever decisions each of us makes regarding her or his own body and gender expression.

It is not contradictory to fight against the institutional enforcement of rigid gender roles while simultaneously advocating for individuals' rights to choose how they live in order to feel safe and comfortable. Nor is it contradictory to provide peer support to each other so that we can build healthy self-esteem while embracing an individual's decision to modify his or her body if he or she chooses to do so. We can each challenge society's arbitrary assumptions about gender and sex without becoming dogmatic. None of us should be expected to reject every oppressive factor in our lives at the same time; it would burn us out and drive us crazy. The sum of our small rebellions combined will destabilize the normative gender system as we know it. Various forms of feminisms, queer activism, transfeminism, and other progressive movements all attack different portions of the common target, which is the heterosexist patriarchy.

VIOLENCE AGAINST WOMEN

Since the 1970s, feminists have identified violence against women not merely as a series of isolated events, but as a systematic function of the patriarchy to keep all women subjugated. Transfeminism calls attention to the fact that trans women, like other groups of women who suffer from multiple oppressions, are particularly vulnerable to violence compared to women with non-trans privilege.

First, trans women are targeted because we live as women. Being a woman in this misogynist society is dangerous, but there are some factors that make us much more vulnerable when we are the targets of sexual and domestic violence. For example, when a man attacks a trans woman, especially if he tries to rape her, he may discover that the victim has or used to have a "male" anatomy. This discovery often leads to a more violent assault, one fueled by homophobia and transphobia. Trans women are frequently assaulted by men when their trans status is revealed. Murders of trans women, like those of prostitutes, are seldom taken seriously by the media and the authorities—especially if the victim is a trans woman engaged in prostitution.

Trans women are also more vulnerable to emotional and verbal abuse by their partners because of their often low self-esteem and negative body image. It is easy for an abuser to make a trans woman feel ugly, ashamed, worthless, and crazy, because these are the same messages the larger society has sent her over many years. Abusers get away with domestic violence by taking away women's ability to define their own identity and experiences—the areas where trans women are likely to be vulnerable to begin with. Trans women have additional difficulty in leaving their abusers because it is harder for them to find employment; they will almost certainly lose child custody to their abusive partner in a divorce if there are any children involved.

In addition, trans women are targeted for being queer. Homophobes tend not to distinguish between gays and trans people when they commit hate crimes, but trans people are much more vulnerable to attack because they are often more visible than gays. Homophobic terrorists do not look into people's bedrooms when they go out to hunt gays; they look for gendered cues that do not match the perceived sex of their prey, effectively targeting those who are visibly gender-deviant. For every gay man or lesbian whose murder makes national headlines, there are many more trans people who are killed across the nation, even though there are far more "out" gays and lesbians than there are "out" trans people.

Trans men also live in the constant fear of discovery as they navigate a society that persecutes men who step outside their socially established roles. Crimes against trans men are committed by strangers as well as by close "friends"; the crimes are undoubtedly motivated by a combination of transphobia and misogyny, performed as a punishment for violating gender norms in order to put the offenders back in a "woman's place."

Because of the danger in which we live, transfeminism believes that violence against trans people is one of the largest issues we must work on. We may be hurt and disappointed that some women-only events refuse to let us in, but it is the violence against us that has literally killed us or forced us to commit suicide far too long. We have no choice but to act.

In this regard, cooperation with traditional domestic violence shelters, rape crisis centers, and hate-crime prevention programs is essential. Some shelters have already decided to accept trans women just as they would any other women, while others hesitate for various reasons. We must organize and educate existing agencies about why trans women deserve to be helped by social service agencies if their domestic situation makes it necessary. We must stress that the dynamics of the violence against trans women is not unlike that involving non–trans women, except that we are often more vulnerable. And we should also advocate for services for trans men.

As transfeminists, we should not just demand that existing organizations provide services to us; we should join them. We should volunteer to assist them in developing effective screening methods in order to preserve safety as they expand their base. We should make ourselves available as crisis counselors and case managers to other trans women in need. We should help them fund trans-specific workshops for their staff, too. We should develop self-defense courses for trans women that are modeled after feminist self-defense programs for women, but which pay special attention to our unique experiences. There may not be enough of us to start our own shelters from scratch, but we can work toward the elimination of the violence against trans people as part of the broader coalition working to eliminate violence against women and sexual minorities.

We must also address the issue of economic violence. Trans women are often in poverty because as women we earn less than men do, because overt discrimination against trans people in employment is rampant, and because of the prohibitively high cost of transitioning. This also means that abusive partners of trans women have more leverage to control us and keep us trapped in abusive relationships. Transfeminism believes in fighting transphobia and sexism simultaneously in the economic arena as well as in the social and political ones.

HEALTH AND REPRODUCTIVE CHOICE

It may seem ironic that trans women, who in general have no capacity for bearing children, would be interested in the women's reproductive rights movement, but transfeminism sees a deep connection between the liberation of trans women and women's right to choose.

First of all, society's stigmatization of trans existence is partly due to the fact that we mess with our reproductive organs. Nongenital cosmetic surgeries are performed far more frequently than sex reassignment surgeries, yet they do not require months of mandatory psychotherapy. Nor are people who pursue cosmetic surgeries ridiculed and scorned daily on nationally broadcast trash talk shows. Such hysteria over trans people's personal choices is fueled in part by society's taboo against the self-determination of our reproductive organs: like women seeking abortions, our bodies have become an open territory, a battleground.

Additionally, the hormones that many trans women take are similar in origin and chemical composition to what non–trans women take for birth control, emergency contraception, and hormone replacement therapy. As trans women, we share their concerns over the safety, cost, and availability of these estrogen-related pills. Trans and non–trans women need to be united against the right-wing tactics aimed at making the means and information for controlling our bodies unavailable, if not illegal.

Of course, reproductive choice is not just about access to abortion or birth control; it is also about resisting the coerced sterilization or abortion of less privileged women. Likewise, transfeminism strives for the right to refuse surgical and hormonal interventions, including those prescribed for intersex people.

During the 1980s, lesbians were purged from some reproductive choice organizations because they were seen as irrelevant to that cause. But the right to choose is not exclusively a heterosexual issue or a non-trans issue, as it is fundamentally about women having the right to determine what they do with their own bodies. Transfeminists should join reproductive choice organizations and demonstrate for choice. A society that does not respect women's right to make decisions regarding pregnancy is not likely to respect our right to make decisions about medical interventions to make our bodies congruent with our gender identity. If we fear having to obtain hormones from underground sources or traveling overseas for a sex reassignment surgery, we should be able to identify with women who fear going back to unsafe underground abortions.

In addition, transfeminism needs to learn from the women's health movement. Research on health issues that are of particular interest to women, such as breast cancer, did not arise in a vacuum. It was through vigorous activism and peer education that these issues came to be taken seriously. Realizing that the medical community has historically failed to address women's health concerns adequately, transfeminists cannot expect those in the position of power to take trans women's health seriously. That is why we need to participate in, and expand, the women's health movement.

Drawing analogies from the women's health movement also solves the strategic dilemma over the pathologization of gender identity. For many years, trans people have been arguing with each other about whether to demand the de-pathologization of gender identity disorder, which is currently a prerequisite for certain medical treatments. It has been a divisive issue because the pathologization of gender identity disorder allows some of us to receive medical interventions, even though it stigmatizes us and negates our agency at the same time. Before the advent of feminist critiques of modern medicine, female bodies were considered "abnormal" by the androcentric standard of the medical establishment, which resulted in the pathologization of such ordinary female experiences as menstruation, pregnancy, and menopause; the women's health movement forced the medical community to accept that these events are part of ordinary human experiences. Transfeminism insists that transsexuality is not an illness or a disorder, but is as much a part of the wide spectrum of ordinary human experiences as pregnancy. It is thus not contradictory to demand that medical treatment for trans people be made more accessible, while de-pathologizing "gender identity disorder."

CALL FOR ACTION

While we have experienced more than our share of rejection within and outside feminist communities, those who have remained our best allies have also been feminists, lesbians, and other queers. Transfeminism asserts that it is futile to debate intellectually who is and is not included in the category "woman"; instead, we must act—now—and build alliances.

Every day, we are harassed, discriminated against, assaulted, and abused. No matter how well we learn to "pass," the social invisibility of trans existence will not protect us when all women are under attack. We can never win by playing by society's rules of how women should behave; we need feminism as much as non–trans women do, if not more. Transfeminists take pride in the tradition of our feminist foremothers and continue their struggle in our own lives.

Transfeminism believes that a society that honors cross-gender identities is one that treats people of all genders fairly because our existence is seen as problematic only when there is a rigid gender hierarchy. It is essential for our survival and dignity that we claim our place in feminism, not in a threatening or invasive manner, but in friendly and cooperative ways. Initial suspicion and rejection from some existing feminist institutions are only natural, especially since they have been betrayed so many times by self-identified "pro-feminist" men; it is through our persistence and commitment to action that transfeminism will transform the scope of feminism into a more inclusive vision of the world.

POSTSCRIPT

I wrote "The Transfeminist Manifesto" in the summer of 2000, only a couple of months after I had moved to Portland, Oregon, where I found transgender and transsexual communities and began exploring the intersections of feminism and trans experiences. I guess I was naïve, but initially I was surprised when I found out that there were anti-trans sentiments among some feminists and antifeminist sentiments among some trans people, because the trans people I had met were the kind of people I respected as both feminists and trans activists. I wrote this manifesto in order to articulate a feminist theory that is decidedly pro-trans, and a trans rhetoric that is rooted in feminism. I think I succeeded.

There are, however, problems with this manifesto. In several revisions I made over the last two years, I fixed some of the minor problems, but larger problems are left intact, because they cannot be fixed without rewriting the entire piece. But I think it is important to discuss what these problems are and why they crept into this manifesto. Two of these larger problems are discussed below:

- Overemphasis on male-to-female trans people at the expense of female-to-male trans people and others who identify as transgender or genderqueer. I take full blame for the fact that this manifesto is heavily focused on the issues faced by male-to-female transsexual people, while neglecting the unique struggles of female-to-male trans people and other transgender and genderqueer people. At the time I wrote this piece, I felt the need to restrict the focus of feminism to "women" because I feared that expanding the focus would permit non–trans men to exploit feminism for their own interests, as some so-called men's rights groups do. Although I still feel that this fear is justified, I now realize that privileging transsexual women's issues at the expense of other transgender and genderqueer people was a mistake.

- Inadequate intersectional analysis. The manifesto focuses mainly on the intersection of sexism and the oppression against trans people, yet it fails to address how these issues intersect with other social injustices. For example, the manifesto refers to women of color's critiques of white women's racism within the feminist movement, but fails to address how trans women can become allies of women of color. Again, I hesitated to move the focus away from sexism at the time I wrote this manifesto, as I feared other (non-trans) feminists' criticisms. Now I agree with the notion that any feminist theory that fails to account for racism, classism, ableism, etc., operating among women is incomplete. I concede that this manifesto is incomplete.

Although I am making two very different critiques, the manifesto's problems both come from the same source: the idea that feminists should focus primarily—sometimes solely—on the oppression that all women experience. In this worldview, issues such as racism and classism can be addressed only when they further the battle against the patriarchy—for example, by addressing white men's racism against women of color—but not when they expose the hidden divisions within the women's movement. This manifesto for the most part plays into this trajectory while failing to challenge its racist, classist, or other implications. I realize now that, at the time I wrote the manifesto, I did not feel secure enough in my own conviction in multi-issue organizing and gave in to the fear that I would be criticized for diluting feminism. Only through camaraderie with other fierce women of color, working-class women, and women with disabilities have I become free from this fear.

I have thought about writing a new manifesto to address these and other insights I have gained since 2000, with the confidence and clarity I have now, but for now I am leaving the task to others. If you write one, please send it to me.

PART FIVE

Doing Feminism

ALANA SUSKIN

Hearing the Daughter Voice:
The *Bat Kol* as Rrrabbi Grrrl

I.

I doubt that as I was growing up, I would have considered myself religious. My family went to synagogue for holidays and on Friday nights, but I certainly did not think much about God. At the same time, I always knew that I was Jewish. I have always been proud to be Jewish, even among people who informed me that it was a shame that I was going to hell because, other than being a Jew, I seemed like an all right person.

Perhaps it should be no surprise that I turned out to be religious, though. I learned at home that the center of Judaism is social justice. I recall one trip to the grocery store, when I was around eight or nine. I wanted my parents to buy a box of prepared fried chicken, but my father refused. He told me that the company that made the chicken was known for its union-busting, and he would not buy anything from it.

It never occurred to me that we should not buy the food because the chicken wasn't kosher (permitted by Jewish dietary law). My family, for the most part, did not keep kosher. No one made the connection for me between Judaism and unions, but somehow I knew: good Jews do not buy products from companies that prevent workers from making a living wage. I knew very little about what Jews were supposed to do ritually, but I knew what Jews were supposed to do ethically.

Even if I didn't think much about Judaism when I was young, I always knew that I was a feminist. Though I grew up during the Reagan era, at a time when the word "feminist" was often used as an insult, I knew that feminism was about making the world a just place. I also knew that justice was required of me as a Jew. I was a Jew and I was a feminist: of course! After all, weren't all Jews supposed to be feminists? I knew that there were people who did not like Jews, people who did not like people of color, people who did not like gays, and people who did not like feminists. I understood that those dislikes reflected the same type of ignorance and prejudice. I did not know that all Jews were not feminists. It seemed obvious to me that if one was a Jew, on the receiving end of prejudice and oppression for so many thousands of years, one should know that all prejudice was alike and avoid it.

By the time I got to college, I barely made it home to observe the major holidays, and I certainly didn't bother to observe them if I didn't go home. Yet, I never abandoned my identity as a Jew, because for me the key to Jewish identity was doing justice. Thus, I was always involved *as a Jew* in working for social justice projects, signing petitions, and going to marches in Washington for women's rights, for gay and lesbian rights, for the poor, for the environment.

Although I did not yet know it, being raised in both Jewish traditions of socialism and of religious observance, and then reinforcing these patterns of justice through my academic life in women's studies and philosophy, destined me to go to rabbinical school. My family's immigrant, socialist roots and our religious tradition say that the world is real, oppression is real, and we need to work for change. Academia had been a haven from the world, a place that taught me how to think well and clearly, how to take arguments apart and put them back together. However, after a few years as a graduate student, I began to see academia's shortcomings. I could no longer live in a world where intellect was a game and argument merely a pleasure. I had always loved the game of argument: I was (and am) very good at it. I used to say to myself that knowledge for its own sake was beautiful. I still believe that, but I realize that this isn't enough. Jewish tradition tells us that the rabbis, arguing about whether Torah learning or deeds were more important, favored the Torah, as long as it leads to deeds.

II.

Oddly enough, it was my work in women's studies that made me re-think Judaism. While completing my master's degree, I had decided that I would work toward the graduate certificate offered by the women's studies department. Although many faculty members in the department were Jewish by birth, I found that many were often subtly hostile to Judaism, particularly traditional Judaism, while being open to diversity among other groups. Sometimes the hostility existed even while these same faculty members were fighting anti-Semitism on the left and within women's movements. I once found myself arguing that departmental meetings shouldn't be scheduled on Friday nights, the night when our Sabbath begins. I once noted the number of confer-ences and meetings that were scheduled on Saturday—our Sabbath—or on Jewish holidays. I found myself defending even the possibility of being both a ritually observant Jew and a feminist. In one class, we read an article that argued that Judaism was so patriarchal that any ob-servance of it beyond the most nominal level amounted to submitting to patriarchal values and rules. It was very frustrating to read article af-ter article that only criticized Judaism. Some of these articles' authors were Jewish women who seemed to know very little about what they were criticizing. Others were Christian authors who used Judaism as a foil for Christianity's own misogyny, attempting to show that early Christianity was a feminist alternative to that shameful patriarchal Ju-daism, despite the fact that this perspective has little historical validity. I felt extremely peculiar: I couldn't defend a religion that I really knew very little about.

I did not even know why I felt the need to defend a religion in which I participated very little. As I grew older, I had certainly come to see that Judaism, or at least practicing Jews, were not perfect. Yet, reading feminist essays that said that Jewish women should throw out Judaism as it was and start over left a sour taste in my mouth. If that was the only solution, why bother calling it Judaism at all? If Judaism was un-salvageable, why do so many of us who are feminist and Jewish want to keep something called Judaism around? I found myself defending Judaism, trying to show a truly feminist side to Judaism that was and always had been a part of the Jewish religious tradition.

This is how I became involved in Jewish women's studies. Every time a secular Jewish woman stated that we needed to reject men's traditions and start our own totally unrelated religion—but still call it Judaism—I thought to myself, what do we know about these traditions? Why do we assume that they are all men's traditions? And how could we simply invent new laws and just throw out the old ones? How could that be Jewish? Where is God in that? So I did what Jews have always done: I studied.

In studying Judaism, I became disappointed and pleased. Within my tradition was a strain of liberation theology, but in many places another strain that rejected modernity had turned a radical tradition into one that was so afraid of its own destruction by assimilation that it had rejected all that was radical within it.

Women's studies gave me the tools to evaluate the strengths and weaknesses of Judaism. I was not alone in this pursuit: since the mid-1980s, a growing number of Jewish feminists have begun to evaluate our traditions. Feminism has grown to a point where it is able to examine itself and its own prejudices. This has made room for more women and more feminisms.

Jewish women's studies, like womanism (African American feminism) and Xicanisma (Chicana feminism), has become a movement in itself. However, because many second wave feminists equate Jews with "white and middle-class," they have not attempted to differentiate Jewish feminism from the broader category of feminism in general. This is a mistake, for within Judaism there are many ethnic groups: Jews of color from Africa and the Middle East, as well as other Jews of color, all of whom have their own critiques of secular culture as well as the Ashkenazi-centric Jewish world. Moreover, even the Ashkenazi—Eastern European Jews—are ethnically differentiated from the "white" culture around us.

It is true that Judaism is not only a religion but also a culture, and not just one, but many; at the same time, all Jews are a single people. These intertwined matrices of identity make it difficult to tease out which feminist critiques of Judaism—even by Jewish women—fairly question women's treatment in Jewish religious life and which of these critiques are something else. Academic feminists, Jewish or not, still struggle with a society that makes women hate their bodies and people of color hate their skin and hair. Jewish women have been disproportionately represented in feminism in every wave, just as Jews are disproportionately represented in all social justice movements. However, despite our numbers, it is only recently that, like other ethnic feminists, Jewish women have begun to see that feminists have not yet weeded out all of their own prejudices against those who are nonwhite and non-middle-class.

Feminist prejudices against religious Jews are part of that struggle. One of the best classes that I ever took examined colonialism and race; the course also introduced me to the work of Karen Brodkin,[1] who talks about the shifting racial identities of Jews (whether we are considered white or not depends upon a variety of factors). Her work points toward other Jewish women's analyses of the rejection of Jewish identity. Evelyn Torton Beck, for instance, analyzes both the misogyny and racism or anti-Semitism of the JAP-bashing that was common in the 1990s (JAP refers to "Jewish American Princess").[2] Inherent in the rejection of our identities as Jewish women are the poisonous attitudes that Jewish women have come to accept about ourselves. When we reject Judaism, we are also rejecting a nonwhite immigrant identity in which we are seen and see ourselves as "too Jewish." Caricatures of Jewish women—as people with hair that is too curly, noses too big, bodies too round, voices too loud (both literally and figuratively), breasts too big, and sometimes skin, hair, and eyes too dark—are also part of these "critiques" of Judaism. Such "critiques" are unfair; they are not really critiques, but rather prejudice beneath the surface. The struggle to be secular is not necessarily different from any other kind of hair straightening or nose bobbing.

The world of activism, to which academic women's studies is strongly tied, teaches us the truths of power dynamics and how to take them on. Indeed, without an activist background gained in women's studies, I would never have learned the primary truth of forcing change in a place that needs it and admits that it needs it, but nonetheless refuses to implement that change. If women are to have a role in the future of Judaism, we have to stop waiting for men in charge to recognize how right our arguments are. As one feminist once said, "What people have to recognize is that no one gives you rights, you just take them." We simply have to do what it takes.

III.

The Jewish world is still largely sexist. This sexism is rooted in the cultures that have been imported into the Jewish tradition. Sexism in Judaism came historically from both Greek and Roman cultures and their descendants; it also came from the reaction within our communities to modernity: the disintegration of the community into the primacy of the individual citizen, the high mobility of individual families, and the erosion of religious education for both children and adults. In our time, fear of these changes has led Jews, along with many other communities, to repress women in the name of returning to an ideal—and imaginary—past. Sexist ideas are entrenched among those who have assimilated and among those who attempt to reject assimilation. Thus, all Jewish communities have adopted sexist norms, at least to some extent.

Within Judaism's ritually observant communities, the main evidence of sexism is the exclusion of women from public roles. A particular problem is that in Judaism great importance is ascribed to prayer in a quorum, in which, for many communities, women are not counted. The inaccessibility of text study in general to those not raised to it—particularly women—is also a problem, as knowledge of the many and varied sacred texts is also considered to be of extremely high value to the community. Finally, the texts of Jewish law itself seem sexist: they lack role models for women, contain misogynist laws, and exclude female voices in the interpretation of those laws.[3]

When I began to learn about my tradition, I found it a daily struggle. It became very difficult to read that historically only men determined the law in those texts, with little or no input from women, thus ignoring the realities of women's daily lives. Sometimes the rabbis would make pronouncements about women's biology that were patently ridiculous; a simple question put to a woman might have provided them with a more accurate answer. However, these men were sitting in male spaces that were "uncontaminated" by women. Their study spaces were sacred and exclusive, a boys' club. Apparently, to ask a woman a question about her body would have been too unseemly. Yet, here and there, one does encounter the individual rabbi who says he must discuss with his wife before taking a position, or a rabbi who rules that a certain law is harmful to women or who takes it upon himself to ask a woman about something on which she is the expert.

Today these texts are records of the divine voice: religious Jews must take them into account. However, as a woman who will be a rabbi, I have the opportunity to take dissenting voices and make them my own, to take minority opinions and show why they are the correct interpretation of law, to make my voice, a woman's voice, a part of that recorded struggle to hear God's voice.

But this is not enough. Our tradition asks us if it is better to study or to do. The answer is that to study is better, when it leads to action. The Jewish world has in many places become alienated from its tradition of textual study. Even in those places where text study (generally conducted primarily among men) is still central to the community, action has somehow slipped away. American life is safe, open, and full of opportunities that have been denied to Jews historically, and in many places still are. In this atmosphere, many observant Jews have forgotten that the point of all those laws is to repair the flaws of the world, to teach us what justice is, to remind us that, in everything we do, our hands should be God's hands. Somehow, the measure of observance has become limited to certain kinds of ritual behavior such as keeping kosher or not driving on the Sabbath. It does not occur to many Jews that preventing women from participating in the public forms of religious life might violate the laws we keep. It is ordained that one must give to the poor, and so we do, because that is justice (indeed, the Hebrew word for giving to the poor means "justice"). I have heard many men say that it disturbs them that women are not counted in all public prayer quorums, but they continue to take honors and go up to lead prayer in places where this is true, rather than try to change the status quo there.

The role of the rabbi in the world needs to become more activist. The rabbi who ensured that our tradition would continue after the Temple in Jerusalem was destroyed knew that the world had been turned upon its head and things would have to change. He made sure that they did, without destroying the tradition itself; we as rabbis have to do this again. The world has changed and is still changing. No longer do constant pregnancies and births prevent women from participating in the public arena. Although being excused from public prayer may have initially relieved women of a responsibility they did not have time for, this exclusion now has become an excuse to bar us from the community. No longer should women alone bear the burdens and joys of childrearing and care. In legislating participation by both sexes in both roles, we ensure a world that is truer to God's vision of justice.

Jews need feminism because without feminism, Judaism ceases to be true to itself. Judaism has always been a religion that resisted the degrading paradigms of the dominant culture. When Palestine was ruled by Rome, the Romans valued the male body as the epitome of all that was sacred. Like today's American culture, the Roman culture was a gymnasium culture, one that viewed human perfection as the perfection of the body, and a very narrow perfection at that. The rabbis rebelled then and said that male sexuality must be reined in and set to God's service. The Romans saw the rebellion of the Jews, our insistence on circumcision for male children and the study of Torah, as defying their belief that Roman culture was the only true civilization. The way of those rabbis was to resist the dominant ideology of power. Today, Judaism is true to its rabbinic roots when we—Jewish women as well as men—are a countercultural force.

Feminism is today the basis of resistance to the dominant paradigm. Feminism is now the method by which we are able to analyze that dominant culture and reject what are accepted universally as truths simply because these truths have been indoctrinated into us since we were born. Judaism has those methods of resistance still embedded in its laws, its hermeneutics, and its traditions, but we need feminism to reawaken us to them. Feminism is what will remind Jews of the traditional flexibility of our method of interpretation of Jewish law and of the radical nature of our resistance to the status quo.

Today, the world needs rabbis who have adopted feminist methods, an ideology of activism that hears the reality of injustice and addresses it, without depending upon "it's always been that way" as satisfactory and sufficient. Feminism made me someone who went out and interacted with actual people, someone who worked in the community to change the world, and not just someone who thought about what was wrong with it without even attempting to conceive of a solution. Truth is important, but it's only a beginning. Feminism taught me that to do God's will means to listen to people's pain, but then to take action to change society so that people do not have to adjust to injustice. To do God's will means to work to see justice ring out across the land.

In my rabbinic training program, we spend five years in seminary, the third year of which is spent in Jerusalem with third-year students from the other seminaries in my movement. We are encouraged to visit many different kinds of synagogues and thus witness different styles of prayer. In the year that I was required to spend in Israel, it became very plain to me how much feminism is still needed to create a role for women in the public spaces of Judaism.

Although male and female rabbinical students set out on a similar journey to Israel, they have radically different experiences once there. No male rabbinical student will ever be turned away from praying at a synagogue. However, female rabbinical students are sometimes not able to enter a synagogue even when dressed in clothing normative to the Orthodox. Why? Because some Orthodox synagogues do not have a space for women at all. Even when they do, it is only in the *ezrat nashim*, an all-woman space that is boxed off and inadequate in size, with a wall that often prevents women from seeing or hearing very much of the prayer service. The most liberal Orthodox synagogues in Jerusalem allow women a bit more space, a way to hear what is going on, and perhaps a slightly lower wall, or a wall made only of an opaque cloth; sometimes these synagogues offer a parallel service, separate from the men's, in which women may actively participate, rather than merely passively watch. However, women are never permitted to lead prayer for the entire community or even to be counted as part of the community. Nine men and a woman are always fewer than ten to the Orthodox, and they would claim that in such a case a prayer quorum—the minimum number of people needed to pray as a community, explained in some of our texts as the minimum number of people who make up a community—has not been reached. Ten women are not even a group; ten women are always private individuals, never a community.

My rabbinical program trains female and male rabbis. However, the question becomes: What is it exactly that those who created the program are training us to do? Are we being trained to go along with the immoral structures that are in the place where we live? Why haven't the men refused to pray at these synagogues?[4] And more important, why haven't those who are training us provided us with an egalitarian place to go on the Sabbath?

The lack of support for egalitarianism indicates a recent shift to the right within Judaism, generally speaking. While many Jews give lip service to the idea that egalitarianism is an "equally valid choice," few—even among the most liberal Jewish groups—use the language of moral obligation. I reject the notion that egalitarianism is an "equally valid choice." It is the only valid choice. Non-egalitarian communities are not following the law of God that says to do justly. We have a tradition that one does not say certain prayers in the presence of the dead because the dead can no longer recite those prayers. In light of this, how can we say that men are permitted to be community members in places where women cannot? Are the dead more worthy of respect than the living?

When we say that egalitarianism is a "choice" and then present our communities, particularly the children of our communities, with a standard of non-egalitarian prayer, we teach them that it is not only acceptable but also correct to be non-egalitarian. The ostensible reasoning for this behavior is that everyone can participate in the "more traditional" mode of prayer. However, those who say this fail to recognize both that half the participants can never participate and that teaching children that non-egalitarian Judaism is the "real" baseline tradition does them a disservice and promotes a falsehood.

The center of our religion is liberation theology. It is the coming out of a narrow place, Egypt, where we served a man, into a wide road—*halacha*, literally—but also the word for our body of law where we serve God. When we serve God, when we obey God's law, we are acting as agents in the world for justice to repair the brokenness of the world. Yet, when we ourselves are broken, how do we begin to repair the world?

The Jewish tradition says, "Love labor and hate honor, and do not seek to be intimate with authorities," and "It is not your obligation to complete the task, but neither are you free to desist from it." The Jewish tradition, especially in Europe and the United States, is embedded in the history of labor and liberation movements. That tradition started with the Exodus from Egypt and continued through the anarchism of Emma Goldman and the traditional observance of the laws of justice by Rabbi Abraham Joshua Heschel when he walked with Dr. Martin Luther King Jr., through the streets of Selma. He said of his marching, "Our legs were praying." Today, the activists of Rabbis for Human Rights in Israel, who work for the rights of foreign laborers, Palestinian Israelis, Bedouins, and non-Israeli Palestinians, as well as for the rights of many other Jewish organizations, recognize our long tradition of radical resistance to injustice.

IV.

While I was in Israel, I worked for the organization Rabbis for Human Rights. This organization does phenomenal work with many different disenfranchised groups. The work I became most engaged in was that for human rights for non-Israeli Palestinians.

At the time I was there, Israel was essentially under siege by Palestinian terrorists, who targeted civilians all over the country. It was not a popular time to be working for the rights of civilian Palestinians, who were regarded with suspicion simply for being Palestinian. Because Palestinians do not live within Israel proper, it is easy to prevent them from coming into the country to work or study. Because the West Bank and Gaza were under military occupation, it was easy to prevent people from leaving even their villages. This meant that women in labor and injured Palestinians could not get to hospitals. It meant that children could not get to school; it meant that people could not get to work, even in other Palestinian towns. The roadblocks, it is claimed, merely prevent Palestinians from coming too close to Jewish settlements, but they often do a great deal more, preventing Palestinians essentially from going anywhere at all.

As a Jew, I could not live for a year in the country of my people while doing nothing to protest the treatment of the stranger who lives among us. As a feminist, I had to do more than simply say it was wrong; I had to go and do something about it.

The first time I demonstrated at a roadblock, it was calm. A classmate, his roommate, and I went to the site together with a coalition of peace activists, including Rabbis for Human Rights; once there, we met Palestinians from a nearby town and began to dig. The soldiers took our shovels from us, so we dug with our hands, with stones, with our folded signs. We dug until both of the roadblocks were level and the pit in front of them was filled in. We knew that in a few hours, our work would be undone by soldiers and a backhoe, but we had shown that Jews (mostly Israelis) and Palestinians could work together peacefully. We had shown the young soldiers who, after all, were just a bunch of teenagers doing their mandatory service, that Jews did not have to be afraid of all Palestinians and could even talk to and joke with their brethren in the army. We were not the enemies of either side.

The second time I went to a roadblock demolition, the demonstration was more difficult. When we began, there were many peace groups on both the Israeli and Palestinian sides gathered together to protest the blocking of roads. Members of Peace Now, Bat Shalom, Rabbis for Human Rights, Christian Peacemakers Taskforce, Rapprochement, and the Women's Peace Coalition traveled together to remove the roadblocks cutting off Karawe, Bidha, and Messha from Nablus and Salfit.

When we arrived at our site, the Palestinians came down the road to meet us, carrying signs and banners. Most moving to me were several women who came up to the women of our group, embracing us and kissing us. The men shook hands warmly with everyone.

We gathered at the first roadblock toward the Israeli side and began, mostly with our hands, to move dirt, huge boulders, and cement barriers. We all worked together, some of us singing, some of us chatting companionably. We worked calmly together to lower the barricades.

After some time, the police and soldiers started to get agitated. They arrested two Palestinians and then began to cart off people from the Israeli side as well. Except for one woman, who is well known to the army for being arrested at these events (her partner is Palestinian, so I was told), they took the men first and then, after a pause, a few women who were calmly sitting and continuing to dig after being told to stop.

After that, the police organized to force everyone back to the second roadblock. We formed a human chain, but after a while people began to straggle out into the space between the two roadblocks, and the women there made a chain with their arms and stood in front of the Palestinians, who were being shoved around. A great cheer went up as an earthmover on the Palestinian side of the roadblock began to clear the roadblock away. Although the protesters remained very calm and peaceful, the soldiers became agitated and suddenly pushed us back toward the Palestinian side. They then quickly withdrew, at which point I realized that they were about to throw gas at us. I turned toward the roadblock and suddenly felt something bounce off my leg. It then exploded in a flash of light, and I ran toward the side of the road. Apparently I have good instincts: without thinking, I held my breath while running, took my bandanna off my head, and put it over my mouth and nose. I got to the side of the road and semi-collapsed.

After a few moments, I lurched to my feet and was seen by a Spanish journalist. He came over, along with an Israeli soldier who told me not to touch my face and to keep my eyes open. The journalist got several excellent pictures of me coughing and spitting, teary-eyed and runny-nosed, confirming that there definitely was tear gas.

This demonstration was entirely peaceful; not a single stone was thrown. There was no violence committed either by the Palestinians or by the Israeli demonstrators. There was no provocation that started the Israeli retaliation. In fact, I suspect that most of the soldiers would have been happy to simply stand, watch, and wait to rebuild the roadblock until we went away. That would have been the smart thing to do, since it would have denied the press their interesting photo opportunities. However, when some higher-ranking men arrived, they seemed to want to show us who was boss and regain control of a situation that was not really out of control.

I have always been very left-wing, even in terms of my feelings about relations between Israelis and Palestinians. During the year I spent in Israel, I saw with my own eyes what happens there. It is not always clear who is in the right and who is not; the international media really do minimize Palestinian violence against Israelis, but official Israeli spokespeople also lie about what's really going on. The danger of terrorism from Palestinians is real. There are good people on both sides— and fanatic loonies on both sides as well. I cannot say that I have a solution to keep Israeli citizens safe from those on the Palestinian side who want to see the eradication of Israel and of all Jews. But the existence of evil is not an excuse for further evil. My responsibility is to my people, and I cannot accept anything less than moral behavior from my own. In the case I just described, things were fairly clear: it was a nonviolent demonstration, to which the Israelis overreacted. As a Jew,

I was proud to see so many of us standing and requiring moral behavior even under the most difficult circumstances. It is no surprise to me that many of the Jewish organizations involved in human rights work for Palestinians and others are openly feminist; even among those that are not, many of the members espouse feminist beliefs. To me, this represents precisely what I see as feminism's contribution to Judaism: the reviving of our radical tradition of social justice.

The roadblock demonstrations did not end roadblocks in the West Bank. It would have been nice if they had, but none of us expected that they would. We knew that our work was somewhat symbolic, a gesture, but it was also very real. What the demonstrations did do was show the Israeli government that it cannot act without Jews of conscience taking notice. Many of the demonstrators were women of the Israeli left, whose feminism is the backbone of the Israeli peace movement. I was proud to have had the opportunity to join them. Their work continues, of course. The ideology that leads people to risk themselves against a state for the sake of conscience is a feminist one. At its root, the struggle to ensure the recognition of Palestinian humanity is the same as the struggle to recognize the humanity of women: fully, without exception, all people deserve to live with dignity, without fear, with access to health care, education, and jobs. This work is central to my life as a Jew and as a feminist.

V.

As always in Judaism, it is the texts that point me in the right direction. When one studies a piece of Talmud, whatever problem one is wrestling with suddenly seems to make a miraculous appearance in the words of the rabbis. In their arguments, I see that the ideology of the Conservative Jewish movement, even when it is not always able to live up to its loftiest ideals, shines through. I am a feminist, and the philosophical methods that underlie my connections to the world and its struggles also underlie the methodologies of Conservative, traditional Judaism. Of course, the texts of Judaism are not uniform, and many of them are misogynist, xenophobic, and so forth. But these texts form a tradition that has always struggled with its worst and best together.

The tradition we have makes us grown-ups. We can no longer run away: we have to understand that God made us Her partner. There is no marriage in which we can have rights; marriages aren't about rights: they are about having respect for what the other person needs. If either partner does not give respect, does not fulfill obligations, then the marriage cannot survive. Feminism is about understanding that both partners must have respect for themselves and their partner. Although feminism speaks in the language of rights, rights are not the fundamental goal. Beneath the language of feminism is the reach toward respect for the other: men meeting their obligation toward women, as well as women toward men. When someone speaks of her or his rights, the underlying matter is that the community has failed in its obligation to listen to what its members—all of them—require. When a community understands that it is a community of obligations, and meets them, then no one needs to speak of rights.

My goal as a rabbi is to make the community hear the voice of the disenfranchised. This is what makes me a feminist: the knowledge that God is present in every voice, and so every voice must have the chance to speak. I am not the first female rabbi; hundreds have gone before me. Similarly, I'm part of the third wave—not the first or second—of American feminists; there has been much feminist movement long before I came along. The struggle still continues. The Haggada, the text Jews read at Passover, says, "In every generation it is obligatory for each person to see themselves as if they themselves had been redeemed from slavery in Egypt." As a feminist, I can add that in each and every generation of feminism, we are all obligated to see ourselves as undertaking the redemption of humanity from inequality. Women, the stranger, the minority, and the poor—none has reached equality. The powerful of humanity still greedily grab all the resources they can and make war, literal or metaphoric, to keep "what is theirs."

There is no doubt that traditional Judaism is now well on its way to including women; what has yet to be discussed at any length are the repercussions for the community as a whole and the fact that men's visions of faith must also be transformed by feminism. What Judaism looks like to outsiders is often the result of the struggle within our community both to change and to resist change. The struggle within Judaism is one mirrored by the wider world, whether within other religious traditions, or politics, or even feminism itself. In the Talmud, there is occasionally a voice that speaks from the heavens, to make known God's will, and it is called the *bat kol*—that is, "the daughter voice." It is time that Her voice is heard.

NOTES

1. Karen Brodkin, *How Jews Became White Folks and What That Shows about Race in America* (New Brunswick, N.J.: Rutgers University Press, 1998). I was introduced to Brodkin's work through her article "How Jews Became White Folks," in *Race,* ed. Steven Gregory and Roger Sanjek (New Brunswick, N.J.: Rutgers University Press, 1994), which became the first chapter of her book.

2. Evelyn Torton Beck, ed., *Nice Jewish Girls: A Lesbian Anthology,* rev. ed. (Boston: Beacon Press, 1989).

3. At least, they have until quite recently. Today, in some communities, and to a limited extent, we are beginning to see women's voices represented in interpretation of Jewish law.

4. To be fair, I know of one who does refuse to pray at non-egalitarian services. Different people have told him repeatedly that he is "cutting himself off from the rich possibilities that are open to him."

Rocking the Gender Order

When you think about feminism, what do you think about? What do you imagine in your mind's eye when you hear the word "feminist"?

Jennifer is wearing faded jeans, combat boots, a black lace bra, and no shirt. Her hair is dyed an unnatural shade of pinkish red, and she is wearing bright red lipstick. She is standing on a stage in a small bar in Chicago. A bass guitar hangs low on her hips, and as she plays, she spreads her legs, throws her head back and forth, and swings her hair wildly. With her onstage are three other women, and together they are creating a tight, pulsing hybrid of punk and hard rock.

Eddie is wearing a faded T-shirt covered by an unbuttoned flannel shirt, army fatigue pants cut raggedly just below the knee, and combat boots. His unkempt hair falls around his face and down to the middle of his back. He is onstage holding a microphone with both hands and passionately belting out angry lyrics about a young woman who was institutionalized because she was too rebellious. With him onstage are four other men pounding out hard, aggressive rock music. Between songs he urges the audience to be careful and take care of each other.

Kim is wearing jeans and a T-shirt. Like Eddie, his hair is very long, disheveled, and complemented by a bushy beard. He is aggressively playing lead guitar as his bandmate Chris belts out some of the cleanest, most versatile male vocals you'll ever hear.

Courtney is wearing a sheer, baby-doll dress, which is very short, loose, and "girly." Under her dress you can see black lingerie; on her feet are platform-heeled, black sandals. She has a guitar resting against her hips, one leg up on the speaker in front of her, and she is snarling and spitting out lyrics about sex, violence, and alienation.

Ian is wearing khaki pants cut off just above the knee, a faded T-shirt, and combat boots. His hair is shaved very close to his scalp. He is playing a guitar and lyrically putting himself in the position of a woman dealing with her fear of and anger about sexual violence. With the other four men in the band, he is rocking a room full of people with edgy, aggressive music. When he notices two men fighting in the audience, he breaks off in the middle of the song and tells them to stop and separate. He and the rest of the band stand there until the two men move to opposite sides of the room.

The people I have described above are Jennifer Finch of the band L7, Eddie Vedder of Pearl Jam, Kim Thayil of Soundgarden, Courtney Love of Hole, and Ian MacKaye of Fugazi. They are all rock musicians, and they have all embraced a feminist sensibility to forge a new kind of rock music culture. Rather than simply reproduce the old, tired, sexist ways of rock and roll, these people, along with many others, decided to do it differently. Unlike songwriters and performers in previous eras, when rockers made their politics about their opposition to the Vietnam War, for instance, explicit in their lyrics, this group of people has brought feminism into their everyday lives by simply doing gender differently as they performed rock music and shaped rock culture.

╳Feminism is, most generally, a set of ideas about the world. While there are many schools of feminist thought, most feminist perspectives begin from the assumption that there is gender-based inequality that works to the advantage of men as a group and to the disadvantage of women as a group. A feminist perspective also asserts that gender inequality is a social construct—in other words, that male dominance is conferred and enacted through social practice and custom, and is therefore mutable, and that women's subordination is a problem and must be eradicated. Feminist politics, then, consists of any action taken to challenge, transform, or eradicate the social conditions that confer dominance and material, political, and social advantages upon men. When I say that these rock artists adopted a "feminist sensibility," I mean that these people were consciously aware and critical of sexism and committed to challenging gender inequality and male dominance in their own lives. Their world was rock music.

In the early 1990s, some women and men decided that the mainstream rules of rock music culture, especially those for hard rock and heavy metal, needed some renovating. On the heels of the decade of Reagan-Bush conservatism and corporate, glam-metal mania, people in Seattle, Washington, D.C., Minneapolis, Chicago, and elsewhere began building a new sort of rock and roll culture from the ground up. Hanging rock and roll authenticity onto a feminist political frame, they simply began doing things differently. They didn't make overt political, pro-feminist statements in their lyrics, videos, or stage performances. Nor did they make explicitly political statements when interviewed. Instead, this feminist sensibility translated into simply behaving differently. Through their everyday activities as rock musicians, including how they presented themselves in interviews, onstage, in their lyrics and videos, and as fans, as well as how they talked about the music and musicians and how they acted and interacted with each other at concerts, they set up a new set of rules for what it means to be a rocker. And in doing so, they were able to construct a rock subculture that did not reproduce the male-dominant boys' club of "cock rock" that had dominated rock since its beginnings. I call this subculture *alternative hard rock* (AHR).[1]

For two and a half years, I spent time with alternative hard rockers in Chicago. During this time, I was able to talk with a dozen fairly well known AHR musicians who were passing through town doing gigs or recording. As I talked with these people and thought about what was going on sociologically, I realized that AHRers were deploying a fairly effective strategy for transforming the gender order and thereby challenging male dominance in their own lives. More important, while the activities of AHRers were specific to rock culture, the general strategy, I thought, could be applied to any social setting. I call this strategy *gender maneuvering*. To gender-maneuver, you examine any social setting to see how gender organizes the positions and the activities of people involved in that specific setting, and then you do things differently.

While one of my goals is to show how feminism was used to transform rock culture, my main goal is to present AHR as simply one example of how feminism can be used in our everyday lives. The main point I would like to convey by describing these rockers is that feminism is not simply a set of academic ideas or collective actions, but is also a tool that can be used to understand, evaluate, and transform the most mundane, simple practices and beliefs in our lives. Each of us, as individuals or as part of a group, can engage in a sort of feminist politics simply by doing everyday things differently; and, as alternative hard rockers have shown, we can have a blast while doing so.

THE GENDER ORDER OF MAINSTREAM ROCK CULTURE

Gender order refers to a network of beliefs about gender difference and rules for how to perform or "do" gender. In contemporary Western cultures, this network includes the assumption that there are two genders—male and female—each with a corresponding set of personality characteristics, desires, and embodied practices called masculinity and femininity. Masculinity and femininity are believed to be opposites, with each biological sex, gender identity, and set of characteristics defined by its difference from the other. Masculinity and femininity are also assumed to complement each other. They make sense as two halves of a whole. This set of assumptions about gender difference and complementarity gets mapped onto all kinds of social positions in different social settings and institutions: husband/wife, father/mother, boss/secretary, doctor/nurse, and so on. The rules for what behavior is appropriate for a good husband, wife, father, mother, boss, and secretary parallel the rules for masculinity and femininity in general. Wives, mothers, and secretaries take care of the needs of others; they are pleasant, nurturing, and other-centered. Husbands, fathers, and bosses are good leaders; they are assertive and authoritative. However, the relationship between masculinity and femininity is not truly complementary because there is an implicit hierarchy in our society that values the masculine over the feminine. Being a good leader, for instance, is valued and rewarded more than being a good nurturer. Finally, the gender order depends on all of us, women and men alike, going along with its rules and requirements. As we occupy different social roles, such as spouse, parent, and worker, we are required not only to perform the tasks associated with that position, but also to "do" gender.[2] That is, we are required to present ourselves to others not just as parents, spouses, and workers, but also as men and as women. As we perform or "do" gender in our everyday lives, we reproduce and support the rules and requirements that set masculinity and femininity up as hierarchical, yet complementary, opposites.

If we take a close look at rock music culture, we can identify how the gender order gets played out in that setting. Rock music culture, like all cultures, consists of a set of social positions, common beliefs, and shared practices. Embedded within rock culture are the ideas about gender difference outlined above; the sorts of beliefs and activities that constitute doing rock reflect and maintain those assumptions. For instance, if we use the lens of gender to take a look at the two most public and prominent social positions that make up rock culture—musician and rock fan—it becomes clear how ideas of gender are implicated in our expectations regarding who and what rock musicians and rock fans are. Rock musicians are supposed to be rebellious, aggressive, and interested in having sex with lots of different women. If one is a rock musician and wants to be perceived by others as a rock musician, one must act out, perform, or "do" rebelliousness, aggressiveness, and sexual promiscuity. These rules for doing the rock musician role parallel the requirements of masculinity more generally, which prescribe that all young men be aggressive, somewhat rebellious, and interested in sex. Because the rules for doing rock musician require masculine behavior, the position of rock musician itself is thus masculinized. By adopting the role, anybody who is a rock musician ends up being masculinized, regardless of her or his gender identity.

Contrast this with the pop star. The pop star is considered less skilled, more conforming, more interested in fame and fortune, and more focused on romance and the world of heterosexual ritual. Think about it—the rock musician (aggressive, rebellious, sexual) is contrasted with the pop star (well-behaved, vain, romantic). Sounds a bit like the bad boy juxtaposed with the good girl, doesn't it? It's no coincidence that one of the worst insults one can hurl at hard rock musicians is that their music is pop drivel. It's sort of like calling a boy a sissy. The pop star serves as a feminized (and thus inferior) opposite to the masculine (superior) rock musician. Rock and rock musicians derive their masculine valence from the degree to which they differ from pop music and pop stars.

Now consider the more explicitly feminine complement to the rock musician—the groupie. Who is the groupie? According to rock ideology, the groupie is a nameless, faceless, and ideally sexually attractive woman who is available for inconsequential sex. She is, in sum, the feminine sexual object. Her role as a nameless, faceless object necessarily situates her as inferior to the rock musician. In many ways, she is perceived as simply one of the rewards for being a successful rock musician. So the relationship between rock musicians and groupies, as defined through rock ideology, reproduces the hierarchical relationship between masculinity and femininity in the dominant culture at large.

Not all rock fans, however, are groupies. What about the "real" fans of rock, those who are serious about the music? They learn how to play an instrument, know about music, and have insider knowledge about rock bands and rock culture. It is a central component to rock culture that serious rock fans are aspiring musicians themselves. The serious fan is, in this way, on the same continuum of rock knowledge and skill as the rock musician. The difference between musician and fan is not qualitative, but quantitative. Thus, the complement or opposite of the rock fan is not the rock musician. Instead, the opposite of the serious fan in rock culture is the teenybopper fan, who is less interested in the music than in the attractiveness of musicians. Rather than aspiring to be a musician, the teenybopper fan dreams of being the wife or girlfriend of a rock musician. The serious fan has aspirations for success and status, works hard at developing the skills and knowledge required, and is concerned with the important matters in rock and roll life, like musical skill and integrity. Sounds pretty masculine, doesn't it? The teenybopper, as rock ideology constructs her, is not interested in skill and knowledge but instead wants a sexual partner who is skilled, knowledgeable, and successful. Very feminine, indeed. Moreover, although girls can work their way into the ranks of both musician and real fan, there is absolutely no room in rock ideology for boys to be groupies or teenyboppers. This reflects the implicit hierarchy between masculinity and femininity—girls gain status by "doing" masculinity, while boys lose status by taking a walk on the feminine side. The constraints on the type of relationship deemed "acceptable" between musician and fan also reflect heterosexism by eliminating any possibility of making explicit any homoeroticism between male rock musicians and real fans who are males.

In sum, the musicians and serious fans embody and exhibit the highly respected, and not coincidently masculine, positions in rock, while the pop star, the groupie, and the teenybopper fan are feminized and at the bottom of the hierarchy. As people go about "doing" rock culture, if they follow these rules as fans and musicians and support the ideological underpinnings that give these positions meaning, they continue to re-create the gender order in the culture at large.

But what if people started to become fed up with this gendered construction of rock? What if they wanted to rock but didn't want to reproduce male dominance as it manifests itself in rock culture? If the gender order of male dominance depends on an ideological matrix that binds masculinity and femininity into a hierarchical embrace, even as they act out their complementary roles, then disrupting that relationship just might disrupt the gender order of rock music culture.

As I mentioned earlier, gender maneuvering refers to any individual or group actions that, in some way, disrupt the relationship between masculinity and femininity in any given setting. Through talk, "body language" and presence, as well as modes of interaction, individuals or groups can "do" gender in unexpected or alternative ways, and by doing so can manipulate how masculinity and femininity articulate or construct each other. In all contexts, the same sort of hierarchical, yet complementary, relationship between masculinity and femininity is encoded in the rules, but the actual behaviors that are required or expected differ. In other words, because the requirements for performing gender roles vary from context to context, the specific form of gender maneuvering will also vary by context. For instance, the normative expectations for how to "do" femininity while hanging out with friends on a Saturday night might differ from those on the job, so breaking the rules for gender performance will be different depending on whether you're out with friends or at work. Gender maneuvering within rock culture, then, would be about disrupting the relationship between masculinity and femininity as it takes shape in the relationships between musicians, groupies, real fans, and teenyboppers.

This is exactly what alternative hard rockers did. Through their talk, their embodied practices, and their interactions with each other, they manipulated the rules for how to "do" musician, groupie, real fan, and teenybopper in ways that disrupted the gendered hierarchy between them. Let me explain how.

"WE'RE JUST HERE TO ROCK": REDEFINING THE "MUSICIAN"

One of the requirements for "doing" rock musician is to participate in interviews. It is often through the interview that rock musicians establish what it means to be a rocker. They talk about their music, their tours, and, in many cases, about their access to women. By talking about their sexual exploits, rock musicians produce the gendered and hierarchical relationship between themselves as musicians and women as groupies. The rocker establishes himself as the masculine musician while simultaneously situating women fans as sexual objects. When I interviewed AHR musicians, the interview itself was consistent with mainstream rock culture. However, the way these rockers talked about groupies and being on tour redefined what it meant to be a musician.

For instance, Ian MacKaye is one of the singers, guitarists, and songwriters in the band Fugazi, a harder-edged band out of Washington, D.C. He talked about trying to "do" sexuality differently and encouraging others to do the same:

> I wrote a song called "Out of Step" that said, "don't smoke, don't drink, don't fuck. At least I can fuckin' think." And it was sort of about guys around me. That was their big thing, to get fucked up and get laid constantly. That wasn't my priority in life. My priority was to be like a person or whatever. . . . [Punk music] was something that gave me access to a whole 'nother world, and I was challenged on so many levels, like politically, sexually. Everything I thought had to be turned upside down and reexamined.[3]

Kim Thayil, lead guitarist for the all-male band Soundgarden, expressed a similar sentiment:

> I think in the last few years there's been a lot of great bands that have killed that stereotype, that male stereotype. . . . Initially when I got into [rock music] I was like, yeah, guys are dicks, rock bands are pretty stupid, and I want to be in a rock band that doesn't patronize the sexist and racist aspects of rock. Like punk in that sense . . . they're normal people. They're not playing some kind of rock dream of dressing up and getting girls or whatever.[4]

Other alternative hard rockers stated their point of departure from mainstream rock's groupie culture more straightforwardly. Jennifer Finch of L7 said, "Groupies are mostly a mainstream rock phenomenon. It's a sexist world, and groupies are just part of that world. [It's] not any different from any other sexist aspect of society. . . . I don't get into that scene myself, but for some people, it works."[5] Although Finch did not condemn the people who do participate in "that scene," she was very clear about her own rejection of that aspect of being a musician. The groupie scene, according to Finch, is embedded in larger patterns of sexism, and she wasn't interested in participating. Though Finch presents her choice to avoid the groupie scene as a personal preference, her bandmate Donita Sparks made it clear that this was a choice made by many AHR musicians: "The groupie thing just doesn't happen. It's not part of the sensibility of what we're doing. And the guys that we tour with—you know, the Melvins and Wool—it's not like there are groupies back here hanging out with them. It's just not part of what we do."[6]

I asked her, "What is this sensibility you keep referring to?" Sparks responded, "It comes out of punk roots. It's about being more enlightened, having a sense of fairness and not being sexist pigs. You know those guys in rock bands with all the groupies. That's fine, but they're usually fuckin' pigs trying to prove something. We're just here to rock."[7]

Eddie Vedder extended this outlook to lyrical and video content when he said:

Music videos are so cliché. They all objectify women. Like I was watching Warrant's video for "Cherry Pie." That just disgusted me. I know some people try to make fun of the whole use of women in videos, but they end up doing the same thing. I quit my last band over a conflict over a song. It was called "She's So Sexual." It was written by someone else in the band, and I just refused to sing it. It seemed like it was from the perspective of a bunch of guys standing around watching a woman go by. It also used words like "baby" and "sweetie." I didn't write it and that's not how I would express myself, so I quit.[8]

As they talked about what they do, these musicians redefined what it meant to be a musician and subscribed to alternative rules for how to "do" musician. By claiming that the groupie scene was not part of what they do, these AHR musicians took groupie out as the opposite of the musician, and consequently, the term "musician" was no longer synonymous with the hypersexualized, heterosexual masculinity of mainstream rock.

AHR musicians also talked about their fans in a way that disrupted the relationship between musicians and groupies. Kat Bjelland of the edgy Minneapolis band Babes in Toyland talked about her fans in order to construct her own position as musician. When I asked her if there was a difference between the ways men and women approached her, she responded, "The guys are never, like, sleazy, groupie-type people. It's always really nice people. We have really nice fans for some reason. They're really smart and cool. . . . You know, [they have] similar minds."[9]

Having "similar minds" meant understanding that being a musician did not include having sex with fans, and that "doing" fan did not include trying to gain sexual access to musicians. According to Bjelland, her fans do not play the part of groupie. Since her fans never played groupie and she didn't play the old role of musician, for her the gendered relationship between musicians and fans disappeared.

One might argue that, when a woman musician turns male fans into sex objects and uses her status as a musician to gain sexual access to men, she is challenging the gender order. After all, it is a woman who is sexually objectifying and exploiting a man. Yet, when individual women embrace and "do" masculinity and when men "do" femininity, the overall gender structure, or the relationship between masculinity and femininity, remains intact. If women musicians enact the musician role in the same ways men have, they become masculinized, and the men or women groupies become feminized as the nameless, faceless sexual objects of the musician's desire. The gendered relationship between sexual subject as masculine and sexual object as feminine is sustained. That is, the gendered meaning of the relationship and hierarchy between musician and groupie does not change, even if the gender identities of those performing the roles of musician and fan do not match up neatly. So changing the gender order is not about switching places; it is about redefining the places and the relationship between them.

FROM "GROUPIE" TO "GROUPER": REDEFINING THE GROUPIE AND TEENYBOPPER

The musician-groupie relationship depends on rules and requirements for both musicians and fans. One could disrupt this relationship by redefining what it means to be a musician, as outlined above, or one could develop alternative rules for the groupie and the real fan. Alternative hard rockers were quite clever in the ways they redefined the groupie.

One of the most interesting gender maneuvers to destabilize the musician-groupie dichotomy in rock culture was the transformation of groupie into rock performer. One evening in June 1993 the opening act was Cynthia Plastercaster. Cynthia Plastercaster is one of the few groupies who has not remained nameless and faceless; in rock culture, she is world-famous, not only for having had sexual relations with rock stars such as Jimi Hendrix and Mick Jagger but also for having made plaster casts of her conquests' penises. Rather than performing music with a band as the opening act at this concert, Plastercaster not only described in detail her sexual experiences with and the sexual adequacy of various "rock guys"; she also related anecdotes about the casting in plaster of their genitalia. As Cynthia Plastercaster brandished the identity of groupie with pride, her descriptions of the practices that led to that identity flag were transformed into rock performance. When

Cynthia Plastercaster's experiences as a groupie became rock performance, the line dividing rock performer and groupie dissolved. She had become both.

Sometimes musicians, especially women musicians, have collapsed the distinction between a musician and someone who is attracted to, has sex with, or develops intimate relationships with musicians. One night I was talking with a local musician in Chicago about a recent article she had read in a fan 'zine about groupies. She said, "I always worried about being called a groupie because I've always dated musicians. But, you know, that's who I'm around. I admire them and what they do. And I wanted to do what they were doing. I'm a grouper, not a groupie."[10]

Her use of the word "grouper" rather than "groupie" signified a conscious rejection of the dichotomy between those who are interested in the music and those who are interested in the people who are playing the music. There is still an attraction to and—as this woman said—an admiration of musicians. At the same time, however, this woman is a professional musician herself. By using the word "grouper," she changed the word "groupie" (a sex object) into someone who acts. The grouper acts as both musician and someone who dates musicians. Unlike the groupie, the grouper is a subject, not an object.

Alternative hard rockers also gender-maneuvered by collapsing ideological divisions between real fans and fans who are sexually attracted to the musicians. For instance, Jennifer Finch talked about being a young woman who is both interested in rock music and attracted to musicians. She said: "When I was young, I remember seeing Mick Jagger and thinking, 'I want to be his girlfriend.' I saw Jerri Hall and how glamorous she was. I wanted to be her. I wanted to be Mick Jagger's wife. Then I got into punk music, and I started wanting to be Mick Jagger, not his girlfriend. It became an option to *be* Mick Jagger."[11] By talking about her attraction to Mick Jagger as inextricable from her desire to become a musician herself, Finch dissolved the line between the real fan who aspires to be a musician and the teenybopper fan who wants to marry a rock star. She was both, and so the mainstream gender ideology that says you are either serious about the music or you are attracted to musicians no longer made any sense.

One evening I watched as a woman approached a man, grabbed his arm, jumped up and down, and said in a shrill voice, "Are you in a band?!" He laughed, and then she said in a lower, matter-of-fact voice, "Me, too." This woman playfully mocked the performance of "groupie" and quickly shifted into the position of musician, thereby exposing and destabilizing the gender construction of the musician-groupie relationship.

The people I spent time with in Chicago also gender-maneuvered to erase the ideological line that separates the real fan from the teenybopper. Though there was a fair amount of discussion about musicians' musical abilities and about the important activities of the band, these conversations always included some banter about how "hot" (i.e., sexually attractive) the musicians were. Rather than "doing" either real fan or teenybopper fan, both women and men simultaneously "did" both. In AHR, the real fans acted as groupie/wanna-bes or as teenyboppers. Sexual desire for musicians did not fall into two neat categories that separated fans along the lines of gender identity, as mainstream rock ideology would have it. Instead, sexual desire for musicians was articulated by both men and women, and people who expressed sexual desire were not considered less-than-serious rock fans. And perhaps most interestingly, the men and women expressed sexual attraction and desire for both women and men musicians. At least in terms of forging new rules for "doing" real fan, alternative hard rockers were fairly successful at undermining not just sexism but also some forms of heterosexism.

There was really no way for me to determine empirically whether individual musicians actually had sexual relations with fans on a regular basis. It is entirely possible that, whereas in their talk and public performance alternative hard rockers constructed themselves as different, less sexist musicians and fans, individually some of the musicians—and fans—might have reproduced the sexist patterns they criticized. Nonetheless, in their interviews and in their interactions with others, alternative hard rockers still forged a new set of rules for publicly "doing" rock that departed from the norms for mainstream rock culture. And these new rules made for a different experience at the rock shows. Men didn't hit on women. Women fans and musicians were respected and taken seriously. I and other women could really enjoy the show and participate fully and safely; women were no longer sexual objects.

We were rock fans and rock musicians. We were, in essence, no longer inferior. And this was accomplished by simply recognizing the problem and deciding to do things differently.

WHAT NEXT?

Alternative hard rockers used feminist critiques to take a long, hard look at rock and roll. Feminism gave them the lens through which they could identify how normal, everyday practices in rock music were embedded in the larger gender order that places men and masculinity above women and femininity. Once alternative hard rockers had identified the sexist rules, practices, and beliefs in mainstream rock culture, they pitched them off the stage, picked up their guitars again, and launched into a different kind of rock culture. With a new set of rules for how to "do" musician and fan, they created an alternative gender organization for their own rock subculture.

There are important lessons that we can take from alternative hard rockers. First, the lesson is that any one of us, alone or preferably in groups, can do the same thing. Take a look around your immediate world and see how male dominance gets reproduced. Think about your scene. Do you play sports? Do you like to hang with your friends? Do you date? Do you have sex? Do you bowl? Do you write poetry, fiction, screenplays? Do you wait tables? Consider how the gender order organizes different parts of your life. What are the masculine positions and what are the feminine ones, and how are they situated in relation to each other? How does this relationship set up complementarity and hierarchies of male dominance? When you have a handle on the workings of masculinity and femininity, think about how you and your friends might undermine or openly challenge them by doing things differently in your daily life.

Second, alternative hard rockers teach us that men and women can gender-maneuver. This sort of feminist practice is not limited to women, for it is the actions of all of us that reproduce the patterns of male dominance. We can all subvert the gender order.

In sum, alternative hard rockers teach us that even the most sexist, male-dominant cultural forms or patterns can be rethought, done differently, and reconstructed. The AHR subculture also teaches us that both women and men can participate. There's no reason why every-body can't gender-maneuver in some small or large way. Imagine the possibilities if we all did this in all of the specific roles and locations in which we move about the world. I'm not suggesting that this is an al-ternative to more traditional forms of collective action. This sort of politics will do little to remedy the wage gap or eradicate the exploita-tion of women workers in developing nations or ensure access to safe and effective birth control. What I am saying is that this is something we can all do right now, right here—wherever "here" might be. We can gender-maneuver *and* work collectively for institutional change. And there is no reason why we, like alternative hard rockers, can't have a lot of fun doing it.

NOTES

1. Although there is much well-founded suspicion of the term "alternative" to describe rock music, I chose this label purposefully. I think "alternative" is a particularly useful word because it always refers to a relationship rather than simply a characteristic. The word "alternative" not only is a referent to the thing being described—a genre of music, for example—but also points to what it is al-ternative to: that is, what is accepted, mainstream, dominant, and hegemonic. The bands to which I am referring were not so much alternative in terms of their hybrid of punk and hard rock, for that is the sound that eventually became the mainstream in the mid-1990s. The people I spent time with were on the ground floor of developing and proliferating an alternatively *gendered* rock and roll. Thus, the relationship that "alternative" connotes in the label as I use it is not about the sound of their music. Instead, it refers to how they *did* rock music dif-ferently from mainstream rock in terms of sexuality and gender.
2. See Candace West and Don Zimmerman, "Doing Gender," *Gender & Society* 1, no. 2 (1987): 125–51.
3. Ian MacKaye, interview by author, Chicago, Sept. 9, 1993.
4. Kim Thayil, interview by author, Chicago, July 2, 1994.
5. Jennifer Finch, interview by author, Chicago, July 1, 1992.
6. Donita Sparks, interview by author, Chicago, Oct. 1, 1994.
7. Ibid.
8. Eddie Vedder, interview by author, Chicago, March 27, 1992.
9. Kat Bjelland, interview by author, Chicago, Nov. 5, 1994.
10. Anonymous musician, interview by author, Chicago, July 31, 1994.
11. Finch interview.

Pranks and Fake Porn:
Doing Feminism My Way

Welcome to the Home of the Big Bad Chinese Mama. THE #1 MOCK MAIL-ORDER
BRIDE/ASIAN PORN SPOOF SITE IN THE WORLD! *Inside are contained the "demure lotus blossoms," the "geishas," the "oriental sluts"—whatever you had imagined
in your patriarchal, colonialist longings. These women will take you by storm
(and will kick your ass). Yeah, you've seen mail-order bride sites before, you
may have even surfed over to an Asian porn site, but never in your wildest, culturally commodifying, sick sexual desires, have you been schooled by women
(womyn) like this!* . . .

—http://www.bigbadchinesemama.com (May 2000)

In May 2000, I created the site www.bigbadchinesemama.
com both as a public art piece and as an Asian American anthology of
voices and personal satire. The site was my senior project as an under-
grad at UCLA. It was a daring project for me because I was taking a mix
of scholarly ideas and annoying frustrations and sharing them on the
Web with strangers in the crude and seemingly amateurish medium of
a mock mail-order bride/fake porn site. The site's content hints that it
is intended to question the mail-order bride industry and to attack all
white males as bigots, but these were only my secondary and least important objectives. As a woman artist who also happens to be Asian
American, I continue to feel pressure from the Asian American and
feminist movements to be "representative" of their political goals—
goals I do not always understand or agree with. The process of developing the site helped me test and renegotiate what I loathed about "feminist" notions and activist politics. This site helped me change what I
thought about feminism and activism by redefining those ideas for
myself and other people.

Why was I afraid of the word "feminism"? I had spent four years at college avoiding using the word to identify my leftist politics. At UCLA, using the word "feminist" is like declaring yourself a political leader. The way I saw it, you couldn't just casually call yourself a feminist and go about your college life drinking at parties and flirting with guys. If you were a self-identified feminist, it was as if you had declared a religious vow that came with responsibilities. A feminist was someone who lacked humor. If I wanted to be what I thought a feminist was, I'd have had to make lifestyle and attitude adjustments according to the Commandments of Political Correctness. In other words, as a self-proclaimed feminist, I would have to develop a supersensitivity to anything that might be somewhat offensive, policing society for every ounce of injustice. "Feminism" was a word that was repellent to me, even as an educated college student.

Until recently, I feared the word. I refrained from declaring myself a feminist when I offered guest lectures about the skewed representations of Asian women on Asian sex sites and about my efforts to subvert these images through www.bigbadchinesemama.com. On one occasion, a student put me on the spot and asked me if I thought of myself as a feminist. I explained, "I don't consider myself so much a feminist as I do an artist who believes that there is political power in the personal voice." The San Francisco State University professor who was hosting me in her classroom corrected me in front of the class. She explained that that was what feminism is about. Third wave feminism is about embracing individual experience and making personal stories political. First and second wave feminisms sought to empower women as a united front. Although they offered a political voice for women as a whole, they didn't acknowledge the varying agendas and experiences of individual women. Third wave feminism was a response by women of color and others who felt homogenized by a movement defined by the goals of middle-class, white women.

This definition of third wave feminism astonished me. Who knew that, according to some odd academic definition previously unavailable to me, I was a feminist? I had two degrees from UCLA and still didn't know that feminism wasn't about man-hating women holding picket signs. Too bad the rest of the world couldn't understand the kind of feminism I was embracing without taking a women's studies class. Was it also possible that the only people who know about this so-called third wave of feminism are the "learned" feminists who have already struggled with the definition in classes and discussion groups? What about John Doe, a fifty-four-year-old accountant who couldn't care less what "feminism" means, just as long as he's out the door by five o'clock? How about Jane Doe, a new immigrant in America who would much rather make ends meet and learn English than know that "feminism" is not a scary word?

Maybe a national billboard campaign needs to be launched. We need giant signs above every campus and freeway that read: "Hey, America! Don't be afraid of the word 'feminist'! It doesn't mean man-hating or being humorless! There is a new thing called 'third wave' feminism that will open the door so you can embrace politics by being who you are!"

The concept of feminism has become so academic that only a select few understand its new meaning. In spite of this, feminist politics can be shared with the world if it is carefully disguised in the mass media. Pop culture provides an effective vehicle to carry the self-celebrating concepts of third wave feminism. The unfortunate downside is that we end up with inane catchphrases such as "Girls Rule, Boys Drool" and "Girl Power." These sound bites are paradoxical in their attempt to inspire women. For example, the gorgeously thin and shapely women of Destiny's Child singing about being independent certainly have no problem maintaining their self-esteem. Feminist catchphrases in pop culture use the term "girl" but rarely, if ever, use the word "woman." It suddenly becomes too serious to say "Woman Power!" instead of "Girl Power!" I wanted to bridge the gap between serious feminism and pop feminism in order to make the idea of feminism less scary. As it turns out, www.bigbadchinesemama.com was the bridge.

Let me set the backdrop for the creation of my Web site by describing my history.

During my freshman year at UCLA, I was vulnerable to the indoctrination of ethnic studies and women's studies courses. I grew up as a third and fourth generation Chinese American in San Francisco and saw the advantages of being "Americanized." I witnessed the subtle effects of liberal white racism in the disguise of "multiculturalism," and I grew up an awkward teenager because I always felt torn between my individual identity as a woman and pop culture's constructions of femininity. I resisted when approached by student groups formed on the basis of ethnic background. I felt such groups were "clannish" because they did not embrace other ethnic groups. Soon, however, I found myself drawn to them as a way to bring me closer to "the motherland." My first women's studies class was like a therapy session; with the help of theory and academic analysis, I was able to examine my experiences. I finally had a place where I could see my own experiences in context and analyze every awkward and uncomfortable moment from my childhood. The women's studies classroom gave me a place where I could redirect my anger and self-hatred—at government, at my culture or lack thereof, at the mass media, and especially at white men and their big oppressive penises.

These were amazing revelations, but instead of feeling empowered, I felt completely helpless. Women's studies almost ruined me. I spent my first summer after college toxically angry back home in San Francisco, unable to reconcile my "new identity" with my day-to-day living. I shaved my head because I didn't want to be the object of the popular gaze. I roamed the streets in search of ex-boyfriends, believing that they somehow owed me an apology for every inequity in our past relationships that might have been rooted in their assumptions about my race and gender. I was unable to watch television or movies, because the overwhelming presence of white actors on screen reminded me that my life was a product of "colonization."

The power that I thought I had been given by my new-found knowledge completely paralyzed me. At the end of that summer, an ulcer ripped through my stomach, and I had a semi–nervous breakdown. I realized that my anger was only hurting me and was doing nothing to change the world around me. From that point on, I acknowledged that I gave racism and sexism too much credit for causing my woes. Though my gender and ethnicity framed my experiences, I was still an active agent in my life. The only thing that was really victimizing me was my own self-pity; the inherent factors of race and gender only posed a challenge. Of course, this is a melodramatic example of what happens in a "self-awakening." During my second year of college, I was able to calm my aggression; I began to make amends with my feelings of cultural displacement through art and performance.

After this point, I felt pressure to make all of the artwork I created "representative" of Asian people. The mass-media stereotypes of Asians I had become acutely aware of were the images of Asian women as exotic and sexual creatures, or conversely, as sexually inert and nerdy. Through my classes, I became overly sensitive to elements in my artwork that were stereotypical and began to censor those elements so that my work would be "empowering." However, I discovered that the more unstereotypical I made my art, the less human and more uninteresting it became. In my attempts at complete political correctness, I wrote about characters who were unreal. It was very difficult to create characters or address themes in my work that were honest. I began to feel resentful of my activism, as it seemed to suffocate my artistic voice instead of allowing me to explore it.

Soon it seemed more appropriate to write a history book than to create art, because the obligation to "represent" everyone's politics accurately was so overwhelming. Why was the act of achieving personal freedom through art so oppressive? Why had the process of making art as an Asian American woman become so drenched in unanticipated responsibilities? Could it be possible that the act of living and creating art freely was protest in itself, and that it was more subversive and more challenging than an overt act of protest? Is it possible that by not caring about the constraints put on me because of my race and gender and by just living my life, I had actually been able to achieve goals similar to those that major political movements would seek to meet? In my case, those goals meant living as if my race or gender was not a constraint.

I knew that politics was indeed constraining the messages of art—and not just my own work—when I attended a poetry reading at UCLA for Asian Pacific Heritage Month. Poet after poet seemed to drone on forever about "identity politics." The poets' works cast away stereotype after stereotype, but rarely revealed who the poets were. A Vietnamese American woman approached the mike. Before reading, she apologized for not having work that was "important and political." It was disappointing that she felt that her work was neither important nor political just because she didn't talk about white oppression or feeling silenced by institutionalized racism. Her poem was about her struggle with weight loss. This was an issue that was very personal to her and very relevant to many people in the room because it confronted issues of body image.

In a way, I connected with this poet because I wanted to create an art piece that appealed to audiences without being too pedantic or too politically correct; I also did not want my art to have its message negated—that is, the way pop culture did—by refusing to get too serious about feminism. I wanted to create an anthology that would be public and that could be understood both by people who were knowledgeable about academic rhetoric and by those who were not. I was wary of reducing my arguments to academic theories that I didn't understand and that I knew were inaccessible to the mainstream. I wanted to express what I thought feminism should be by creating an unpretentious and simple work that didn't bog audiences down with theory but used theory in an accessible way. I didn't want to negate the idea of strong women by carrying my message through bikini-clad women. Nor did I want to "de-program" the female image by making my participants asexual.

Art has the potential to be more broadly accessible than other forms of communication, but the problem with most anthologies, art events, and chapbooks made for Asian American women is that audience potential is limited to how many seats are available or how many copies can be produced and sold. While live performance and literature can play a role in a cultural critique, the demographics of their audiences limit their potential. When people participate in an Asian American–themed event or purchase a literary work by an Asian American, they generally are already interested in Asian American issues. I wanted to reach people who had neither an existing interest in nor a concern for Asian American women and their politics.

The solution to this dilemma came to me through my work with Mimi Nguyen, a Ph.D. candidate in gender studies at UC Berkeley who showed me how to make academia relevant in day-to-day events. After a draining quarter in her Asian American Women's Literature class, with endless readings that seemed to take the same point from a different angle, her Web site (http://www.worsethanqueer.com [March 10, 2000]) was offered as the last assignment of the term. Mimi's site is self-declared "critical theory for handy everyday use." Mimi is a queer Vietnamese refugee and a participant in punk rock culture. Her writing demolished my stereotype of academics as dry, intimidating readers of ancient books. Her site is an archive of journal reflections on daily events, magazine articles, and drawings, all of which reflect her studies in postcolonial and poststructural theories. With her sassy writing style, Nguyen was able to awaken my interest in academia. What I found very interesting was one entry in which she stated that people had found her site by doing a search for Asian porn.

It dawned on me that locating "safe spaces" for Asian women to meet and converse on the Internet was virtually impossible because doing a search for "Asian women" almost always yielded mail-order bride and pornographic sites. In addition, I was tired of "safe spaces"—I had spent four years in classes, at art events, and at poetry readings that were so safe I felt insulated—and I began to feel awkward because I wasn't as upset as the people around me. I yearned for reality; I was tired of feeling like I was preaching to the choir.

I decided to build a Web site, not as a discussion space for Asian American women, but as a space that would examine my conflicting politics. I also decided not to take on the burden of trying to please or represent an entire population. I wanted to reach people who were knowledgeable about Asian American politics and those who weren't. I thought that intercepting traffic would be the best way to reach those who most needed to see my message. I quickly realized that this tactic would target the gross guys who accost me at places like the 99-cents store and ask me if I speak English; the people who ask me why it is that Asians are so docile; the men who come up to me at clubs and tell me it is their "fantasy to be with an Oriental woman." Through a highly arbitrary and unscientific survey of this sample, I deduced that this group is probably part of the same population that visits Asian porn sites or mail-order bride sites.

And thus my format for www.bigbadchinesemama.com was born!

I chose my domain name before I knew the site would be a mock porn site, because I wanted to subvert the *Joy Luck Club*–esque notion of a Chinese Mother as a weak, pained, and silenced woman who was set against the backdrop of mythology and ghosts. Instead, I wanted to move toward what I saw as the future of the Chinese Mother—a more aggressive, down-home "mama" similar to black mothers or mothers from the Deep South. "Big," "bad," and "mama" are also words used to describe women in black porn sites. Asian porn sites emphasize the smallness, shyness, and coyness of women; by using dramatically different adjectives, I intended to subvert a dominant trend. Just try typing the stereotypical adjectives used to describe Asian women—words such as "exotic," "petite," and "demure"—into a search engine, and typically you'll get Web sites on Asian porn or Asian themes. The pictures of the women on Asian porn sites emphasize shyness, and many women pose in a "naughty but nice" way. Type words that stereotypically describe black women—words such as "big booty"—into a search engine and you'll get black porn sites. In those sites, the fonts are inflated and gaudy, with the photography emphasizing the overt sexuality of black women; sometimes there are jungle prints in the background. Type in "Latina," and you will find naked Latin ladies and potential brides.

Before I built the site, I spent many late nights in college doing unofficial research. As I surfed the Web, I discovered that the general format for Asian sex sites was begging to be mocked. These sites made me laugh more than get upset because the emphasis on "orientalness" was so extreme that it was ridiculous. The exoticness of Asian culture was emphasized ad nauseam. The Web designers overused things such as decorative oriental fans, chopstick fonts, lanterns, and clickable gongs. In the Frequently Asked Questions (FAQ) section on almost every mail-order bride site, I found pertinent questions for potential "buyers," such as "Will my bride speak English?" and "Why will an Asian bride be a better wife than a Western bride?" and "What will a visa cost to bring her over?" Both the questions and the answers emphasized the apparently inherent subservience of Asian women and spoke of women as commodities instead of as humans. Although we would like to think that stereotypes of Asian women as "dragon ladies" and subservient "lotus blossoms" are long since passé, sites like these not only keep those images alive but also profit from customers who believe the stereotypes to be true.

In trying to encourage women who weren't hard-core activists to participate in this project, I assembled a harem of mail-order brides from my UCLA friends and classmates; these women, I thought, would represent a broad spectrum of empowered women who enact their politics at different levels. Some are political organizers; some participate in Asian American community events; others are considered "sellouts" or "apathetic." I had each woman create a mail-order bride bio to parody the bios on real mail-order bride sites. I wanted the bios to respond to what these individuals had experienced as women—and not just to their lives as Asian Americans. I had the women pose for pictures that responded to the images of Asian women in sex sites. In these pictures, some make funny faces, while others cover their faces; one chose not to be pictured at all. All of these images were subversive responses to the commodifying gaze placed on most Asian women on the Web.

I tried to get a large spectrum of experiences and demographics in the pool of "brides" for the site without attempting to make the diverse participants reflect the population at large. The participants come from different ethnic backgrounds; some are mixed race, some are queer, and all come from different economic backgrounds. I acknowledge that to represent every experience and demographic would be impossible, and I am not responsible for representing everyone. I hope to encourage visitors from all walks of life to explore bolder forms of expression by seeing the broad range of women who participate in my site. I have since received new bride submissions from visitors to my site. I have three brides who are Asian men; in their bios and photos, they poke fun at issues such as Asian male emasculation and being a gay Asian man constantly picked up by "rice queens" (slang for old white men who prey on gay Asians).

For my Web site, I parodied the FAQ section on other sites by creating a "FUQ" ("Frequently Un-asked Questions") section. I took questions from the mail-order bride sites and answered them on own my terms—slamming the answers found in traditional mail-order bride sites with my own Riot Grrrl sensibilities. My answer to whether the brides on my site speak English is an adamant "Of course we do. Why the fuck wouldn't we?" The pictures framing the sides of this section are of the "brides" beating and hurting white men. I intentionally made these pictures over the top, both to spoof the idea of "the angry Asian American feminist" and to show how rallying cries like "Bring down the White Man!" can be translated into ridiculous images. It was my personal response to the occasional fanatical antagonism in revolutionary movements.

I also included prank calls made to massage parlors and porn studios to set an example of what I see as "armchair activism." In one call to a massage parlor, Randy, our caller, pretends to be an eighty-five-year-old white man who would like to be massaged by "an Oriental." In the call, he asks such ridiculous questions as "Is there a senior discount?" and "Can my twenty-five-year-old wife watch?" The woman on the other line takes every laughable concern very seriously, as if she is used to getting weird calls like this all the time. In this parody, she also explains that "it's all the same" when he asks if he can have a Chinese instead of a Korean masseuse. Although she first answers the phone in a sexy voice, the woman becomes increasingly suspicious of Randy's motives during the call; by the end, her real voice is blaring through the receiver as she questions his age. I have received responses from visitors who feel that the prank calls are juvenile and do nothing to change the current state of politics. This is true: prank calls are juvenile and do not do what petitions and rallies do. However, posting these calls publicly gives visitors a glimpse of the sex industry as well as the male, eurocentric values it caters to and works under. It also gives an example of subversive action that even the laziest of activist types can take. I also want to show that it's okay to laugh at certain injustices instead of feeling constantly offended and disempowered by them.

One link on bigbadchinesemama.com is called "Memoirs of an Anti-Geisha"—a deliberate play on the title of Arthur Golden's best-selling novel, *Memoirs of a Geisha*. For the months that this novel about the geisha with the silver eyes (ahem) was all the rage, I put up with people (always white) trying to talk to me about this book. They acted as if they were so much more familiar with me and "my people" after reading the novel. (Never mind the fact that China and Japan are different countries or the fact that I live in America.) Golden's book was released in 1997, when Asian trends were all the rage in fashion, food, and beyond. Barnes and Noble packaged the book with tins of green tea to provide readers with an "authentic" cultural experience. And Madonna morphed into a geisha after reading the book. In my spoof of *Memoirs,* I celebrate the facets of my life that are ugly because they make me who I am, not because they are exotic or trendy. I describe crude habits such as nose picking and booger flicking that all humans secretly participate in. The section entitled "Big Feet, Loud Mouths" responds to subtly oppressive beauty standards for Chinese American women, using my big feet as a metaphor. My big feet were regarded as ugly when I was growing up; I was told that men prefer women with small feet. I grew up feeling uncomfortable about the size of my feet, always wishing that I could have feet that were more petite and less stinky. In my critique, I point out that I should have been proud of my big, stinky feet because they symbolize the freedom that my ancestors never had during the subjugating era of foot binding. The point of my critique is not to throw out Golden's book as inaccurate or poorly written but to embrace a less fanciful representation of Asian American women that pop culture tends to overlook.

I sought traffic in unorthodox ways because I wanted to get hits from people who were not familiar with Asian American women's issues. I cut and pasted a meta-tag from a porn site into my site so that when people searched words for porn, they would be led to my site. I placed ads for the site in the back of the *New Times LA* where the ads for escorts are, advertising my site as a porn site to see Asian women. I would also go into chat rooms and spam my Web address. Occasionally, people would try to kick me out of their chat rooms, though most times I would get curious visitors to bite the bait. I found clubs at different Web sites dedicated to fans of Asian women (ironically, many of these sites were housed at Click2Asia.com, a site intended for an Asian American audience). Most of these clubs were visited by men looking for a quick lay; the clubs were essentially porn-swapping clubs. I linked my site to these clubs, promising people who clicked on the link a gorgeous Asian woman. I used suspiciously alluring copy: "Wanna see hot and naked Asian women holding eggplant for free? Click here!" The descriptions I used were intended to entice men who were used to seeing Asian women as commodities. I tried to make the descriptions sound slightly subversive so that perceptive women might catch on that something wasn't quite right.

I also found much support by linking my site in nonsubversive ways to other sites on the Web. I found fan bases in sites for Asian and Asian American women. I was linked to academic sites, Asian American women's sites, feminist sites, and personal sites. I also received press from publications such as the *Village Voice,* the *LA Weekly,* and the Asian Pacific American magazine *Pacific Ties.*

I was nervous when I first launched the site. I felt vulnerable because visitors could access and interpret my thoughts and images whenever they wanted. However, it was liberating to have this presence on the Web because all the work is accessible twenty-four hours a day, and this approach is not as exhausting as day-to-day activism. It was exciting to know that my words and ideas could be found even when I was sleeping. This was a change from what I was used to thinking of as activism: a demanding effort that required participation by my "live" self.

I monitor the progress of the site and reactions to it across the Web through my guestbook. This is how I learn about people's reactions to the site. Many sites will censor and delete entries that condemn the Web site in order to protect their image to their loyal visitors, but for me, it is very important that the guestbook remain unaltered, because I want people to see that racism and sexism are alive and well. I was especially concerned about the reaction from other Asian Americans who might see my representation of Asian American women as crude. Soon after the launch of the site, I had obsessive visitors who would sign and start conversations in my guestbook daily, if not hourly. This was interesting to me because I immediately noticed how defensive my opposition was. They tried to take control of my Web site through my guestbook. They questioned every image and idea that was presented and then refuted anyone who signed with a note of appreciation. Some looked right past the obvious and accused me of not properly "representing" their image of an Asian woman.

Almost two years after I launched the Web site, I am extremely jaded. My guestbook entries are e-mailed to me daily, and I have slowly numbed my social conscience under the onslaught. Can you imagine what it is like to receive and file away daily e-mails that proclaim "FUCK NIGGERS!" hundreds of times, that inform me that I am a "dick-sucking cumbag," or even tell me that I should die? These guestbook entries, the public reactions to the site, prove that my site has reached its intended audience; my tactics have attracted both those interested in Asian American politics and those who are "oppressors." Because their positive and negative responses all appear within my site, they can be read only within the context of my site. There are those who live under the illusion that the world is much more progressive. The negative re-actions that I leave posted on the board reveal the extent of real igno-rance that still exists.

Reactions from Asian Americans are usually empowered. Occa-sionally, I get letters saying that my site offered both a new way to think about challenging oppression and the confidence to try activism in different ways. Other Asian American visitors criticize my site as not a "good representative" of Asian Americans and complain that I am making "us" look bad (as if "we" were a baseball team).

Unfortunately, these viewers fail to see that I wanted to challenge the idea that any public Asian American figure is obligated to stand in for the entire Asian American community. It's virtually impossible for one person to represent all political concerns, since the Asian Ameri-can population is so huge and varied. Because the issue has been broached publicly, other visitors respond and get the chance to gener-ate a public dialogue on the subject. Some visitors tell me that they cannot understand that my site passed as an "academic" project be-cause the bright colors and images seem so juvenile. My response to them is that my site is more catchy and accessible than pie charts and long, convoluted thesis projects. I want to challenge traditional modes of academia and to explore how dialogue generated in a classroom can be transported into the rest of the world.

Through a special hits counter, I discovered that some unorthodox traffic finds me in ways that I did not anticipate. I have been linked to some sites that cater to men with foot fetishes because of the pictures of my feet in the "Memoirs of an Anti-Geisha" link. I get at least two e-mails a month from men who want me to rub my feet on their faces so they can worship them. Yes, this is disturbing, but it comes with the territory. These are the visitors who, despite my blatant attempts to show that my site is a farce, still believe that my intention is to provide myself and the harem of mail-order brides as a commodity. It's quite shocking that some visitors fail to see through the heavy-handed satire I have created. This public display of ignorance is important because it wakes up visitors who respond to my site by saying, "So what? People aren't this dumb. Your message is old hat." Sometimes I respond to vis-itors who seem unconvinced that my site is serving any purpose, but the task can be overwhelming, as I receive so many negative responses a month. My goal is not to convert anyone to my way of thinking but just to share my ideas with them.

The site has served its purpose. It took me out of anger; now I am working on new art that my anger and frustration were hiding. I don't feel so reluctant when I take on new performance projects because I have already been to such an extreme with www.bigbadchinesemama. com that I know how to handle good and bad feedback. It is easier to do new projects that explore facets of identity. The project finally gave me a chance to use knowledge that I thought would forever be confined to a college classroom and would have no outside applications.

Recently, I have been much more comfortable calling myself a feminist when people ask me to describe the work that I do. Feminism has become something to which I have given my own interpretation, and I have taken the responsibility of not letting the word feminism "name me." Instead, I believe that I can take the reins and redefine the word for myself. This is the attitude that I would like to pass on to others; I hope that they, too, will change their attitude toward the word. Feminism is a proactive, creative act that you can do in your backyard. It is anything that will change the state of women for the better or open new dialogue on the state of women. Through my Web site, I tackled many of my fears about the inaccessible and impersonal nature of feminism. What I didn't realize until later was that, in challenging what I thought was wrong with feminism, I was actually doing feminism.

Afterword: A Correspondence between Katha Pollitt and Jennifer Baumgardner

Dear Katha,

As you know, I am invested in claiming that there is a third wave and that younger women are taking feminism forward, toward greater freedom if not always toward stronger laws or more organized protests. Intergenerational dialogues are useful—in print and in person—because they clarify era-related differences in how we were raised and thus what we are reacting against or fighting for. Although feminist conversation between second and third wavers is just beginning, already there are huge snags. Using just my own experience (in order to cut down on generalizations), I have felt that the feminism I am "inheriting" doesn't represent me or my life. My most profound development as a feminist occurred when I realized that older women didn't have an obligation to expand "their" feminism so that it defined me, but that I had the right and responsibility to create a feminism that was relevant to my life and my values. I think the second wave (not a monolith) had to do the same thing—or I get that impression from reading the histories and knowing a lot of older women who were and are active. Black women didn't feel represented in white groups, so they created their own feminist groups and owned the term for themselves.

Younger women don't reject feminism—as in equality and dignity and civil rights—out of hand. The Betty Friedan stuff makes sense, even to guys (equal pay, job opportunities for women, etc.). The Helen

Gurley Brown/Erica Jong stuff makes sense, too—women are allowed to have sex and like it, to have big appetites, to want to do important work, to be neurotic or insecure or want a man for companionship. The feminism that younger women are afraid of, it seems to me, is the feminism that assumes there is one pure way to be and it is anti-capitalist, super-serious, and hostile to bikini waxes and Madonna. I have met women at various "Veteran Feminists of America" events who think that they invented feminism and scoff at younger women as hopelessly mired in patriarchy and man-pleasing. I find this kind of radical feminism troubling because I think my generation was raised to be much less affected by men than the previous generation was. What I mean is that some older feminists' single-minded focus on patriarchy is as much a reflection of how large men loom in their eyes as it is an accurate sense of the "root" problem.

What the finger-pointing about who's a more politically correct feminist obscures is a deeper and more personal crisis of responsibility. For instance, you and I have worked together and there probably is a positive "feminist" side to our dynamic and a more typical "human" side to it. The positive side is that you are older and more accomplished but have been open to working with me and championing me over the years; we have done a fund-raiser or two as well as that press release about emergency contraception with relative ease, and we are friends. The human side is that I do more of the grunt work because . . . because I think I should and it's easier and I know more about computers, but also because I fear you won't do it if I leave it to you. I mean, I wouldn't necessarily be confident enough to own up and ask you to do something more grunty.

I think the thorn in my side (and that of my generation, if it's possible to extend my righteous anger that generally) is that I see younger women doing a majority of the work and older women doing a majority of the complaining. At the speak-outs and fund-raisers that you and I have coordinated intergenerationally, two or three younger women always take the bull by the horns even though they are outnumbered tenfold.

I think this points out a central issue for all oppressed types, which is that we wish things would just be equal without our having to take the scary step of asking for what we want or standing up for ourselves in individual moments; the big general moments aren't quite so scary, somehow. It's easier to say, "Older women don't listen to younger women!" rather than "Katha, I'm tired of doing all the typing." The same applies to feminists' relationships with men: when our oppression is portrayed as systemic, then we don't have any individual responsibility to have more honest relationships with men individually in our lives, whether it's our dad to whom we don't tell the whole truth or our boyfriend whom we resent for not making the bed.

But then what do you do?

Dear Jenn,

Take the feminist movement—please! In fact, pretty soon, you'll have no choice—the second wavers are getting on. You and I have been discussing the issue of feminist generations for a number of years, and I am glad to see that you are moving away from focusing on the transfer of power within existing organizations. That always struck me as unrealistic—older people rarely give up power because young people want their turn. You might as well expect tenured professors to retire at sixty so that young scholars can get jobs. Of course existing organizations should be more flexible and open and willing to transform themselves—but they have a history and a culture and a personality, much as families do, and as in families change is very difficult. At a certain point it makes more sense to move out and get your own apartment. Why spend your life complaining? I'm glad to see young women are taking that energy and using it to start their own groups, raise their own funds, write their own books, start their own publications. This is, after all, what those older feminists did back in the day.

When you and I talk in public or in larger discussion groups about generational shifts, I tend to take your side, but this familiar talk of passing the torch makes me inclined to agree with the older feminist who said, "Get your own damn torch!" More interesting than the question of power transfer is that of changing the accent or focus or style or even content of feminism to appeal to younger women. The women's movement has been culturally marked by the period of its rebirth—say 1967–1975—and yes, some of the traces left by that era seem rather dated today. Folk songs, herbal tea, clunky sandals, poems about menstruation, posters of women of many colors dancing in a circle or holding up half the sky—there's nothing wrong with any of this (I like folk songs!), but it feels a bit embalmed. (Of course, in writing this I realize how few older feminists I know who actually have these tastes.) One of the exciting things about feminism—indeed the whole left in the 1960s and 1970s—was the sense that it was on the cultural cutting edge, saying new things in new, daring ways.

So many feminist revelations have been absorbed into the culture that it's hard for me—but maybe not for you—to see another such moment coming along any time soon. You mentioned Erica Jong, whose *Fear of Flying* shocked and delighted the nation with its heroine, Isadora Wing, who enjoyed casual sex and who described her adventures in a graphic, down-to-earth, irreverent way. (I remember how shocked I was by her humorous description of her husband's unappealing genitals.) Today, Isadora's way of life sells millions of copies of *Glamour, Cosmo, Elle,* and *Marie Claire* and has its own hugely popular set of TV shows, *Sex and the City, Friends, Will & Grace.* Similarly, concepts that weren't even named until the 1970s—sexual harassment, acquaintance rape, marital rape—are now household words.

And yet, the fact that feminist ideas are part of the culture doesn't necessarily mean that they have significantly transformed the way life is actually lived by most people. Here I think is the bone of contention you and I worry over and gnaw at in our intergenerational discussion group. How much have things really changed? Acquaintance rape is part of the public discourse now, and a few men in publicized cases have been found guilty in court or kicked out of their colleges. But does date rape actually happen less? Are there fewer men who think a woman who wears a short skirt and has a couple of drinks too many is asking for it? Fewer women who blame themselves and absolve the guy? Is there more justice for victims? Similarly, the idea that household chores should be shared when both the man and the woman have jobs is very widespread today. But all the studies show that women do most of the work in the home whether or not they work outside it, and that men haven't increased their share of the scut work by more than a few nanoseconds since the seventies.

Millions of young women today have grown up with feminism, as you've written, "in the water." (Don't forget, though, that millions have grown up with Christian fundamentalism or Ronald Reagan or

Rush Limbaugh in the water. There are large tracts of America where feminism, word and concept, is still anathema.) But that doesn't necessarily mean that they can live according to those ideas. How many women, young or old, left the Southern Baptist Church when it banned women ministers and declared that the husband was the head of the household to whom his wife should "graciously" submit? Surely many made sarcastic quips and rolled their eyes, but they still fill the pews and put their money in the collection plate. Women still gravitate toward, and are pushed toward, female-stereotyped jobs with pay scales that assume a husband's greater income, they still change their names when they get married—and they still get married. I'm not blaming them—I'm just observing that society places rather serious limits on the ability of most women to live differently, even if they think differently. Those limits are subtler now—everything looks like a free choice. But how freely does a woman decide to become a beautician instead of a firefighter? To take her husband's name rather than keep her own, much less offer him hers?

You write that young women reject "radical feminism"—the highly ideological, rather rigid feminism that came out of the 1960s and 1970s left—while embracing the basic vision of women's equality. I would put it differently. I doubt many young women know much about those older feminists or think much about them. I think what they have in their heads are media stereotypes—the hairy-legged, "man-hating lesbian," the PC-spouting "feminazi," the castrating, childless "career woman." I'd say that when women (of whatever age) say, "I'm not a feminist, but . . . ," what they are signaling is that they like men and want men to like them, that they believe they can rely on their own efforts to get where they want to go in life, and that they are not about to make a fuss about the sexist background noise that infuses—still!—daily life. Or am I wrong, Jenn?

Dear Katha,

Despite the media stereotypes and general ignorance about the second wave, many young feminists are taking ownership of feminism, I think. And you are right that we will have to take it soon enough, anyway. The torch metaphor cuts both ways: younger feminists have gotten their own torches, only to be told, "You call that a torch?!"

YOU—or older women—don't need to change the content or style of feminism to attract younger women. WE have already changed it. For instance, you only have to look at the essays in this book to realize that feminism's style has changed—we're hooked into pop culture, the Internet, and hip-hop. I think *that* is more the issue—that feminism has changed, and younger women who are involved in more institutionalized feminism sometimes wish that that would be acknowledged. Instead, we often hear "Where are all the younger women?" and "Why aren't younger women feminists?" and "How can we reach out and motivate these [idealized form of young woman who doesn't resemble young feminists actually in the room]?" Of course, as I write that, I remember that plenty of young women are into the "embalmed" version of feminism you describe. On our travels to women's studies departments, Amy Richards and I have received more than our fair share of oversized purple T-shirts featuring goddess imagery.

Dear Jenn,

In its brief, intense heyday, the women's movement won some very quick victories: access to contraception and abortion rights, the integration of innumerable all-male precincts from McSorley's tavern to Yale University, the end of sex-segregated want ads, divorce reform, access to credit, recognition of domestic and sexual violence as social problems, welfare rights, admission to high-paying blue-collar jobs, not to mention a transformation of the discourse of sexuality and relationships—it's quite an amazing list. Yet the underlying structures of male privilege proved surprisingly resilient. I think some older feminists are caught between those two realities—"So much changed in an instant! Your generation could be making that happen, too" and "Nothing really changed, women are just as screwed over as ever." Feminists who came out of the 1960s left have the added burden of ambivalence about some feminist victories—if you're a socialist, how happy can you be that women are becoming corporate lawyers and stockbrokers in droves? And if you think politics is supposed to be a grassroots, handmade business of sit-ins and demonstrations and leaflets, the professionalized electoral feminism of Emily's List or NARAL can look like a betrayal of principle.

Dear Katha,

Let's talk more about the book, because it represents something about the movement. *Catching a Wave* begins by riffing on a famous Fannie Lou Hamer line. "We are tired of waiting. Sick and tired," the editors write. (Hamer said she was "sick and tired of being sick and tired," which sums up being an activist and being oppressed in a few words.) Rory and Alison then go on to describe different situations in which women's raised expectations have not translated into more power for our gender as a whole—more women graduating with honors than men doesn't mean more female tenured professors than men, for instance. This seems to be what you are saying with your comment that younger women have confidence and feminist values but aren't analyzing or waking up to the sexist background noise that holds us back as a group. Maybe this is the case, but what is this sexist background exactly? I see it more as in the foreground. After all, date rape and workplace discrimination are visible and understood as wrong— but solving the problem is infinitely harder than naming it, however key that first step of acknowledgment is. When I am on college campuses, for instance, it's clear that date rape is prevalent but also that people don't know how to identify or deal with it. Men often don't feel that they have a part in the conversation, and women don't know whether to include men or how to change their own behaviors. Many college kids like to get really wasted at school and a lot of bad, passed-out, and nonconsensual sex occurs.

I feel that feminist women today—not just women who are young, either—have a different task than second wavers did. The first and second waves beat open doors that were firmly closed to women and named injustices that had been invisible because there were no words to describe them. I think this is sort of similar to knocking down the Berlin Wall. Currently, feminists are in the position of the former East Germans: of building something new after the barrier is knocked down. You ask, "How much have things really changed?," implying that we all have our work cut out for us and also that younger women are perhaps delusional in their sense of confidence. So, let's really look at how things haven't changed.

You cite systemic and institutional ways in which women are far from equal to men, as do Rory and Alison in their introduction. Important, of course, but I am also interested in the personal ways in which things haven't changed. For instance, in light of your recent romantic travails, you have said to me (and I thought it very funny and true) that so much of feminism is not "digestible." We eat our feminist carrots, we swallow our theory like bran, we exercise our brains in women's studies classes, but you still gave your ex-lover the bigger study even though he didn't make his living as a writer and work from home and you did. Why? Because it seemed fair or at least reasonable within the context of your home and relationship. After all, he left his cool apartment to move in with you; you wanted to make him feel at home—is that so wrong? Meanwhile, my sexual relationships with women have a lot to do with me trying to find a new way of being in love, one where I don't feel the urge to coddle a man. My coddling side (and the self-hatred that comes with it) has crept into my life, despite my being fortified by feminism. I guess I'm sensing that the personal frontier is where my generation is doing most of its work (I see this in the essays in this book—all about culture and TV and hip-hop and porn) and that is important work. Just as important as the law-changing/tenure/first-woman-president stuff, because how we conduct our personal lives (what speaks to us, what we value) represents us directly—this is why the personal is political.

A couple of weeks ago you and I were talking about the introduction to this book. Both of us mentioned the passage where Rory and Alison cite a young feminist writer, Merri Lisa Johnson, "complaining" about bell hooks's "demand that feminists must relearn desire so that they don't get turned on by hypermasculine, oppressive men." Johnson balks at hooks's advice, declaring that she "won't do it. I am not that feminist," meaning she's not that kind of feminist, she's not that exhaustively and almost self-hatingly critical of her own motives. Rory and Alison seem to read Johnson as saying that she won't follow hooks's dictum, not because it's rather stupid and abstract (like saying, "I demand that writers relearn accounting so that they stop being so poor"), but because she is afraid of the "work." You agreed with hooks, Rory, and Alison, but I agree with Johnson. There is nothing inherently feminist about changing your real desires—whether it's for a rakish guy or Mahnolo Blahniks. Feminism is about getting in touch with your true desires—whether it's your ambition or your sexuality or your maternity. Feminism might mean realizing that you never wanted to be a stay-at-home mom who canned her own tomatoes; it was just expected of you. Or feminism might mean that you leave your job on Wall Street because you want to raise your kids and do the PTA. hooks's thesis assumes that there is some Real Feminist (yes, a platonic form) that we should aspire to. I believe in a feminism that strengthens my connections to my own desires.

Dear Jennifer,

I am all for following one's star and embracing one's "true desires"—but who arranges the constellations in one's personal firmament? Where do those "true desires" come from and in what social context does one pursue them? Sometimes we want things—really, really want them, as the Spice Girls would say—that are ill-advised, foolish, wrong, that are more than likely to end in a bad place. To pick up on your example, I hope women who really want to stay home with kids (not the same as "raising" them, which working mothers and fathers also do) and spend their energies on the PTA, have loyal, faithful, healthy husbands, or trust funds because exempting oneself from paid employment is a very risky choice to make. It may look like freedom when you quit your boring, stressful, meaningless job, but ten years later you can find yourself in deep trouble: dumped with no money or stuck in a bad or okay-but-unequal marriage. Or, the marriage may be fine, but you're living an isolated life in a town you hate because you have to follow your husband's job—the male breadwinner calls a lot of shots in a marriage. And what about when you do go back to work? Women who stay home with kids are handicapped in the job market for life—they never catch up in salary, promotions, or pensions, and they often have to take jobs way below their capabilities. A feminism that doesn't raise these issues isn't worth much. Surely the job of feminism isn't merely to say, "Sure, whatever you want, sweetie! As long as you really, really want it."

The great insight of the women's movement was to see that individual choices are socially shaped and socially constrained. Would your Wall Street mom want to stay home with the kids if her husband wasn't working eighty hours a week at his Wall Street job? If she didn't secretly believe the daily dose of propaganda we all get that working mothers are selfish bitches whose children grow up to be drug addicts with low SAT scores? Why are her options either/or, anyway? Why is the family happiness balanced on her back? (And why is she on Wall Street? Because socially useful jobs pay so little and get so little respect?) I wish I had a dollar for every time I persuaded myself that I really, really wanted to do the thing that was easiest to do, that would preserve a relationship instead of challenging it, that avoided a confrontation or a risk of failure. My point about Merri Lisa Johnson was not that she was afraid to do the "work" of "relearning desire." It's not that she's lazy, although she phrases her refusal in a flip way. I don't even know if it's possible to change one's deep sexual nature by analyzing it politically—to understand that women internalize sexist values and eroticize male power doesn't mean those things stop being erotic. Perhaps, if Johnson looked deep into her heart, she would only end up ashamed of her desires but still having them, longing for "hypermasculinized, oppressive men" while dutifully going through the motions with a nice guy she found pallid and unsexy. The light bulb has to want to change, and it sounds as if Johnson hasn't gone far enough down the road with Mr. Macho to have a problem with her choices; maybe she's having too much fun to imagine what it would be like to be a middle-aged woman with a hypermasculine, oppressive husband or (more likely) ex-husband.

My point was less about her than about feminism. I think feminists have to raise those uncomfortable, unsettling, infuriating questions about intimate relations and personal choices: it's not enough to say, "Whatever floats your boat." The wave that floats your boat today can swamp it and even drown you tomorrow. If a woman can become sexually excited only by a man who feels superior to her, can love only someone who is emotionally unavailable, that's going to be a problem for her—one she shares with plenty of women, by the way. How can a movement that fights women's inequality not talk about the ways inequality feels right, inevitable, good? About the ways we go for men who possess the qualities we repress in ourselves? About the ways society undermines women's sense of self-worth and then nudges them toward conventional, disempowering choices? (And what is more conventional than wanting a "manly" macho man, a bad boy, a rake? It's only in the mini-world of feminism that this looks like a daring and original preference!)

It's very hard to raise these issues in ways that are not alienating, moralistic, know-it-all, hypercritical (and hypocritical), nitpicky, and drenched in disapproval. God knows, there is a mile-wide streak of puritanism in second-wave feminism, and a tendency toward overkill and overstatement—not to mention suppressed competition and hostility! Nobody likes being made to feel guilty because she enjoys high-fashion shoes. One distinction I think doesn't get made often enough or clearly enough, however, is that between choices that may be a little sexist in origin (shaving one's legs—that old perennial!) but are basically harmless, and choices that have serious implications for the course of one's life and for the lives of others. "You go, girl!" is a good slogan. But it's not the only thing women need to hear. They also need to hear, from time to time, that old, infuriating, favorite saying of the hairy-legged ancients: the personal is political.

Bibliography

Abu-Lughod, Lila, ed. *Remaking Women: Feminism and Modernity in the Middle East*. Princeton, N.J.: Princeton University Press, 1998.

Allison, Dorothy. *Bastard Out of Carolina*. New York: Dutton, 1992.

———, ed. *Skin: Talking About Sex, Class and Literature*. Ithaca, N.Y.: Firebrand Books, 1994.

Badran, Margot, and Miriam Cooke, eds. *Opening the Gates: A Century of Arab Feminist Writing*. Bloomington: Indiana University Press, 1990.

Baumgardner, Jennifer, and Amy Richards. *Manifesta: Young Women, Feminism, and the Future*. New York: Farrar, Straus and Giroux, 2000.

Beauvoir, Simone de. *The Second Sex*. Translated by H. M. Parshley. New York: Vintage, 1952 (orig. French, 1949).

Bogard, William. *The Simulation of Surveillance*. Cambridge: Cambridge University Press, 1996.

Bondoc, Anna, and Meg Daly, eds. *Letters of Intent: Women Cross the Generations to Talk about Family, Work, Sex, Love and the Future of Feminism*. New York: Free Press, 1999.

Bordo, Susan. "The Body and the Reproduction of Femininity: A Feminist Appropriation of Foucault." In *Gender/Body/Knowledge: Feminist Reconstructions of Being and Knowing*, edited by Alison M. Jaggar and Susan R. Bordo. New Brunswick, N.J.: Rutgers University Press, 1989.

Brodkin, Karen. *How Jews Became White Folks and What That Shows about Race in America*. New Brunswick, N.J.: Rutgers University Press, 1998.

Brown, Lyn Mikel, and Carol Gilligan. *Meeting at the Crossroads*. Cambridge, Mass.: Harvard University Press, 1992.

Bulbeck, Chilla. *Re-Orienting Western Feminisms: Women's Diversity in a Postcolonial World*. New York: Cambridge University Press, 1998.

Chesler, Phyllis. *Letters to a Young Feminist.* New York: Four Walls Eight Windows, 1997.

Coker, Cheo, dream hampton, and Tara Roberts. "A Hip-Hop Nation Divided." *Essence,* August 1994, 62–64, 112–15.

Davies, Bronwyn. "The Problem of Desire." *Social Problems* 37, no. 4 (1990): 301–16.

Davis, Eisa. "Sexism and the Art of Feminist Hip-Hop Maintenance." In *To Be Real: Telling the Truth and Changing the Face of Feminism,* edited by Rebecca Walker. New York: Anchor, 1995.

de Lauretis, Teresa. *Alice Doesn't: Feminism, Semiotics, Cinema.* Bloomington: Indiana University Press, 1984.

Deming, Caren. "For a Television-Centered Television Criticism." In *Television and Women's Culture: The Politics of the Popular,* edited by Mary Ellen Brown. London: Sage Publications, 1990.

Denfeld, Rene. "Feminism 2000: What Does It Really Mean (to You)?" *Sassy* 9 (May 1990): 60.

———. *The New Victorians: A Young Woman's Challenge to the Old Feminist Order.* New York: Warner Books, 1995.

Douglas, Susan J. *Where the Girls Are: Growing Up Female with the Mass Media.* New York: Random House, 1994.

DuCille, Ann. *Skin Trade.* Cambridge, Mass.: Harvard University Press, 1996.

Edut, Ophira, ed. *Adios, Barbie: Young Women Write about Body Image and Identity.* Seattle: Seal Press, 1998.

Ehrenreich, Barbara. *Nickel and Dimed: On (Not) Getting By in America.* New York: Metropolitan, 2001.

El Saadawi, Nawal. *A Daughter of Isis: The Autobiography of Nawal El Saadawi.* Translated by Sherif Hetata. New York: Zed Books, 1999.

Epstein, Barbara. "Ambivalence about Feminism." In *The Feminist Memoir Project: Voices from Women's Liberation,* edited by Rachel Blau DuPlessis and Ann Snitow. New York: Three Rivers Press, 1998.

Estrich, Susan. *Sex and Power.* New York: Riverhead Books, 2000.

Faludi, Susan. *Backlash.* New York: Anchor, 1991.

Findlen, Barbara. *Listen Up: Voices from the Next Feminist Generation.* Seattle: Seal Press, 1995.

Firestone, Shulamith. *The Dialectic of Sex: The Case for Feminist Revolution.* New York: Bantam Books, 1970.

Fiske, John. *Television Culture.* London and New York: Routledge, 1987.

Freeman, Jo. "The New Feminists." *Nation* 24 (February 1969): 241–44.

Fudge, Rachel. "The Buffy Effect, or A Tale of Cleavage and Marketing." *Bitch: Feminist Response to Pop Culture* 10 (1999): 18–21, 58.

Fuss, Diana. *Identification Papers*. New York: Routledge, 1995.

Gore, Ariel, and Bee Lavendar, eds. *Breeder: Real-Life Stories from the New Generation of Mothers*. Seattle: Seal Press, 2001.

Greer, Germaine. *The Female Eunuch*. London: Paladin, 1970.

Grossberg, Lawrence. *We Gotta Get Out of This Place: Popular Conservatism and Postmodern Culture*. New York and London: Routledge, 1992.

hampton, dream. "Free the Girls; or, Why I Really Don't Believe There's Much of a Future for Hip Hop, Let Alone Women in Hip Hop." In *Vibe Hip Hop Divas*, edited by Rob Kenner. New York: Three Rivers Press, 2001.

Heywood, Leslie, and Jennifer Drake, eds. *Third Wave Agenda: Being Feminist, Doing Feminism*. Minneapolis: University of Minnesota Press, 1997.

Hirsch, Marianne. *The Mother/Daughter Plot: Narrative, Psychoanalysis, Feminism*. Bloomington: Indiana University Press, 1989.

Hochschild, Arlie Russell. "Coming of Age, Seeking an Identity." *New York Times*, March 2000: D1.

Hollibaugh, Amber. *My Dangerous Desires: A Queer Girl Dreaming Her Way Home*. Durham, N.C.: Duke University Press, 2000.

Holt, Maria. *Half the People: Women, History and the Palestinian Intifada*. Jerusalem: Palestinian Academic Society for the Study of International Affairs, 1992.

hooks, bell. *Feminism Is for Everybody: Passionate Politics*. Boston: South End Press, 2000.

———. *Feminist Theory: From Margin to Center*. Boston: South End Press, 1986.

Hourihan, Margery. *Deconstructing the Hero: Literary Theory and Children's Literature*. New York and London: Routledge, 1997.

Hull, Gloria, et al., eds. *All the Women Are White, All the Blacks Are Men, But Some of Us Are Brave*. New York: Feminist Press, 1982.

Jayawardena, Kumari. *Feminism and Nationalism in the Third World*. London: Zed Books, 1986.

Johnson, Merri Lisa, ed. *Jane Sexes It Up: True Confessions of Feminist Desire*. New York: Four Walls Eight Windows, 2002.

Kamen, Paula. *Her Way: Young Women Remake the Sexual Revolution*. New York: Broadway Books, 2002.

Kearney, Mary Celeste. "'Don't Need You': Rethinking Identity Politics and Separatism from a Grrrl Perspective." In *Youth Culture: Identity in a*

Postmodern World, edited by Jonathon Epstein. Malden, Mass.: Blackwell Publishers, 1998.

Kellner, Douglas. *Media Culture: Cultural Studies, Identity and Politics between the Modern and the Postmodern.* London and New York: Routledge, 1995.

Kolodny, Annette. "Dancing through the Minefield: Some Observations on the Theory, Practice, and Politics of a Feminist Literary Criticism." *Feminist Studies* 6, no.1 (1980).

Lentz, Kirsten Marthe. "*Quality* versus *Relevance:* Feminism, Race, and the Politics of the Sign in 1970s Television." *Camera Obscura* 15, no.1 (2000): 45–93.

Looser, Devoney. "Introduction 2: Gen X Feminists? Youthism, Careerism, and the Third Wave." In *Generations: Academic Feminists in Dialogue,* edited by Devoney Looser and Ann Kaplan. Minneapolis: University of Minnesota Press, 1997.

Lorde, Audre. *Sister Outsider.* Trumansburg, N.Y.: Crossing Press, 1984.

MacKinnon, Catharine A. *Feminism Unmodified: Discourses on Life and Law.* Cambridge, Mass.: Harvard University Press, 1987.

———. *Toward a Feminist Theory of the State.* Cambridge, Mass.: Harvard University Press, 1997.

Maglin, Nan Bauer, and Donna Perry, eds. *"Bad Girls"/"Good Girls": Women, Sex, and Power in the Nineties.* New Brunswick, N.J.: Rutgers University Press, 1996.

Mannheim, Karl. "The Problem of Generations." In *Essays on the Sociology of Knowledge,* edited by Paul Kecskemeti. New York: Oxford University Press, 1952.

McRobbie, Angela, and Mica Nava, eds. *Gender and Generation.* London: Macmillan, 1984.

Mitchell, David. "Modernist Freaks and Postmodern Geeks." In *The Disability Studies Reader,* edited by Lennard J. Davis. New York: Routledge, 1997.

Moi, Toril. *Sexual / Textual Politics: Feminist Literary Theory.* London: Routledge, 1985.

Morgan, Joan. "The Bad Girls of Hip-Hop." *Essence* 77 (April 1997): 132.

———. *When Chickenheads Come Home to Roost: My Life as a Hip-Hop Feminist.* New York: Simon & Schuster, 1999.

Orr, Catherine M. "Changing the Currents of the Third Wave." *Hypatia: A Journal of Feminist Philosophy* 12, no. 3 (1997): 29–45.

Pipher, Mary. *Reviving Ophelia.* New York: Putnam, 1994.

Pollitt, Katha. *Reasonable Creatures: Essays on Women and Feminism*. New York: Vintage, 1995.

Quinn, Rebecca Dakin. "An Open Letter to Institutional Mothers." In *Generations: Academic Feminists in Dialogue*, edited by Devoney Looser and Ann Kaplan. Minneapolis: University of Minnesota Press, 1997.

Rich, Adrienne. *Blood, Bread, and Poetry: Selected Prose 1979–1985*. New York: W. W. Norton, 1986.

———. *Of Woman Born: Motherhood as Experience and Institution.* New York: W. W. Norton, 1976.

———. *On Lies, Secrets, and Silence. Selected Prose 1966–1978*. New York: W. W. Norton, 1978.

Rich, B. Ruby. "Feminism and Sexuality in the 1980s." *Feminist Studies* 12 (Fall 1986): 525–61.

Roberts, Tara, and Eisa Nefertari Ulen. "Sisters Spin Talk on Hip Hop: Can the Music Be Saved?" *Ms.* (February/March 2000): 70–74.

Roiphe, Katie. *The Morning After: Sex, Fear, and Feminism on Campus*. Boston: Little, Brown, 1993.

Rose, Tricia. *Black Noise: Rap Music and Black Culture in Contemporary America*. Hanover, N.H.: Wesleyan University Press, 1994.

Russo, Mary. "Aging and the Scandal of Anachronism." In *Figuring Age: Women, Bodies, Generations,* edited by Kathleen Woodward. Bloomington: Indiana University Press, 1999.

Scott, Joan, et al. "Conference Call." *differences* 2, no. 3 (1990): 52–108.

Siegel, Deborah L. "Reading between the Waves: Feminist Historiography in a 'Postfeminist' Moment." In *Third Wave Agenda: Being Feminist, Doing Feminism,* edited by Leslie Heywood and Jennifer Drake. Minneapolis: University of Minnesota Press, 1997.

Smith, Kemba. "Pardon Me." Interview by Stephanie Booth. *Honey* (September 2001): 86.

Snitow, Ann. "A Gender Diary." In *Conflicts in Feminism*, edited by Marianne Hirsch and Evelyn Fox Keller. New York: Routledge, 1990.

Sorisio, Carolyn. "A Tale of Two Feminisms: Power and Victimization in Contemporary Feminist Debate." In *Third Wave Agenda: Being Feminist, Doing Feminism,* edited by Leslie Heywood and Jennifer Drake. Minneapolis: University of Minnesota Press, 1997.

Talhami, Ghada. "Women under Occupation: The Great Transformation." In *Images and Reality: Palestinian Women under Occupation and in the Diaspora*. Suha Sabbagh and Ghada Talhami, Series Editors. Institute for Arab

Women's Studies Monograph Series, no. 1. Washington, D.C.: IAWS, 1990.

Tucker, Hannah. "High School Confidential." *Entertainment Weekly* 505 (October 1, 1999).

Vance, Carol, ed. "More Danger, More Pleasure: A Decade after the Barnard Sexuality Conference." In *Pleasure and Danger: Exploring Female Sexuality.* Boston: Routledge & K. Paul, 1984.

Walker, Alice. *In Search of Our Mothers' Gardens.* New York: Harcourt Brace Jovanovich, 1983.

Walker, Alice, and Rebecca Walker. "The Two of Us." *Essence* (May 1995): 172–73.

Walker, Rebecca. "Becoming the Third Wave." *Ms.* (January/February 1992): 39–41.

———. "Being Real: An Introduction." In *To Be Real: Telling the Truth and Changing the Face of Feminism,* edited by Rebecca Walker. New York: Anchor Books, 1995.

———, ed. *To Be Real: Telling the Truth and Changing the Face of Feminism.* New York: Anchor Books, 1995.

West, Candace, and Don Zimmerman. "Doing Gender." *Gender & Society* 1, no. 2 (1987): 125–51.

Wolf, Naomi. *The Beauty Myth: How Images of Beauty Are Used against Women.* New York: William Morrow, 1991.

———. *Fire with Fire: The New Female Power and How It Will Change the 21st Century.* New York: Random House, 1993.

Woolf, Virginia. *A Room of One's Own.* 1929; reprint, New York: Harcourt Brace Jovanovich, 1991.

Contributors

Jennifer Baumgardner and *Amy Richards* met at *Ms.* in 1992, while Amy was working with Gloria Steinem and Jennifer was interning (and later editing) at the magazine. Together, they wrote *Manifesta: Young Women, Feminism, and the Future* (Farrar, Straus and Giroux, 2000) and have traveled to bookstores, universities, and high schools across the country, talking about feminism today. Baumgardner writes for various magazines, from *Harper's* to *Elle;* she is writing the introductions to a series of reissued "feminist classics" (including Germaine Greer's *The Female Eunuch* and Shulamith Firestone's *The Dialectic of Sex*), and is writing a new book called *Look Both Ways: Girls and Sex* (forthcoming, 2004). Richards is a contributing editor to *Ms.* magazine and the cofounder of the Third Wave Foundation, the only national organization for feminist activists between the ages of fifteen and thirty. She is also the voice behind "Ask Amy," an on-line activist advice column located at http://www.feminist.com that has been going strong since 1995. Baumgardner and Richards are both very active with the Third Wave Foundation. They are co-authoring a follow-up to *Manifesta* called *Recipe-Tested: An Idea Bank for Real Activism.*

Sarah Boonin graduated from Duke University in 1997, where she received her B.A. in women's studies and psychology and was an active member of Duke's feminist student organization. Boonin then spent four years working at the Feminist Majority Foundation (FMF) in

Arlington, Virginia. While at FMF, she helped to build and later direct *Choices,* FMF's national Campus Leadership Program. She also played a major role in organizing Feminist Expo 2000 for Women's Empowerment, the largest feminist convention in the United States in two decades. Boonin left FMF in August 2001 to attend Harvard Law School, where she remains actively engaged in issues of women's rights and civil rights. Boonin plans to use her law degree to continue her work in the feminist movement.

Michele Byers is an Assistant Professor at Saint Mary's University in Halifax, Nova Scotia. She wrote her doctoral dissertation on *Buffy the Vampire Slayer* and, though she continues to try, she can't seem to stop writing about *Buffy.* She has published articles in *Signs, Higher Education Perspectives,* and *Studies in Popular Culture* (forthcoming), and has forthcoming book chapters in *Canadian Eh?* and *Surviving Sprawl.* She has written about *Beverly Hills, 90210,* reality TV, Brandon Teena, suburbia, and the mediated city. Byers is involved in a project on Canadian identity and the youth-oriented TV series *Degrassi;* she also continues to look for more ways to actively study and promote the third wave.

Susan Muaddi Darraj earned her M.A. in literature from Rutgers University and is continuing her graduate studies at the Johns Hopkins University. She is a freelance writer whose work has appeared in *Sojourner, Calyx, Baltimore Magazine, Pages Magazine, Monthly Review, Al-Jadid,* the *Philadelphia Inquirer, New York Stories, Phoebe,* and elsewhere. She lives with her husband in Baltimore.

Rory Dicker is Assistant Professor of English at Westminster College in Fulton, Missouri, where she teaches courses in American literature and women's studies. She received her Ph.D. in English from Vanderbilt University, where her emphasis was on nineteenth-century American women's writing; currently, she is revising her dissertation, which discusses domesticity and the fiction of the American 1860s. In the spring of 2002, she felt less like a third waver and more like a second waver as she taught the first Introduction to Women's Studies course ever to be offered at Westminster.

Nancy Gruver lives in Duluth, Minnesota, with her husband, Joe Kelly. They visit their adult twin daughters, Mavis Gruver and Nia Kelly, as often as possible. Nancy is the founder and publisher of *New Moon: The Magazine for Girls and Their Dreams*. To learn more about *New Moon*, go to http://www.newmoon.org.

Alyssa Harad is a Ph.D. candidate in twentieth-century American literature at the University of Texas at Austin. She is currently finishing her dissertation on American trauma, everyday life, and literary testimony. She is a cofounder of Grrl Action, a summer outreach program held at the University of Texas, Austin, that brings together girls from diverse socioeconomic backgrounds to write creative autobiography and transform it into a collaborative performance. She also teaches an annual workshop on 'zines at Girlday, a free festival of hands-on workshops that she also helped to found. Before entering graduate school, she taught creative writing and held creative arts therapy groups at a private psychiatric hospital, where she worked primarily with adolescents.

Erin Harde is a graduate student in journalism at the University of Western Ontario. She intends to work as a music journalist and a free-lance writer about pop culture. She has presented a paper to the Canadian Women's Studies Association and has an essay forthcoming in a collection entitled *Strobelights and Blown Speakers: The Music and Art of Radiohead*.

Roxanne Harde is a doctoral candidate in English at Queen's University. Her dissertation research examines the operations of feminist theologies in the work of early American women poets. She has presented papers at interdisciplinary conferences in Canada and the United States. She has published articles in the journals *Critique, Contemporary Verse II*, and *Legacy*, as well as in several edited collections. Currently, she is guest-editing a special "girlpower" issue of *FEMSPEC*.

Astrid Henry is Assistant Professor of Women's Studies and English at Saint Mary's College in Indiana. Her forthcoming book on generational relationships in U.S. feminism will be published by Indiana

University Press. The book examines the relationship between contemporary feminism and 1970s U.S. feminisms, the ways in which generational struggles are currently being played out in feminism, and the centrality of the mother-daughter trope in describing these struggles.

Emi Koyama is a multi-issue social justice slut synthesizing feminist, Asian, survivor, dyke, queer, sex worker, slut, intersex, genderqueer, and crip politics, as these factors, while not a complete descriptor of who she is, have all affected her life. She is currently most active in intersex, sex workers' rights, and anti–"domestic violence industry" activism. Koyama lives in Portland, Oregon, and is putting the "emi" back in feminism through her on-line propaganda at http://www. eminism.org.

Susannah B. Mintz is Assistant Professor of English at Skidmore College. She is the author of the forthcoming *Threshold Poetics: Milton and Intersubjectivity* (University of Delaware Press), and is currently completing a book-length study of contemporary autobiographies by women with disabilities.

Alison Piepmeier is Senior Lecturer in Women's Studies at Vanderbilt University. Most of her scholarly work focuses on nineteenth-century American women's writing; she has published on Mary Baker Eddy and Sojourner Truth, and she is currently working on a book called *Out in Public: Configurations of Women's Bodies in Nineteenth-Century America*. She's involved in feminist activism and antiviolence work on the Vanderbilt campus and is thoroughly enjoying the opportunity to design and teach courses on women in the world, gender and violence, and third wave feminism.

Gwendolyn D. Pough is Assistant Professor of Women's Studies at the University of Minnesota, Twin Cities Campus. She completed her B.A. in English at William Paterson University, her M.A. in English at Northeastern University, and her Ph.D. in English at Miami University in Ohio. She is currently working on a book-length project that explores black womanhood, hip-hop culture, and the public sphere.

Media critic *Jennifer L. Pozner* is the founder of Women in Media & News (WIMN), a new media monitoring, training, and advocacy non-profit that seeks to transform public debate by promoting positive, accurate portrayals of women in news and entertainment media. Previously, she was Women's Desk Director for the national media watch group FAIR. A contributing media editor to the national feminist newspaper *Sojourner*, Pozner's freelance work has appeared in *Ms.*, *Extra!*, *Newsday*, *Bitch*, and the anthology *Uncovering the Right on Campus*, among others. Pozner lectures and conducts media trainings to help women's campus and community groups learn to use media outlets. Her tiara-wearing alter ego, "Mya Cash," is the informal coordinator of the political satire group NYC Billionaires for Bush & Bloomberg. She can be reached at jenn@jenniferpozner.com.

Mimi Schippers is Assistant Professor of Sociology at Albion College. She received her Ph.D. in sociology from the University of Wisconsin at Madison. Her work focuses on theorizing and researching gender and sexuality in everyday interactions. Her most recent book is *Rockin' Out of the Box: Gender Maneuvering in Alternative Hard Rock* (Rutgers University Press, 2002). She is currently working on a comparative ethnography of queer subcultures in Paris and Chicago.

Alana Suskin will be (God willing) ordained as a Conservative rabbi in May 2003. Her work has been published in a variety of journals and anthologies, including *Bridges* and *Lilith*, as well as on-line at socialaction.com. Her writing often focuses on the social action work that she does as a feminist, a Jew, and a human being. She can be reached at alanamscat@yahoo.com.

Kristina Sheryl Wong is a performance artist, actor, writer, and educator. Most notoriously known as the Webmistress of the mock mail-order bride Web site www.bigbadchinesemama.com, she was recently published in *Yell-oh Girls*, edited by Vickie Nam (HarperCollins, 2001). Currently, she is working on her first full-length novel, *Between the Peaks*, thanks to the 2002 Emerging Voices Fellowship from PEN USA. She is also in the process of reworking her solo show, "Miss Chinatown 2nd

Runner-Up," which premiered and sold out at Highways Performance Space in Santa Monica. Wong is the Artistic Director of the Asian American Community Teen Theater (AACTT) Company, where she works with high school students on plays that educate other teens about AIDS/HIV.

Index

Activism: armchair, 303; art as, 294, 297–99; challenges of, 19, 299; examples of, 11, 19–20, 36, 52n19, 150, 286–92; and Judaism, 25, 269, 270, 272–78; need for, 3, 8, 25; parody in, 302–3; redefining, 153; and women's studies, 267; and World Wide Web, 53n19, 299, 300–307

Adolescent girls: and activism, 107–8, 111; being ignored, 108–10; development and, 87, 103, 173; "Girl Power," 36, 108, 174, 296; Girls' Movement, 101; justice and, 106, 107, 108, 110, 112, 113, 114; media and, 104, 109; "natural feminism," 22, 106–7, 110; and relationships with older women, 103–15; and relevance of feminism to, 82, 83, 101, 102, 106, 108; and repressing aspirations, 111; and self- perception, 103, 108; sexuality, 22, 81, 82, 83, 85, 87, 90, 94–95; voice, 90, 103, 105. *See also* sexuality

Afghanistan, 39–40; women in, 189, 191–92

Africa, 191, 266; Algerian women, 196, 198; Egyptian women, 196, 202, 272, 277

AIDS, 75, 96, 147, 237, 242

All the Women Are White, All the Blacks Are Men, But Some of Us Are Brave (Hull et al.), 234

Allison, Dorothy, 84, 90–91

Ally McBeal, 33, 119, 132

Anthony, Susan B., 33

Arab American women, 24, 191, 192–93, 199

Arab women, 24; assimilating to Western culture, 193; and coalitions with other women of color, 199–200, 201, 203; and family life, 195; feminism, 190, 191, 192–93, 194, 199, 202; feminism, history of, 192–94, 195–96, 198; misunderstandings about, 191; and nationalism/colonialism, 195–96, 197–98, 200–201; and organizing, 197–99; as other, 200; stereotypes of, 189, 190, 201, 203

Asian American women, 25, 296; and mail-order brides, 294, 300, 301–2;

Feminism *(cont.)*
144; and media, 15, 121; and multiplicity, 117, 147; organizing, 23, 141, 142, 151–54; and otherness, 136n13; public vs. lived, 118, 120, 122, 131, 282, 291, 310–312; radical, 123, 129–30, 131, 248, 310, 313; redefinitions of, 24; self-identifying as, 22, 23, 95–96, 116–17, 119, 120, 134, 295, 307; stereotypes of, 119, 121, 295, 313; and theory, 83, 124, 300. *See also* feminist generations

Feminism, first wave, 8–9, 140, 213, 295, 315

Feminism, second wave: and activism, 50, 167; critiques of, 15, 16, 139, 179, 209, 310; and friction with third wave, 14, 15, 119, 123, 148; goals of, 9, 58; history of, 9, 50, 84–85, 165, 167, 217, 311–12; marginalization of women of color and lesbians, 9, 179–80, 248, 309, 319; radicalism of, 129–30; seen as archaic, 118; stereotypes of, 119

Feminism, third wave: and activism, 11, 13, 19–20, 119, 120, 151–54; and apathy, 11, 13, 219; continuity with the second wave, 5, 10, 16, 19, 127, 135, 149–50, 222, 226, 309; critiques of, 14, 130; definitions of, 12, 119, 122, 135–36n5, 295; and distinctions from second wave, 11, 14–15, 16–17, 18, 119, 215–17, 222, 225–26, 309, 310; and diversity, 12, 17; feminism "in the water," 11, 144, 163, 219, 312; and feminist free-for-all, 17–18; and girls' movement, 101; history of, 9–11; and individualism, 220; as inheritance, 219, 220, 309; key texts, 12–13, 27n27; and leadership, 159–60, 163–64; and multiplicity, 8, 10, 16, 17, 77, 159–

60, 164, 167; and popular culture, 16–17, 77, 126, 132, 296, 314, 316; reinvention of feminism, 118, 119, 135, 148, 220, 222, 224, 225–26, 227, 309; taking on the personal, 119–20, 122, 131, 295, 316; and U.S. third world feminism, 9

Feminist EXPO, 154–56

"Feminist free-for-all," 17, 18

Feminist generations, 211–12, 215; as coherent/unified, 214, 309; dutiful daughter of feminism, 210, 211, 222–24, 225; familial model, 214, 218–19; feminism as a mother figure, 24, 209–13, 218, 219, 221, 224, 225, 227; feminism as motherless, 216, 217–18; generational split in feminism, 14–15, 96n1, 123, 148–49, 216, 309–11, 313; matrophobia, 221; "matrophor," 211, 212, 213, 215, 216

Feminist literary criticism, 84, 124–26, 136n13, 201, 203

Feminist Majority Foundation, 138–56

Findlen, Barbara, 12

Firestone, Shulamith, 212

Flanders, Laura, 34, 50

For Colored Girls Who Have Considered Suicide/When the Rainbow is Enuf (Shange), 236

Friedan, Betty, 9, 33, 167, 194, 309

Fuss, Diana, 215, 221

Gender maneuvering, 281, 285–86, 290, 291, 292–93

Gender order, 252, 281, 282–83, 285, 288, 292

Gilligan, Carol, 103, 106, 195

Girls' Movement, 101

Global trade, 40–41

Greer, Germaine, 129–130

Gulf War, 189–90